For my family and friends.

EAST *to* WEST *to* EAST

Journey of a US Trained Chinese Financier

Randolph Kwei

FOREWORD BY JESSE FRIEDLANDER

PORTLAND • OREGON
INKWATERPRESS.COM

Copyright © 2009 by Randolph Kwei

Cover design by Umi Cavallo
Interior design by Masha Shubin

All rights reserved. No part of this book may be reproduced or transmitted in any form or by any means whatsoever, including photocopying, recording or by any information storage and retrieval system, without written permission from the publisher and/or author. Contact Inkwater Press at 6750 SW Franklin Street, Suite A, Portland, OR 97223-2542. 503.968.6777

www.inkwaterpress.com

ISBN-13 978-1-59299-425-0
ISBN-10 1-59299-425-3

Publisher: Inkwater Press

Printed in the U.S.A.
All paper is acid free and meets all ANSI standards for archival quality paper.

Contents

Foreword vii

Preface xiii

PART I: Formative Years 1
   1. Growing Up 3
   2. A U.S. Education 18
   3. From Salary Man to Entrepreneur 32
   4. Father's Forgotten Legacy 44

PART II: New Careers and a Family 51
   5. My First Venture 53
   6. On the Road to Banking 64
   7. Second Career in a Desert City 79
   8. Height of My Banking Career – From Europe
      to Asia 94
   9. The Big Transition 114
   10. My Private Equity Years 131
   11. Starting My Investment Advisory Business 151
   12. Building My Business – the Early Years 164
       Photos 183
   13. The Crisis Years in Asia 193
   14. Rising from the Abyss 209
   15. Coping with the U.S. Bear Market 224
   16. Return of the Bull Market in Asia 243
   17. Merger for the Future 263

PART III: Roots, Recreations, Reflections 279
    18. In Search of Family Roots..281
    19. My Life-long Hobbies 299
    20. Reflections...322
Postscript...339
List of Photographs..347
Index 349

Foreword
By Jesse Friedlander

子曰：知者不惑, 仁者不憂, 勇者不懼

孔子說：聰明人不受欺騙, 品德高尚的人
沒有憂慮, 勇敢的人無所畏懼

"A wise man is never cheated, a virtuous man is never worried, and a courageous man is never afraid."

-Confucius

It has been a pleasure and an honor to know Randy Kwei for almost two decades. Our friendship has enriched and broadened me in countless ways. So, I relish the privilege of offering a few observations to usher readers into his remarkable life story.

Randy Kwei reached seventy years of age a few years ago, but our 35 years' age gap never seems to matter when we are together. We first met through my grandfather Elliott Goldstein, who introduced us in Atlanta, Georgia, in 1994. We later began to play tennis during my occasional travels through Asia. Our sporadic encounters blossomed into a weekly routine following my relocation to Hong Kong in 2002. Our sporting camaraderie and illuminating post-match dinner discussions have become an invaluable part of my life. Any twinge of embarrassment at competing against someone so much older than me is overpowered by a sense of admiration towards my friend for whom age means little.

The way a man leads his life is a reflection of his character and Randy's book codifies this truth. Rather than presenting a self-gratifying list of achievements, this memoir – which clearly expresses Randy's distinctive philosophical view on life – is a genuine gift to others. Through his modest account, Randy reveals his numerous successes and occasional setbacks as his nomadic professional life takes him through three careers and four continents. He also describes the historical backdrops that supported and propelled him through life. Meanwhile, we experience with him the sweet taste of satisfying personal relationships formed through his roles as father, husband, friend, and benefactor. The phrase "I cannot" is not in Randy's vocabulary and this book shows how he accomplished great things while maintaining his characteristic quiet sense of confidence.

Randy invites us on an immigrant's journey traversing vast cultural differences and material realities. He also instructs us in the tectonic historical shifts of the late-20th-century; a China steeped in history, re-emerging from isolation and eager to reach its potential; and a United States that is wealthy and welcoming to new comers.

His story exemplifies the importance of both roots and wings. I am pleased he decided to share it with the world.

As Randy's no-frills, modest personal style has led him to leave out any self-promoting descriptions of himself, I want to add a few of my personal observations here so readers will have a better sense of who they are going to read about:

East Meets West 中西融合

Nobody I know embodies both the ancient values of the East and the modern ideals of the West more seamlessly than Randy. His family traditions and upbringing helped shape his world view. Grandfathers who served as mandarin scholars and public servants during China's dynastic era transmitted to him Confucian values. Growing up in pre-World War II Shanghai, a city that embraced Western culture and technology, Randy's early childhood was influenced by his father who had been educated in the United States and who had adopted many Western customs.

Randy's sojourn in the United States, including first-rate educations at a preparatory school, Yale, and Columbia, helped nurture in him a high degree of self-assuredness. He also developed an unselfconscious sense of individuality, playfulness and authenticity. Randy's career flourished in various management roles in technology and finance industries. He steadily rose through the ranks to senior positions and later founded his own firm. Buddhist practices helped cultivate in him acceptance, gratitude and detachment from personal desires along with freedom from the Asian preoccupation with face-saving and social status. What one finds in Randy is a successful business professional who radiates a refreshing openness to human relationships and the full richness of life.

A Gentleman 君子

I can think of no better characterization of Randy than as a gentleman in the finest meaning of the term – that is, a man who displays dignity and virtue, serves his community, cares for his family, values education and hard work, keeps his word, listens to others, helps the needy, and makes time for friends.

In recognition of his contributions to society, Randy recently received the "Outstanding Service Award" from the Yale Alumni Association for his long and dedicated service, including being a co-founder of the club, serving as the president in its early days, and acting as a trustee of New Asia College, which is affiliated with the Yale University.

Investor 投資家

Randy is a passionate investor who applies deep knowledge of the principles of finance, economics, political science, history, and behavioral theory to managing investment portfolios.

Randy travels tirelessly across Asia to assess and receive updates from corporate management. His stock-picking track record is enviable. Since its inception in 1994, Randy's fund has outperformed its benchmark MSCI Asia Pacific ex Japan by over 100% as of the end of 2008.

Equally noteworthy, Randy has remained loyal to his investment style even during periods of underperformance. He steadfastly focused on companies with strong management, quality earnings, free cash flow, and franchise value. In essence, Randy never looks for the "quick buck"; he follows the same investment philosophy based on the Graham and Dodd methodology favored by Warrant Buffet. This approach, grounded in reason and responsibility, is perfectly compatible with Randy's education, experience and character.

Consistent with his native prudence, he began to build up a large cash position in mid-2007 in anticipation of a sharp fall in global markets. Even more exemplary (and rare), he strongly discouraged clients from increasing their investments towards the end of the bull period. In an industry where some fund managers have been known to pursue fresh capital, even at the most inflated stage of a market bubble, Randy continually displays a rare combination of wisdom and integrity.

Family Man 一家之主

It is a pleasure to watch Randy in the role of husband and father. He demonstrates unfailing patience, devotion and respect for his wife Teresa, who leads a busy life shuttling between her own business and family matters in Hong Kong and New York.

Randy's approach to fatherhood is based on Chinese-style quiet support and unending dedication for his children, Kathy and Clarence. This is combined with American-rooted compassion, respect, and acceptance of their lifestyles and personal choices. A parent's tendency to fret over his children is genetic, but Randy's positive, philosophical view on life and the fact that he raised two extremely capable children have spared him from this burden.

I never saw Randy interact with his parents, but it is clear that the relationship with his father and connection to his heritage are profoundly important to him. After having visited his ancestral homeland in Sichuan Province, he recounted, with palpable joy, his experiences of reconnecting with distant cousins. He later helped one of them with the treatment of her cancer.

Friend 朋友

An interesting aspect of Randy's persona is the vast scope of his friendships. He has friends in business, government, the arts, alternative medicines, and science and from various countries and backgrounds. I would characterize Randy's guiding principles in relationships as generosity, acceptance, and loyalty.

Randy never imposes an arbitrary demarcation between business relationships and friendships. Many of his investors have become friends who travel with him and become acquainted with his family. He communicates sincere concern for his clients and their families' well-being. Often times, he lends a helping hand, including offering career-enhancing networking contacts to their children. There is never the slightest hint of selfishness for doing this; he genuinely enjoys helping others.

Final Comments

Randy's story, like his character, is straightforward and fact based. It didn't surprise me that his memoir is organized in a unique manner. He has divided his story between his work and his interests. Together, the two parts enable the reader to gain a full appreciation of his inspiring career and his endearing character.

I have enjoyed reading Randy's memoir. I am sure you will too.

Preface

"A man's reach should exceed his grasp, or what's a heaven for?"
— Robert Browning

Years ago, when my father was in his 80s, I often urged him to write about his life. I knew very little about his youth or his family. Further, he never had much interest in talking about all that he had done in one of the most tumultuous periods in Chinese history. I found his reticence especially sad since he had been a journalist who spent much of his life documenting the lives of others – but not his own.

I am writing my story so that future generations of my family will have some knowledge of where our family came from. My story is about the exciting but turbulent careers I have had, particularly my investment career in the financial markets of the past decade. Additionally, I hope to leave behind something meaningful and, perhaps, something useful to anyone who may happen to read this book.

I have read many biographies about people who have made a difference in the world. I am not one of them. Still, I think I have an unusual story to tell. It is rare to find someone who has had three careers, lived in several different cultures, and, on top of that, has had such good fortune in health, friends, and family.

Looking Back to Begin

"To look backward for a while is to refresh the eye, to restore it, and to render it the more fit for its prime function of looking forward."
　　　　　　　　– Margaret Fairless Barber, The Roadmender

Many years ago I read a quote from the French writer and philosopher Jean-Paul Sartre. His remark was about memory and perception, and that late in life we look back as if from the rear window of a fast-moving car: Our most recent experiences are a blur, while the images of our lives in the distant past come into sharp relief. As I began to write my memoir, the truth of Sartre's insight rang clear and true as I was taken back to my life as a boy growing up in a turbulent China; to life during the Japanese invasion of Shanghai; and to my family's escape to the British colony of Hong Kong from that great pulsating metropolis just before the Communists captured the city in 1949.

Fast forward with me to my 70th birthday. I got up at 6 a.m. I looked in the mirror and considered the signs of increased aging: thinner, graying hair; eyes now perched atop baggy folds; creases on my face. I had ringing in my ears, and my eyesight was slowly getting worse. On the positive side, my skin was relatively taut and healthy-looking and my posture erect. My cholesterol and hypertension were under control thanks to modern medicine. These days, I dreamed a lot but generally got sufficient sleep. For someone at 70, I suppose it's not a bad scorecard.

For this special day I chose to go to work as usual. In fact I have always worked on my birthdays. After putting on my tan trousers, a plain blue shirt, and a blue blazer, I had my usual breakfast – orange juice, hot oatmeal with soymilk, whole wheat toast, and a cup of hot tea, which is so typical in the average Chinese diet. I quickly scanned the *South China Morning Post* headlines before heading off to work.

Our apartment, located in Repulse Bay, Hong Kong, has a wonderful view over the South China Sea, the spectacle of which I never grow tired. I admired it again as I walked briskly downhill to catch the bus, acknowledging smiles and greetings from the guards, drivers, and two workers cleaning the gutters down the hill. I reminded myself to feel grateful for both being able to run my investment company and feeling excited about it at the same time.

Seventy years, and I've seen changes that boggle the mind. One such change is mobile technology. As I boarded the bus for Central, where my office is, I carried with me a BlackBerry device and one mobile phone equipped with FM radio.

It was a typical day at the office: a morning meeting with my staff on stock ideas and trading decisions, then a strategy meeting organized by JP Morgan, followed by a trustee meeting in the afternoon, and then dinner with my wife and daughter. After dinner, I worked on personal emails and made a call to a business prospect in the United States.

On this special day, I was in bed by 11 p.m. As I closed my eyes, I concentrated on my breathing with a few minutes of meditation. Focusing the mind is difficult, for the mind tends to wander. Buddha said the human mind is like a monkey, and I think he was right on the money.

I gave thanks for all the wonderful moments of the day and the blessings of my family and all the people in my life for whom I care. I contemplated death, too, and what it means. I am hopeful that when the moment comes, I will face it with calm and quiet anticipation, rather than with fear and anxiety.

About This Book

This book is a chronicle of my life's experiences. Because I have had such a long life and three distinct careers – first in computing, second in banking, and third in investing – the book is probably longer than one would normally expect from a memoir of a person like me. In addition, I have written several chapters that included my hobbies, a reflection on what I have learned in my life, and on my discovery of my family roots, a process that has been distinctly rewarding.

In fact, during the course of writing this book, I came upon surprising results in my attempt to trace my ancestry. Several years ago, my brother found a book that belonged to our parents. It was written a long time ago – and in classical Chinese, no less. Curious about its content, I asked a scholar in Fujian, China, to translate the book. To my surprise, it was written by my great-great-grandfather.

The Kwei family's history can be traced in official records all the way back to the Tang Dynasty (618–907). Several earlier records of my family have been found in the form of stone carvings. From these carvings, it was known that in the late Zhou Dynasty (1100 B.C. to 220 B.C.), a family member, who was a court scholar and teacher, was given the name of Kwei for the first time in the family's history. Previously, the family's name was "Ji" – the same family name of the Emperor of the Zhou Dynasty. The mystery remains whether this Ji was a member of the Emperor's family.

Of all my ancestors, I know most about Kwei Wen Hui. He was the father of the author who wrote the book my brother located. In that book, I found my great-great-grandfather's writing about his father. According to the book, this gentleman was a very prominent scholar and officer who served the Emperor in many important assignments. He was also a great scholar who wrote many books, all of which were later preserved in the Emperor's private library.

I don't know why my grandfather wound up in Sichuan. If my family's history is any guide, he probably left Hubei to go to Sichuan on the order of the Emperor. According to my findings, my grandfather was serving as the treasurer of the city of Kaixian when my father was born.

The Kweis were a mobile group of scholars, writers, and middle-level government officers. They were known for their honesty and integrity. Before the world had become integrated or "globalized," our family members were already moving around within China, depending on the prevailing political winds of fortune. Fortunately for me, my father made the biggest move of his life when he left China in 1949 for Hong Kong – then a British colony – and eventually settled in the United States in 1953. In many ways, my life reflects our family's tradition of mobility as well as the times I live in.

Before I begin my story, I wish to mention a few people who have made a big difference in my life's journey. My wife, Teresa, has supported me through the good times and the bad. I am grateful that my children, Kathy and Clarence, have given me so many years of pure joy. Without them, I would probably not be who I am today. I am thankful to my parents who gave birth to me in the first place, steered me to Yale for an extraordinary educational experience, and had the wisdom to let me work out my own problems in my own way.

Bob Stern financed my first business venture in Philadelphia in 1968. Ed Hoffman offered me a job to run the Citibank branch in Dubai in 1974 even though I didn't know the first thing about banking. Dick Bliss appointed me to be the Asian regional head for American Express Bank when I had only six years of banking experience. Dick later encouraged me to organize a private equity fund in 1998 though I had no background in that then infant investment industry in Asia.

I wish to thank all my investors in JK Asian Invest, LLP. They have been extremely patient and loyal through so many ups and downs in the market swings since 1994. I am grateful to Tom Chrystie, who made one of the first commitments in the current fund and has continued to be supportive; Bob Varn, who had the confidence to introduce me to his circle of influential friends in Atlanta; and Jamie Nuland and Guli Arshad in Boston, who decided early on to use our firm as the Asian investment manager for their clients. And, last but not least, I wish to mention Bela Chu, my highly capable and dedicated office manager and company administrator since 1994. Bela has dedicated many years of her career to assisting me with dedication, humor, compassion, cheerleading, insight and hard work.

This book is made possible only because I have had the support and assistance of friends and family. In particular, I wish to thank Patrick Caviness and Louisa Wah Hansen, both of whom spent weeks editing my manuscript. I wish to thank Jesse Friedlander, my young friend with whom I have had a long friendship, for writing the Foreword.

In writing this book, I primarily used materials from my diaries that I have kept for many long years. Where I needed additional materials, I used the Google search engine to locate the relevant information. If there are any factual errors in the book, they can be traced directly to the fact that I lacked a fact checker to validate my story. What I can state here is that I did not fabricate anything in this book. I wrote it as close to what I could accurately and correctly remember as possible.

As I reflect on the past 70 years, my life's journey seems to have embodied both a mission and a destiny. The mission, for me, is to keep striving for new knowledge, to solve new problems, and to reach new horizons. My destiny is to play a constructive role in bridging the divide between the East and the West while enjoying the fruits of the ongoing inevitable wave of globalization.

PART I

Formative Years

1

Growing Up

SHANGHAI, 1935 TO 1948

I was born on October 25, 1935, around 10 a.m. in Shanghai, China. Ten minutes later, my twin brother was born. My family name is "Kwei." In Chinese, Kwei is the name of both a flower and a kind of fish. It is a rare surname, and when I am introduced to another Chinese person, they almost always remark on the fact. Once I looked for my name in the Manhattan telephone directory. There were pages of Lees, Chens, and Wongs, but less than a dozen Kweis.

My parents named us Chen Chi (me) and Chen Ling (my brother). Chen (it is now spelled "Zheng") is a verb and means "to acquire." In Chinese mythology, Qilin (pronounced: chi ling) is a mythical beast similar to a dragon that represents power and strength. My parents split the two characters and gave me the first character as part of my name and the second character as part of my brother's name (the difference between the English spelling of our names and Qilin is due to the Pinyin system of romanizing Chinese words which is now standard). At the age of 15, we would also acquire English names, so that I became Randolph (Randy) and my brother became Thomas (Tom).

In the Chinese lunar calendar, 1935 was the Year of the Pig. Pigs are a symbol of prosperity in Chinese folklore. But at the time of my birth, the world was anything but prosperous. It was a time when the world trembled at the verge of an imminent war – the biggest and most horrible that human beings were yet to witness.

Despite being a battlefield of the Chinese Civil War, at the time of my birth, Shanghai was at an apogee of wealth and influence. Called the "Paris of the East," its style and energy during that period are legendary. Many Chinese of my father's generation used to look back at Shanghai in the 1930s with much nostalgia and pride. They lived well and were in touch with the Big World. My father was no exception. He was a successful lawyer and publisher. I guess that is why my brother and I felt a sense of unquestionable safety even though China was going through a tumultuous period and the world at large was suffering – from the Great Depression to the deprivations of the Jews in Nazi Germany.

Father (named Kwei Chung Shu) came from a long line of prominent scholars and mid-level government officials. Born in 1897 in a small village named Kaixian, Sichuan, into a wealthy family, Father often said that his family had the biggest house in the central square of the village. In the summer, theater troupes would go there to perform for the family and townspeople.

My paternal grandmother died early, so father grew up with a stepmother and her two daughters and two sons. Apparently, she gave him a tough time so that he did not have a very happy childhood. At the age of 11, he passed the scholar examination to go on to advanced education in Beijing.

Father often told us the story of how he traveled in a sedan chair, crossing several mountains before arriving at the capital. Once, during his long journey, he was confronted by bandits. In his storytelling, he would get excited about how his bravery was the main factor for surviving the attack and, presumably, keeping the money he had with him. There were no further details of this incident and how he reached Beijing. As things turned out, he never went back to his hometown.

Beijing was the capital of the Qing Dynasty. It was a time of great turmoil. Foreign powers were keen on dividing the country for commercial gains. After the failed Boxer Rebellion, the Chinese government had to make enormous reparation payments to foreign powers. The U.S. government decided, in lieu of cash, that the Chinese government should support selected students to receive a university education in the United States. My father was one of the first students who left China to be educated in the US.

He did not choose the popular San Francisco, where many Chinese migrant workers lived, but went to the University of Wisconsin instead. He enjoyed his years there and told me he worked in a dairy farm in one summer. After graduation, he enrolled in Columbia University's Graduate School of Journalism. By then, the world was engulfed in the First World War. Being a journalism graduate, he became one of the reporters representing *The New York Times* in covering the peace treaty of Paris between 1920 and 1922.

Although a brilliant career awaited him in New York, Father chose to move to Shanghai in the 1920s. There, he started the first English-language magazine in China, the *China Critic*, which became very well known in those days. A few years ago, I found a copy of the magazine on a website and bought it. The edition was dated January 16, 1936. The magazine, printed on high quality paper, was priced at 20 cents a copy, or US$7 a year. I paid US$25 for a copy 69 years later. On the cover were the titles of four featured articles: "Down with the Quacks," written by my father, who was also editor of the magazine; "As an Oversea Chinese Thinks," "Depression in Peiping," and "Is a Russo-Japanese Non-Aggression Pact Possible?" The inside front cover had four advertisements, three of which were for hotels, while the fourth was for the Shanghai Power Company, which pleaded "Protect your profits by protecting your workers eyes!"

The magazine only had 20 pages. My father had 14 contributing editors, including Lin Yutang – the famous writer in the

1930s who later designed the system that enabled students to find characters in a Chinese dictionary. In addition to editorials mainly written by my father, there were the two special articles cited on the cover. There was a book review and a "forum" contributed by a reader. The contents were all political topics of the day and the articles were well written and serious in tone. The last page of the magazine had a column of airline flight schedules. The back cover had a full-page ad taken by Wills' Three Castles Virginia Cigarettes.

I can imagine how the high quality of this magazine had built up Father's reputation in Shanghai in the 1930s. I would venture to guess that the magazine's circulation was not great, although the number of ads suggests it must have had a reasonable circulation among Western-educated, well-informed, and politically active scholars as well as business people in Shanghai and other cities.

Father's first marriage was to an American woman whom he met in the United States. Inter-racial marriages were extremely rare in those days. In that sense, he already showed that he was an unconventional soul. At that time, Japan had already occupied Manchuria and was clearly intent on taking over the rest of China. The Nationalists were fighting the Communists for control of the country. One can imagine how unstable and volatile the city was. Father was holding down a job and, at the same time, getting a law degree at the Suzhou University. He never explained to me why he decided to pursue another career path, but I suspect his decision was influenced by the opportunities he saw in the business world. Because of the dual business and scholastic commitments, he was probably frequently absent from home. It wouldn't be a surprise to anyone that his American wife decided to divorce him. They had by then a baby daughter, June, who would be my half-sister.

After receiving his law degree in 1928, my father opened his own law office. He practiced law during the day and worked on his magazine in the evening. His law practice flourished and, according to him, included most of the U.S. firms trying to penetrate China's market for their products and services. He befriended C. V. Starr, a young man from New York, who founded American International Assurance and later hired him as AIA's lawyer in China. They became very good friends and I remember Mr. Starr while growing up. AIA would later become the AIG Group, one of the largest insurance companies in the world.

In 1933, Father married Mother, Linda Lee, who was only twenty-one at the time. At thirty nine, Father was 18 years her senior. Mother was born into a prosperous family in Shanghai in 1914. Her father was an early cotton trader–turned–textile industrialist, whose factory was located in Changsha on the Yangtze River, in the province of Henan. He had three wives, and mother was the only daughter of his second wife. His first wife was a Japanese woman and he married the third wife when he was middle-aged.

Mother was a real beauty, as shown in her early pictures. She was taller than Father, being around 5 foot 3 inches – not short among women of that period.

I don't know my maternal grandmother because she passed away when I was an infant. At that time, Japanese troops were invading Shanghai and daily battles were going on. My grandmother was shopping downtown when the Chinese air force dropped bombs on the crowd in a mistaken effort to bomb Japanese ships in the city's harbor. She was hit with shrapnel and died in a hospital a few days later.

When my parents married in early 1934, it was perhaps the most successful period of my father's career. He had two jobs and was highly regarded in the city. They lived in the best neighborhood, in the French Section. But the good times did not last. Japan attacked the United States on December 7, 1941 and declared war on the Allies. Its troops marched into the foreign-occupied areas of Shanghai.

When I was born, Shanghai had already been carved up by the foreign powers into British, French, international, and local zones. Many prosperous Chinese families – including mine with some foreigners – lived in the French zone, along with some foreigners. Our home was in an apartment building at the corner of Petain Road where it intersected with Kao Un Road. The building had eight stories and was served by an elevator with an attendant on duty. There were two apartments per floor; ours was on the third floor.

Father worked long hours, and we rarely saw him. Mother had no need to work, so she spent her time visiting friends and relatives and taking care of her children. Our family had a faithful servant from Anhui, who stayed with us until we fled Shanghai in 1948. She did the cooking and cleaning. We had another helper who washed clothes and ran errands for everybody. After the Second World War, father bought a Studebaker and we had a driver who became my close companion.

My recollection of our home is that it was always clean. But still, there were constant sightings of insects. As a kid, I would catch and examine ants crawling on the windowsills and watch cockroaches slip out of hiding. During the summer months, the beds were draped with mosquito nets that hung from the ceiling and reached down to the bottom of our beds. I would lie on my bed and take pleasure in squeezing insects landing on the net to their untimely demise.

Mother used to buy live chickens and the cook would kill them on the balcony behind the kitchen. He would catch the bird, squeeze the neck below its wings, and then use the knife to slice its neck, with the blood dripping in a bowl. My brother and I would watch the act of slaughter with a mixed sense of excitement and dread. After the bird died, the smell of its plucked feathers would fill the kitchen. Later, the chicken would be boiled and cooked.

In my neighborhood, I remember a grocery store at the corner and several large, stately houses nearby on Kao Un Road. The streets were wide and tree-lined. My earliest memory is of walking with mother and my brother on Kao Un Road and admiring the willow trees in gardens alongside. Mother used to take us to a big public park on Petain Road, about 15 minutes away. She always reminded us that, prior to the Japanese occupation of Shanghai in 1937, there had been a sign in this park that read: "No Chinese or Dogs Permitted." Her voice would clearly show the humiliation shared by millions of Chinese under the Treaty Port system.

As a boy, I was excited whenever I rode in a rickshaw, a chair with wheels attached to two long poles joined by a bar in the front. On weekends, mother would take us shopping by rickshaw in the big department stores (two, namely Sincere and Wing On, are now established names in Hong Kong) in the central part of the city. The rickshaw coolie would lean on the horizontal bar in the front and run. Once the vehicle got going, I suppose it was not so hard to pull. Most of the coolies were lean and middle-aged. It is amazing that they could run for such a long time, even on hot summer days. Each sedan chair was wide enough for only one person. So, mother and one son would squeeze into the chair while the other son would sit on her lap. Whether or not it was legal to fit three people into one chair, I don't know. The coolie certainly had to pull harder but then, he probably got more pay.

Later on, when they became available, we would ride in rickshaw cycles. Instead of running, the driver would ride a tricycle with the passenger carriage resting on the two back wheels. On rainy days, the front of the carriage was covered by a thickly varnished canvas with a distinct odor. That odor and the sound of raindrops are still fresh on my mind.

When I was about four, my first memories of listening to recorded music were formed. At that time, we had a big RCA radio and record player standing on the floor of our living room. Back then, records were made out of shellac and were 12 inches in diameter. To play a record, one had to wind up the turntable. The playing arm was equipped with a sharp needle that tracked the record grooves. My parents had strictly forbidden us to play the records, but there was too much temptation for us not to do so when our parents were away.

We had only a few records of popular songs of the time. My parents kept both American and Chinese records. Bing Crosby was my favorite singer. In one of our experiments, we found that we could obtain sound by using tightly folded paper and keeping the paper edges in the record tracks. We had also cracked one record to see what the material was like. This incident brought a spanking even as we tried to say that it was an accident. That was one of the very few spankings we ever received. We considered ourselves lucky as physical punishment was a norm and frequent occurrence in other Chinese families.

In many ways, our family was westernized so that we had abandoned many traditional rituals. However, there was one ritual that we practiced throughout our childhood. This was to kneel down on our knees and touch the floor three times with our heads to honor our parents on special occasions. These occasions included my parents' birthdays, our birthdays, and New Year's Day.

Another sign my family was westernized could be found on our breakfast table. Instead of congee, the standard Chinese fare, we had toast with butter, milk, and scrambled eggs. This was supposed to be the reason why my brother and I both grew to a height of five feet ten inches. Other than breakfast, our diet was very much the Chinese style with four courses including soup and rice. I remember eating was always a pleasant experience, except during war years when food was rationed and we rarely had meat.

In December 1941, Japan bombed Pearl Harbor and declared war on the United States and other Western nations. We expected the Japanese to put Shanghai under military rule, including the French Section of the city. We were right, and they came to our building in early 1942. Fortunately, the soldiers took over only the first two floors of our apartment building, which meant that we did not have to move.

One day, the Japanese soldiers marched into the quadrangle of our apartment. My brother and I stared at them from our room, frightened by their fearsome demeanor. Their swords were drawn and they looked ferocious. After their arrival, the lift stopped working and we had to use the stairs to go in and out of the building. Every day, I passed the guards on duty on the lower floors with a sense of trepidation.

To our surprise, the soldiers never bothered us. Occasionally, they would even smile and make friendly overtures. I suppose there was no reason for them to be hostile to young children in the building. Their treatment of street children was entirely different, however. The soldiers would kick and chase away children who tried to scavenge rice from the bags that the military delivered to the front door of the apartment building. When I witnessed these scenes, I felt a deep sense of bitterness.

Growing up, I was not a particularly healthy child. I wonder if that had anything to do with the fact I weighed less than 4 pounds at birth. There was a period when I missed a lot of school. Still, I was a good student, just as my brother was, and we both scored high marks in all the subjects. Our parents engaged a tutor to teach us the Chinese classics, which we would study after school and on weekends. We read the Tang poets and had to memorize and recite the Confucius Analects. These exercises probably helped develop my retentive memory even if I no longer remember what I learned then.

One summer, my best friend, my twin brother and I decided to publish a weekly magazine. We wrote the articles and copied them by hand. We then sold the magazines to our parents and a few friends. Another fun thing we did was making planes with small pieces of wood and paper. But this must have been after the end of the Second World War because the parts were imported from the United States. The propeller was attached by a rubber band to the rear of the plane. We all marveled at our beautiful creations. But when we tried to fly the planes, they would soar momentarily and crash. At one time, our room was filled with these out-of-commission planes hanging down from the ceiling, like trophies of our innocent childhood.

The Second World War ended in the summer of 1945. By that time, we had moved from our apartment to the home of my maternal grandfather's third wife. We had to move because the Japanese installed an anti-aircraft battery on top of an apartment building near our own home. There were often air raids during which we had to stay in the hallway inside the apartment because it was supposed to be the safest place. Once, I rushed into the living room's window and saw warplanes flying past our building. Father would inform us of news that he heard over a shortwave radio he had hidden somewhere. When we heard that U.S. planes had firebombed Tokyo, we cheered at the news.

In the early summer of 1945, we knew hostilities would soon cease. The European War had ended few months earlier. Even so, afraid that the Americans would bomb Shanghai, Father decided to leave the city and move inland. I was told very little about what was going to happen to our family except that we would ultimately reach Chongqing, the wartime capital of the Nationalist government, 1,500 miles to the west.

Before we could leave for Chongqing, I got sick and our departure was postponed. When I had almost recovered, Father told us the news that the United States had dropped the first atomic bomb on Hiroshima. For days, he and Mother and everybody we met talked about this unbelievably devastating historical event. Father knew it would have profound consequences on the outcome of the war, and that there was no longer a need to take flight.

He was right. The Japanese surrendered in mid-August, less than a week after the atomic bombing of Nagasaki.. Before long, life got much better. No more rations. No more air raids. No more soldiers. At nine, I was old enough to know what was going on, and appreciate the difference between wartime and peace.

I could clearly see how dramatically Father's spirits lifted. He opened his law practice again and a steady stream of new clients signed up. He bought a new Studebaker and was very proud of it. Not long afterwards, he bought a piece of land west of the city, and hired an architect to design a vacation home for us. One day, we drove to the site and we all fell in love with it. The property included a stream and a groove of trees. The plot was big and in my excitement, I picked out a spot for my own private basketball court. After many years of hardship under Japanese rule, our family enjoyed the newfound sense of liberty. We were free from both colonial and Japanese rule. We were now living under Chinese authority, which we considered legitimate. And my family's fortune gradually improved.

At this time, my brother and I started to learn to play the harmonica and the accordion. Since then, music has become an important part of my life. Later when I was in high school, I was found to have "perfect pitch." I grew to love music of all kinds, from classical to folk to rock.

The prosperous days, unfortunately, didn't last long at all. In less than three years, Shanghai was confronted with a new crisis. Civil war between the Communists and Nationalists had resumed as soon as the Japanese left China. The government tried to maintain order, but with little success. Its attempts to control inflation met with total failure.

I was then in my first year of high school at the Shanghai Model High School, one of the best preparatory schools for boys. My parents were very proud that my brother and I got in. However, it was also a very political school. In the fall of 1947, the government's heavy-handed attempt to control civil unrest led to bloodshed. I remember sitting in a big hall listening to speeches by radical students and shouting in defiance. Emotions ran high as my brother and I joined the other students, marching together through the streets, singing and shouting slogans. Somehow, my parents found out what we were doing and had a servant fetch my brother and me from the demonstration. Soon afterwards, my parents decided to transfer us out of the school and put us in one that was less prestigious but undoubtedly less political.

By fall 1948, inflation was rampant, and paper money became virtually worthless. At that time my mother gave me paper money to pay my tuition. Instead of giving the money to the school, though, I gave it to another student who promised to double my money in three days. Little did I know that this would be the very first investment that I would ever make. In those days, the police would shoot people in the streets for engaging in currency speculation activities. Father, thinking it unpatriotic, steadfastly refused to convert his savings in Nationalist currency to gold or U.S. dollars. As a result, he lost virtually everything he had saved in those few years of good times.

In December 1948, the Communists were grouped across the Yangtze River outside of Nanjing. The United States made a final effort to draw up a peace treaty or ceasefire between the two sides. Almost everyone in Shanghai knew it would be fruitless. Father, who believed strongly in capitalism and democracy, was a staunch anti-Communist. He was warned to leave the country. So, one cold day in early December, Mother took my brother and me and boarded a flight to Hong Kong. We didn't fully understand the far-reaching consequences of this singular flight on our lives until much later.

Leaving Shanghai marked the end of my childhood. Despite hardship and perpetual unease during the Japanese occupation and the turbulent time during the final years of the Nationalist rule in China, I remember my childhood as being a happy one. Having a twin brother to play with and fight with was a blessing, and so was having loving parents who not only took pride in us and pampered us but also disciplined us with the best of intentions.

Hong Kong, 1948 to 1952

When we landed in Hong Kong in December 1948, I stepped out onto the tarmac with a great sense of relief and excitement. The weather was hot and sunny. We had to take off our heavy clothes. A good friend of Father greeted us and later took good care of us for the first few weeks after our arrival. He certainly made our transition to a completely different city far less traumatic than otherwise it would have been.

There were two things about Hong Kong that I noticed immediately. One was cars were driven on the left side of the road instead of the right. The second was I didn't understand a word of Cantonese.

Even after we moved to Hong Kong, there was hope that the Communists and the Nationalists would be able to strike a compromise, with Shanghai in the Nationalist camp. The United States had brokered a truce and Father returned to Shanghai to handle his business affairs. This he did until April 1949 when the truce broke down and war resumed. Father closed his law practice in Shanghai and dismissed the family servants. He would never set foot in China again. My parents became exiles in every sense of the word. They could not accept Hong Kong as their real home or view Hong Kong – a colony of Britain – as part of China.

Our financial circumstances deteriorated, as father, who was already over 50, had lost most of his life savings and had no job. At first, we lived in a single room, in a small flat that we shared with the landlord. The building was located on King's Road in North Point, in the eastern part of the Hong Kong Island. We shared a bathroom and kitchen with the landlord. One of the landlord's sons was mentally retarded, making this arrangement very difficult. Mother's elder stepbrother had also moved to Hong Kong and lived nearby. We would spend many hours together.

In May 1949, my brother and I were admitted to a high school named Chung Chi College on Kennedy Road in Wanchai. At this time, I went through a transformation at school, from being indifferent to wanting to excel. Perhaps, the change of family circumstances made me realize that life was not going to be easy from now on. Perhaps, I was just going through a maturing process to shed the old childish ways. In any case, I managed to move quickly to the top of my class. My essays were regularly featured in special citations. My brother and I were also recognized as very good harmonica players and regularly performed in duos at school functions. We were even periodically featured on a public radio program and that was very exciting. For sports, I took up soccer and boxing. I think I had a big advantage in boxing because of my height. It was a time when I was beginning to like being who I was.

By late 1949, the family's fortunes had begun to improve. Sally Aw, owner of the *Hong Kong Standard*, hired father as the English-language newspaper's editor-in-chief. Father found an apartment with two bedrooms in Happy Valley, an area surrounded by green rolling hills, at the bottom of which was a horse-racing course. It was evident that our hard times were over.

In September 1949, my brother and I were admitted to Wah Yan College, a Catholic high school run by the Jesuit priests. For the first time, all my classes were taught in English. Although not used to it in the beginning, I quickly adapted and even became a favorite of the English teacher. A few of my essays were published in the school papers. Although my brother and I did well, my parents wanted to make sure we would excel in the English language. So one summer, they hired a tutor, who assigned us to read selections from the *Reader's Digest*.

The political situation in Asia remained tense. In 1950, war broke out in Korea, and China moved towards war with the United States. Father decided to send us overseas for schooling, to protect our future as well as our safety. The Xavier Brothers at Wah Yan College introduced us to St. John's Preparatory School in Danvers, Massachusetts. In the summer of 1952, my brother and I were told that we would leave Hong Kong and study there. We were very excited about the prospect of going to the United States, which promised a future that could not be equaled in poor Hong Kong.

Before we left Hong Kong, we each had to apply for student visas. For that purpose, my father asked my brother and me to choose English names. I didn't object to the idea, because it reflected the custom of the period when Chinese people would adopt English names to be more accepted in the West. I chose Randolph because I admired Winston Churchill and his eldest son's name was Randolph. My brother chose Thomas. I quickly took on the nickname of Randy shortly after I reached the United States.

In September 1952, Tom and I sailed on the USS *President Wilson*, bound for San Francisco. I remember waving goodbye to my parents, who stood on the docks and waved back at us. That same evening we had a small farewell party with my uncle and his family before we went on board. The ship then sailed into the night, leaving Victoria Harbor far behind.

At the time I left Hong Kong, I knew some English, but I had never spoken it outside class. My father had two friends who would look after us when we got to the States. I had US$4,000 in my pocket, which, as things turned out, would be more or less the total sum of money I received from my parents to start my new life in a new country. I was not quite 16.

Looking back, Father's decision was consistent with our family's tradition of moving from one place to another in search of work and opportunities. The voyage that my brother and I took was the longest by far, but it reflected an early sign that the world was already becoming a global village.

2

A U.S. Education

The United States embraced my brother and me on the 19th day of our sea voyage onboard USS *President Wilson*. Having sailed endlessly on the Pacific Ocean, passing cities like Yokohama and Honolulu, we were thrilled to see the Golden Gate Bridge passing above us in its bright red color against the pale blue of the Pacific. Just about all the passengers – hundreds of them – were on deck to see this fantastic sight. All of a sudden we all forgot where we came from or what our social backgrounds were. It didn't seem to matter anymore. We were all unanimous in our thoughts, even if only for a split second, we were here to strike out upon a new life.

At the end of our sea voyage, another journey awaited us. A friend of my father met us at the pier, took us to a hotel, and fetched us the next morning to board a train to New York. I was fascinated by the sight of the Rockies as the train struggled slowly up one mountain slope and down another. We stopped in Chicago for half a day and then went straight, overnight, to Grand Central Station in New York City. The trip took three days, and in those three days, my brother and I had the first taste of the "Beautiful Country," or what the United States was known to us in Chinese. I kept my eyes open, absorbing all the sights and sounds of this strange land. Tom and I couldn't wait to share our impressions with our parents, so we spent some of our time on the train writing long, Chinese letters to them.

Finally, the train pulled into Grand Central Station, and a lawyer friend of my father greeted us with a big smile. He was very friendly and his first act of welcome was to take us to Radio City Music Hall to see a movie playing on the giant screen. Then, he drove us to St. John's Prep in Connecticut. I couldn't stop gazing at the New England scenery during the five-hour drive. It was like nothing I had ever seen – the landscaped highway, the houses, the vast expanse of space and the people. The trees were beginning to change colors and that, too, was a brand new experience, as trees back home were green all year round. I was excited about the new life unfolding right in front of me. At that age, I didn't know or contemplate how my life would be changed by coming to the United States and leaving my family and friends in Hong Kong behind.

For the next two years, St. John's would be my home. When I arrived, I could read and write some English, but I had no experience speaking English. I was shy and it took courage for me to communicate with my teachers and students in a foreign language. However, I was determined to overcome this handicap and fit in. I was at the age when social acceptance played an overwhelmingly important role in my self-esteem.

As I would quickly learn, I felt Americans and I were kindred souls. I felt very much at home in the boarding school as well as during visits to classmates' families. Many Chinese students in the United States kept far more to themselves and mixed less with Americans. In that sense, I was different. My parents had warned me about confronting prejudice in the States. There were minor incidents, yes, but none that ever really bothered me. In the years to come, I would become thoroughly American, according to my Chinese friends. But to Americans, I know that I retained enough Chinese traits not to be considered one of them.

School had started by the time we arrived on campus. We were admitted to the junior class and lived in the dorms. When we became seniors, my brother and I were allocated our own shared room. Even though there were two other Chinese boys in the same dorm, they kept their distance. Somehow this didn't bother me. My attention went to the Americans and I made several good friends – a boy who played trumpet in the band; one who took me out in his car on weekends; and another who introduced me to opera. All three frequently invited me to visit their homes nearby, which was how I became familiar with small-town American family life.

It was not long before I found that my rigorous training in the English language back in Hong Kong gave me many advantages over native speakers. Ironically, my knowledge of English grammar was probably the best in my class. Other students often asked me to read their papers and correct the grammar. I excelled in mathematics and physics as well. Soon, I became one of the top students in our class, and Tom was one of my chief competitors.

Of the various after-school activities I engaged in, I was most involved in music. I performed harmonica in concerts, scored music for the school band, and occasionally played drum. I knew I had a talent for music. Even without any formal musical training, I could read piano scores and intuitively understand harmonics. I would spend afternoons reading simple scores and trying to play the piano without a teacher's help.

While living in Hong Kong, I had met a brilliant harmonica player and teacher by the name of Chamber Huang. By now, he had immigrated to the States and was living with his wife in New York City. Often, my brother and I would visit him and he became my mentor. At one point, I was able to play a Vivaldi violin concerto on my harmonica.

My love of music, which Huang helped instill in me, would continue to grow in my college years and beyond as one of my life-long interests.

In late 1952, my parents decided to relocate to the United States, settling in New York City. I spent my first Christmas in the States with them at the Greystone Hotel on West 91st Street. Father, known in some circles as a staunch anti-Communist editor from Hong Kong, was able to find work giving lectures in colleges about the Communist threat across the country. He also had a syndicated column for a short time. Despite his popularity, the family's financial situation grew tight once again.

Like most teenagers, I was nearly completely self-centered. Therefore, I can't remember much that transpired between my parents and me during this period. I was, however, aware of the gradually growing cultural gap between us. I no longer read anything in Chinese. Over time, I began to write letters to my parents in English rather than Chinese, losing much of my ability to read or write my native language.

In 1953, my father found work in the Chinese Language Institute of Yale University, so my parents moved to New Haven. When I started thinking about college, I had a couple of discussions with father. My first instinct was to study music because I was good at it and very interested in the field. But he shot me down in no uncertain terms. He explained to me that there were limits to the career paths of Chinese in America, and almost every Chinese student went into engineering or sciences because it was easy to find jobs in those disciplines.

Persuaded, I decided to join the pack to study electrical engineering, although I wasn't certain if I would like it or be any good at it. I applied to the Massachusetts Institute of Technology, Yale, Princeton, and a couple of other colleges. Because I had friends at MIT, I had already decided to go there. Naturally I was extremely pleased when MIT accepted me. But in the end, I went to Yale because it offered me a scholarship. Given our financial circumstances, the choice was obvious. At the time, I was not sure going to Yale would be a great experience. In this, I was proven totally wrong.

Before I went to Yale in September of 1954, my brother and I had our first summer job, digging ditches at the Maryknoll Seminary in Ossining, New York. Landing that job was a small triumph because, in the previous summer, I could not find any work even after spending days making the rounds to midtown Manhattan employment agencies. I had been willing to work as a clerk or a busboy or as just about anything that would pay something. But I got turned down everywhere.

My labor work that summer was the first of a series of summer jobs for me over the next six years. I enjoyed the company of the student priests. They were young and came from different parts of the country and had very different backgrounds. They were friendly and never tried to talk religion to us. I learned to enjoy Italian spaghetti when I was invited by one gardener to meet his family one Sunday. It was the first time I experienced the Western noodle with tomato sauce and cheese. I didn't like cheese at the beginning but tried it out of courtesy. I think it must have been their warmth and their persuasive personalities that turned my taste buds to become ones that would love spaghetti.

Yale University, 1954 to 1958

My four years at Yale turned out to be the most exciting and the best years of my young life. In 1954, Yale was strictly a male institution. I enrolled as an Electrical Engineering major. Foreign students were not common on Yale's campuses back then. In the class of 1958, my brother and I were the only Chinese students. Besides us, there was a Korean boy who majored in philosophy.

During my freshman year, I lived at home and walked 20 minutes to classes every morning. I soon found myself struggling to keep up. Homework was a heavy load and it kept me up most evenings. My peers had come from top preparatory schools such as Andover and Exeter, and I knew I was playing in a different league. I found it particularly difficult to read Shakespeare. I couldn't keep up with chemistry. On the other hand,

I did well in physics and mathematics. And Music 101 was a course that I thoroughly enjoyed.

To avoid placing any financial burden to my father, I worked part-time jobs five days a week to supplement my scholarship and loan. Throughout my four years at Yale, I held a part-time job at the Yale Audio Studio, which I treasured immensely. My task there was to tape live sessions held in the studio as well as concerts in Woolsey Hall. Working with professional sound equipment was a great experience and it nurtured my interest in the reproduction of sound as a lifelong hobby. I was also sent to different lectures to operate the slide projectors. The professor would push a button and my job was to change the slides. It was an opportunity to listen to lectures on all kinds of subjects, from art to history to medicine.

In those days, every freshman had to meet a minimum level of physical competence. For example, one had to be able to do at least eight chin-ups, swim 50 yards, do 25 push-ups, and so on. I didn't know how to swim and had to learn the sport in the afternoons after classes. I made frequent trips to the Yale Gymnasium for about six months before I was able to pass all the tests. I tried out for soccer along with my brother and made the team. The team had two sets of twins that year. The other twins were David and Carl Lindskog, who would become our good friends in later years. I played goalie but was a second to a boy who was better than I. We practiced every afternoon and the physical conditioning did me a lot of good. I got to play some matches and was happy to play the last minutes in the final game against Harvard.

In social life, I used to go to many "mixers" or dances. Many of them were in New York City and I would take a train to get there. If the mixers were at Wellesley or Mount Holyoke or Smith or Vassar, I would hitchhike. I met many different types of people on these trips, and never felt unsafe. Often, it would take several rides to get to my destination, but I never had any trouble getting where I wanted to go.

Freshman year ended quickly. I thought I didn't do that well. Surprisingly, I was placed on the Dean's List. I managed to make it on the list all four years of college.

Summer came and it was time to look for a job again. Back in the 1950s, Chinese students on the East Coast typically worked as waiters or busboys in resorts in the Catskill Mountains in upstate New York. I didn't fancy doing that kind of work. I was looking for more exciting experiences. So I applied for work at the Westport Country Playhouse, which was famous for its plays and had a restaurant attached to it. I was too young to be a waiter, so I was accepted as a pantry helper. My most important job was to prepare clam chowder, New England style, every evening. This was actually the first time I had ever heard of this kind of soup. Initially I disliked it, but over the course of the summer, it became one of my favorites.

The most famous person I saw at the Playhouse was Marilyn Monroe. She came to the theater one evening with several friends and had dinner at the restaurant. She was the most glamorous person I had ever met and I realized why so many considered her to be a "heartthrob." Of course, I got to see many plays – and for free. Some were pre-Broadway tryouts but others were already popular Broadway shows. It was the first time I attended plays in the States and I thoroughly enjoyed them.

At the beginning of my sophomore year, I wanted to try out for the varsity soccer team. When I got to the field, I realized that my old teammates had put on at least 20 pounds during the summer. I definitely felt I was too small to play and dropped out. This turned out to be a blessing because I found a job as an usher at Woolsey Hall. Not only was I paid for taking patrons to their seats, but also got to hear the greatest music in the world – piano concerts by Arthur Rubinstein, violin performances by Jascha Heifetz and Nathan-Milstein, and the Boston Symphony under Charles Munch, to name but a few. Together with my work at the Audio Center, I spent most of my spare time in music and I was happy in both jobs.

During the school year, academic work became increasingly difficult, challenging, and competitive. Students in my major had to do laboratory work two afternoons per week. Life was intense, demanding and fun. The year ended quickly.

In summer 1956, I got a job working in the assembly plant of Square D Co., an electrical motor manufacturer in Cleveland. I stayed in a fraternity house and worked side-by-side with blue-collar workers putting huge electric motors together. It was mostly physical work and boring. But I needed a job and it was the only work I could find. Looking back, I think the experience gave me respect for factory workers. I also realized how their counterparts in Asia would not come anywhere close to what the American workers enjoyed in the way of living standards and material comforts. It was no wonder that people in the developing world would do anything they could to migrate to the States, even to take up jobs lower in rank than those they held back home.

That same summer, my parents moved back to New York City where my father was again associated with the American International Group, the insurance business established by C. V. Starr, his old client back in Shanghai. From 1956 until father returned to Asia in 1961, he acted as a legal advisor to the company, but pretty much had total freedom to do what he liked.

Going into our junior year in the fall of 1956, Tom and I were assigned to live in Timothy Dwight College, one of the residential colleges at the university. Living in the college dorm made a huge difference to my life at Yale. I was now truly part of the student body. Our roommate was Peter Blake, who later became editor-in-chief of the *Denver Post* and, for many years, was a columnist at the *Rocky Mountain News*.

My circle of friends expanded. I joined a Chinese fraternity called Rho Psi, for Chinese students in the United States. Rho Psi was one of the three major organizations of this type that attracted Chinese students to network with each other. It offered lots of social programs, including dances, picnics, and camping trips. It had a chapter in New York City, which meant that I went to New York a lot. In a typical trip, I would travel to the city in the morning, meet friends and go to a party, and then take a late night train from Grand Central and return to the college when the sun was rising.

The summer of 1957 was spent at Electro Voice, an audio equipment maker in Buchanan, Michigan. This was the first time I actually worked at a job I had wanted. I was assigned to work with an engineer on a microphone project. Then, I was assigned to work on a new product, which was an outdoor loudspeaker. I got to know the use of the acoustic anechoic chamber, simply a chamber with fiberglass wedges mounted in the interior to absorb echoes. The chamber is used by engineers to measure sound levels across the audio frequency spectrum of a product being tested. I got to know how loudspeakers were made. Before I left the job, I assembled a pair of the most advanced loudspeakers and shipped them to Yale. In those days, Electro Voice was a highly respected name, as its products included the best speakers in the business, using the famous Klipsch design to produce the deepest bass reproduction on the market.

Being a senior was an immensely satisfying experience. I added another economics course, and had also decided to go for a master's degree in business administration after graduation. At Woolsey Hall, I was promoted to head usher and had a number of ushers reporting to me. That fall, I listened to Adlai Stevenson make a campaign speech. I heard Billy Graham preaching gospels to a spellbound audience that was on its knees at the end. I heard all the concerts performed by the New Haven Symphony. During the spring of 1958, President Harry Truman was invited to be a fellow of Timothy Dwight. Every morning, he, along with his guards, would walk by my window on his morning stroll.

The weather was perfect for our graduation ceremony in early June, 1958. It was the biggest event in my life to date. I looked forward to it with immense pride and joy. How exciting it was to wear the gown and smoke the obligatory pipe after the ceremony! All the kids were in high spirits. My parents came up from New York. There were a number of lectures but I can't recall any words of great wisdom. The next morning, the local paper featured my brother and me as the pair of twins who received degrees. My parents were thrilled.

When I was a college student, I was treated more or less as a foreigner. I wasn't one of "them." But life has a way of leveling the playing field. Over the years, many of my classmates and I experienced the same kinds of trials and tribulations in work, relationships, and other priorities. Or, perhaps, we have all mellowed to the extent that we value each other simply because we have managed to survive the years behind us. So, when we met in class reunions every five years, I would feel a deep sense of comradeship with them, which has been very rewarding.

In college, I was more or less a typical young man. My life revolved around studies and some social activities. I had virtually no interest in politics and vaguely kept track of events that were unfolding in the world. The United States and the Soviet Union were engaged in a global struggle against each other. The Korean War had resulted in a stalemate and troubles had already started in Indochina. Being the son of an anti-Communist, I was vaguely in support of U.S. policies that espoused the so-called "domino theory" to stop Communism's expansionary moves. In the Middle East, conflicts were escalating between Arab states and the newly created state of Israel. Being ignorant of world politics, though, my youthful life was unperturbed by these developments. Instead, I was busy with my own little priorities in school and in organizing weekend activities, confident that life would hold lots of future opportunities for me. In those days, I was carefree and had no thoughts whatsoever of risks and setbacks.

Columbia University, 1958 to 1960

I made the decision to go to Columbia Graduate Business School at Columbia University because I wanted to live in New York City. There were many reasons for my choice, but the principal one had to do with my perception that New York was the most vibrant city in the nation, with unparalleled opportunities and challenges. I also chose Columbia because its teaching approach blended case studies with traditional lectures. I was determined to succeed in a career, even though it was still undefined.

Unlike the time I started college, I was by now feeling more comfortable with American life and less like a foreigner. I majored in marketing management at Columbia as I thought marketing was the most important function in a business. I was also drawn to finance, an interest that I would capitalize on much later in life.

I lived in John Jay Hall, in an extremely small room with another student. John Jay was located next to the journalism building, where my father used to study. It felt both strange and fascinating for me to spend my days in such proximity to my father's past. The typical MBA student had worked for a few years before going to the business school, but I wasn't one of them. While I did not get a scholarship this time, I decided not to work part-time during the school year but to try to earn enough during the summer to get me through the rest of the year.

In the first year, I was very active in extracurricular activities. I was the business manager for the school's newspaper. This meant I had to go out to obtain advertisements. There were days when I would walk along Broadway, Amsterdam, and Columbus Avenues and solicit ads from every store in the neighborhood. The results were mixed but I learned how difficult it was to be a salesman.

I also joined the Toastmasters, which would meet for lunch once a week. Each participant was given a topic two minutes before he had to speak and he had another two minutes to present his thoughts. Among the students was a young Japanese man who could barely speak English. I admired his self-confidence even though he stumbled in his delivery and obviously had difficulty adapting to the U.S. extemporaneous way of speech. Eventually, this awkward student became the chairman of a well-known Japanese multinational company that had plants in the States.

A major surprise came when, one day in spring 1959, I received a notice that I had been awarded the Rosewell C. McCrae Scholarship, given to the best all-around first-year student. This financial award helped me through the second year of my studies. The following semester, another surprise landed at my door: I received the McKinsey Scholar award. For that, I was invited to have lunch with a number of chief executive officers of major corporations. The CEOs of US Steel, General Motors, and Dupont were present at the lunch. They asked me about China and I felt surprisingly at my ease with the leaders of the U.S. industries. My picture was featured in *Business Week* a few months later.

I knew by then that I wanted to meld my passion for music with my knowledge of business. By now, I was an expert in audio recording and tape editing. So the next summer I found part-time work as a recording engineer at various summer camps. I was to record musical performances by the kids in the camps and sell the records to their parents. Since I was paid only by sales proceeds from records sold, I considered myself an entrepreneur. It was an added bonus that my name ended up on the record jacket. Thanks to this experience, when the fall semester began, I was able to persuade the Columbia University Chorus to allow me to record its music and produce the record for sale on campus.

I was hell-bent on pursuing a career in music recording. I wrote to all the record companies in the States for a job – RCA, Capitol Records, Columbia, and Verve. Unfortunately, I received no offers and virtually no replies from any of the companies. Meanwhile, I interviewed with several big corporations that regularly sent recruiters to campus, including IBM and Citibank. The year 1960 was a tough one for the job market. The fact that I was a foreign student who needed sponsorship for a work visa did not help my case at all.

In June 1960, I graduated from Columbia with an MBA degree and a smattering of knowledge in marketing and finance. I was 24, single and unattached, ready to join the work force and become a taxpayer. Although I knew that I was not the brightest in my class, I was confident that I could do reasonably well in life. The job search was not particularly smooth, but I got three offers, one of which came from IBM in Poughkeepsie, New York, where my brother Tom had been working since the previous year after graduating with a master's degree in electrical engineering from Yale. Tom wanted me to join him, and the idea was attractive. It didn't take long for me to make the choice, as computers were at the cutting edge of technology at that time and I already had experience working with computers in graduate school.

Looking back, I had come a long way from my birth in China during the late years of the Great Depression, and from my childhood under the shadow of the Second World War. As a teenager, I and my family escaped Communism and migrated to the United States. Since I turned 14, I had lived in three different countries (counting Hong Kong as part of the United Kingdom) but never stayed anywhere longer than four years in a row.

But now, the United States had become my home. I had decided to build my career in this country and eventually become a U.S. citizen. I had made good friends with Americans of my age. I no longer read Chinese books or newspapers. I had slowly but inexorably changed my "native tongue" from Chinese to English. This assimilation process had been a natural one. I was comfortable moving between Chinese and American circles.

Unlike the time when I graduated from college, I was more aware of and affected by world affairs. The world in 1960 was in the grips of the Cold War and on the verge of a nuclear war.

In those days, the picture of a nuclear mushroom cloud rising thunderously from Earth had been a regular visual on TV and in newsreels. The free world was faced with aggressive challenges by Communist states masterminded by the USSR. These geopolitical tensions played constantly in my mind and convinced me that the world was a dangerous place. Within the United States, the Civil Rights Movement was creating huge social tensions. I sided with the blacks in their struggle for dignity and equal opportunity. I couldn't vote yet but I was attracted to President Kennedy's youth and eloquence. But while there were many uncertainties in the world, the immediate need to make a living overwhelmed all my other concerns.

3

From Salary Man to Entrepreneur

I am sometimes amazed when using my Panasonic Toughbook notebook weighing a little over two pounds, at how fast the computing industry has developed since the day I entered IBM as a trainee in June 1960, almost 50 years ago. What I hold today in my hand is a machine that has vastly more computing and storage power than a whole room full of computers in 1960 could replicate. And yet, the essential guts of a computer today are not all that much different from the old vintage machines. What has brought the enormous improvement is attributable to revolutionary miniaturization of virtually every component that makes the machine work.

Since 1960, tremendous progress has been made to make every component lighter, faster, more reliable, and less power consuming. What's more, we are now using a computer not only to write, to make graphics, or to compute. We use computers today to connect ourselves to the rest of the world through the Internet, at the great speed of the broadband and through wireless convenience.

The new applications we have experienced in the last decade are truly the stuff dreams were made of. When I started working in the computing field, it was just at the threshold of a major takeoff. At that time, I was a wide-eyed young man just out of graduate school. When I arrived at Poughkeepsie, IBM's engineering and manufacturing center in upstate New York, the company was already a major multinational corporation. It was the biggest, most profitable manufacturer of computers, tape drives, disk drives, and application software in the world. The company had worldwide sales of US$1.8 billion and profits of US$205 million.

I quickly discovered what an exciting time it was to be in the computing world. The hulking vacuum tube computers had been replaced by transistor-based machines. Now, IBM was ready to build computers with semiconductor chips that would hugely expand processing speed and memory capacity. A new series known as the IBM System 360 was in the works. The system would revolutionize the way computers were made and used. It was the first so-called "third generation" computer system in the world. Today, the IBM System 360 is part of computer history, enshrined at the Museum of Science and Technology in Chicago.

As a trainee, I was placed in the product-planning department of the computing division's engineering group. There was no specific job definition. My assignment was to be involved in planning for new equipment being developed in the IBM laboratories. I was assigned to a market planning unit. Later, I learned the company had decided to hire three MBAs as an experiment to determine whether recent university graduates could be useful to a group dominated by seasoned veterans. I ended up being the experiment's only survivor. The other two MBAs were transferred to other work areas after just a few months.

I moved into a garden apartment with my brother Tom. The apartment was on the ground floor and had two bedrooms, a living and dining area, a bathroom, and a tiny kitchen. It was a very modest beginning. We bought the cheapest furniture we could find. I got a car loan to buy an inexpensive Morris Minor which I held onto for three years. My salary was US$6,500 a year – the most I'd ever been paid. From the very first month, I started giving my parents a share of my salary – beginning with US$50 per month.

I still remember my first day at work. It was June 6, 1960. At a welcoming seminar, Dr. Fred Brooks, the world-famous architect of the System 360 series and head of the Poughkeepsie laboratories, told us how lucky we were. "I want you to know that you will be working on some of the most interesting projects in the computing world. You should be glad that you are being paid to do this," he said. "In my opinion, people with the most boring jobs should be paid more than people with exciting work. The janitors of the world should earn far more than we engineers."

"Lucky" was the right word to describe how I felt that moment. I was fully aware I was surrounded by the giants of computing. Until the System 360 series came along, every computer model was designed independently. The breakthrough that Brooks made was to design a family of modular, compatible computers that used the same instruction set and could run the same software at different combinations of speed, capacity, and price. Unfortunately, he was not at IBM for long. Later, he became dean of the computing department at the University of North Carolina. His successor was Gene Amdahl, who later founded Amdahl, a maker of supercomputers.

My first boss was Bill English, a friendly young man who had spent several years in the field as a systems engineer. Unlike today, IBM provided ample support to its customers. The computing industry was in its infancy and IBM was ready and willing to do whatever it took to make its customers happy. This meant that its staff would help design applications, set up programs, and test and install computers on site. The specialists who did this work were called systems engineers. They supported the sales staff in the field. System engineers were familiar with their customers' needs. In fact, they frequently knew more about the customers' needs than the customers knew themselves.

I was not given any specific assignment for some time, but rather simply instructed to educate myself on computers and how they worked. However, reading books about computing was boring and paled next to working with real-life situations. After several months of relative inactivity, I decided to propose a marketing survey. To my delight, my boss readily accepted my idea.

The survey consisted of a series of questions seeking field input on how certain computing functionalities ought to be designed. Later, it was published for internal circulation. By then, Bill English had been transferred and I had a new boss. In fact, I had a whole series of bosses during my four years in Poughkeepsie.

IBM based its human resources strategy on the notion it would have sufficient depth at every management level to handle any contingency. A team of five engineers were in a cubicle next to mine but had nothing to do for at least six months. They spent their time playing cards. This cozy culture lasted many years until the 1990s when competition and innovation posed unprecedented challenges to this behemoth leader and turned it into a lean and mean organization like the rest of the pack in the industry.

On the personal front, I became a U.S. citizen in 1961. Uncle Sam's welcome was an enthusiastic one. I was almost drafted into the Army that same year. I was told to take a test in Hartford, considered a prelude to a one-way ticket to Army barracks. To my relief, IBM was able to obtain an exemption, arguing they needed me in the laboratory.

My brother Tom's life was moving full steam ahead. He married Amy Chen, a graduate of St. John's University in New York, and moved into his own apartment. So I got myself a new roommate, Jack Moreschi, a former classmate from Columbia University.

After working for two years in the IBM laboratory, I was feeling stuck in my career and thought about leaving. Suddenly, a major project landed on my lap. IBM had decided to develop a brand-new external storage device, code named MARS, which stood for Massive Archive Retrieval System. My job was to liaise with financial, production, and marketing departments to support a scheduled launch date some 18 months ahead. Jesse Aweida was in charge of the engineering team. A few years later, in 1968, Aweida would leave IBM to found Storage Technology, Inc., which for many years was immensely successful in making tape drives and selling them for 20 percent less than comparable IBM drives.

For those who are too young to know the state of technology in the 1960s, let me just explain a little about how a computer worked in those days. Input data were stored on specially made cards of stiff paper that had columns of holes punched by a card-punching machine. Reading card data into a computer was a slow and cumbersome process. Just carrying around boxes of sequentially ordered punched cards was physically demanding. And God help you if you every dropped a box. Output from the computer was printed by machines that were noisy and prone to problems. Data in the computer were stored on either tape drives or disk drives. The room that housed the computers had to be air-conditioned and built with raised floors to accommodate a mass of wires and cables underneath. Rows of cabinets stood along the walls for storing tapes and packs of disks. All this made working in a computing center a physically demanding job.

There are major differences between tapes and disks. With tapes, data have to be stored sequentially because tapes move in one direction. So, files on a tape have to be found by searching the entire length of the tape. Searches were very time consuming. Data stored on disks could be retrieved randomly or directly because the disk drive has an arm with recording heads that moves across the diameter of the disk looking for the appropriate data location. Retrieval and updating were much faster than tape but data transfer rate was slower and disk capacity was limited compared with that of a reel of tape. The choice depended on the needs of the application.

The objective of the MARS project was to develop a storage machine that had the capacity of a tape drive but the random access features of a disk drive. The concept was to use tape strips mounted around bins that rotated against its center. One drive could store up to 100 million bytes of data – a huge volume in those days. Corporations and government entities requiring immediate access to storage of vast data and rapid data access were the target users. Prime applications included airline reservation systems, insurance policy files, and social security data files. I was the sole project planner. The experience gave me extremely useful insights into managing major development projects for multinationals.

I worked on the MARS project for two years until 1964, charting every major step along the way from development to target product release. Each task had its own time horizon and a deadline. My job was to work with every department affected by the project and make sure key issues were addressed and resolved. I traveled to the IBM branch offices, presenting the project to skeptical sales people. Ultimately, the project was aborted, because management decided that it could not sell the machine at a profit. The lesson I learned was products that push the envelope technologically are commercially risky. Aweida, who had thrown himself into the MARS project, was deeply disappointed, as was I.

In July 1964, IBM formally launched its System 360 series of computers, which took the world by storm. The new product line was launched in 165 cities in 14 countries. Later, commentators would say that IBM had bet the kitchen sink on this product line. It had invested US$5 billion in the series at a time when its annual revenue was only around US$2 billion. The new system succeeded because it permitted customers to upgrade computer hardware without having to write new software. Even though the MARS project had gone by the wayside,

I felt my contributions were recognized and was proud of the company's achievement.

In 1965, after the MARS project was aborted, I was asked to join a team to work on another advanced project to develop the world's first time-sharing data processing system. This was the IBM Series 360, Model 67, which was called a "virtual memory computing system." The aim of the project was to develop a huge computer to service up to 300 terminal users simultaneously. A system of this magnitude had never been attempted before.

Conceptually, the new system would allow each terminal user to do his work as if he were the only user on the system. In reality, though, there would be many sharing the system simultaneously. Further, instead of having a limited amount of storage, the user would have "virtually" any amount of storage needed. To accomplish this, a new software architecture known as "virtual memory" (VM) was designed. VMs of different users would be swapped in and out of the physical memory space based on a decision algorithm held by the central processing unit. As development progressed, we discovered that the technical challenges were exceptionally daunting.

The software development work took place in a small one-story building in Mohansic, New York. Mohansic is an hour's drive from New York City, or halfway between New York and Poughkeepsie. I moved into a cottage on a farm nearby. Amid this semi-rural setting, I began to learn about the software by supporting the programmers. My job was to debug coding of the software operating system. To do this I needed to learn machine code and how to count in binary numbers or hexadecimal numbers. At one point, I was able to add faster in hexadecimals than in numerals. The work was extremely challenging because there were so many ways that things could go wrong in a program. What happened in one line of code on one page of programming could affect the operation of another line of code on a different page. Because different sections of a program were coded by different work units, identifying and fixing bugs was no simple task.

A year later, I was asked to head up a systems engineering team to install the Model 67 at Lincoln Laboratory, an important IBM client, outside of Cambridge, Massachusetts, the test site for the product. I moved to Boston and shared an apartment with Jack Moreschi, the same roommate I had in Poughkeepsie after my brother got married. Our apartment was at 120 Beacon Street, in the most desirable neighborhood in the city. The Charles River stretched out in front of our living room window, with Harvard University and the Massachusetts Institute of Technology on its north shore.

There were many problems associated with the Model 67 project. To begin with, the operating System was still under development and there were constant changes to be dealt with. Another big problem was the hardware, including the CPU and memory boxes, was brand new and wasn't completely stable. A third problem was that communication between software programmers in Mohansic and those of us in the front line were not always effective. Progress was extremely slow, to put it mildly. Often, it was one step forward and two steps back. The concept of virtual memory was extremely innovative (it would form the basis of today's operating system) but the implementation of such an advanced concept was bogged down because the hardware memory capacity was inadequate and the speed too slow.

After almost a year's effort by IBM and its customer, the project was aborted. Instead, Lincoln Laboratory settled on a far simpler operating system that had many limitations on the number of users and the type of work that could be undertaken. For the second time, I was involved in a project that did not achieve its objectives. I wondered if the old saying, "failure is the mother of success," would apply to my career.

Though the Model 67 project was ultimately aborted, it led to my quick promotion to the leader of a software engineering team for the medical industry in Boston. I assumed some managerial responsibilities in terms of liaising with clients and allocating work among the team members. Our team served all the major hospitals in the greater Boston area, our most important client being Massachusetts General Hospital. Over the next two years, I learned how hospitals worked, from nursing stations to payroll, billing, and even laboratory testing.

At that time, IBM was promoting the so-called teleprocessing system, which allowed remote terminals to feed data and to receive reports from a central processing unit located in a different physical location. This could be between floors of a building or between buildings using telephone lines. It was the beginning of an entirely new way of processing data, and response time sped up immensely. Finally, I felt I was in the forefront of something that was actually working!

By then, I was over 30. My brother had been married for three years. I was still single but had many new friends who were all young professionals and recent graduates from Harvard or MIT. They were mostly Chinese from Taiwan or Hong Kong and we struck a tight social circle. We had dancing and movie parties, and went to concerts and restaurants as well as some outdoor sports outings. Boston was a wonderful and exciting place for young people. The fact that two of the world's great universities were close together gave it a special vibrancy. I rate this time as the best period of my bachelorhood.

The world around me, however, was in deep turmoil. The United States was in the midst of two great historical movements. It had entered into the Vietnam War to contain the spread of Communism. At the same time, the government was struggling to respond to the escalating Civil Rights Movement. By 1967, the war efforts were going badly. The U.S. armed forces were having trouble defending themselves against the Vietcong and the growing presence of the North Vietnamese armed forces.

In domestic affairs, three leaders were assassinated in short order: President Kennedy, Martin Luther King, Jr., and Bobby

Kennedy. Protests by students and the general public against government policies were widespread. One day, I turned on the TV and saw South Boston burning. It dawned on me that in a not-too-distant part of the city where I lived, there was basically a civil war going on. It was completely surreal to me.

At the same time, American society was changing rapidly. Long hair, drugs, and rock and roll became forms of protest against old values and traditions that had held firm for many years. To me, the breakdown of these values was a disturbing development. It was clear that I would need to adapt to the new wave of social order, and I began to harbor doubts about the U.S. policy of containing Communism at all costs.

Looking back, I would say it was during the 1960's that the United States shifted from an age of innocence to an era with a new paradigm yet to be defined. Old morals and old values were challenged and thrown away. New values were being tested but by no means proven. The Vietnam War piled up so much debt the U.S. dollar would soon cease to serve as the anchor of a global system of fixed exchange rates. In 1973, when the dollar was finally allowed to float, it symbolized to me a world adrift.

Against this backdrop, my own small world appeared calm and untouched. I focused on excelling in work and expanding my social network. I paid off my debt to Yale and my first car loan. Over several years, I had saved sufficient funds to invest in the stock market. For much of the decade, markets had been rising and I made more money than I had anticipated. In short, I was quite happy with the progress I was making.

In 1967, I went to visit my parents, who had left New York six years earlier and now were living in Hong Kong. The city was experiencing the spillover effects of China's Great Proletarian Cultural Revolution. Because Hong Kong's water supply was from the mainland, the latter's authorities decided to "humiliate" the colonial government by strictly controlling the water supply to Hong Kong. As a result, water had to be rationed. Each family had access to water for just four hours every four days, a policy which led to every family installing big tanks for water storage.

During the two weeks I was in Hong Kong, I had to go to a friend's place for a shower every few days. I witnessed riots in the streets. Supposedly, the instigators had been paid by mainland authorities to create social disturbances. The tram cars were shielded to protect the drivers. One evening, while I was having a drink with a friend at the Foreign Correspondents' Club, then situated on the top floor of the Hilton Hotel in Central, I heard blasts of gunfire echoing from the streets below. Looking back, this period was perhaps the most traumatic for residents in Hong Kong, many of whom began to migrate to Canada and other foreign countries that would accept them as "refugees."

While the Vietnam War and civil right struggles were raging, the US stock market was advancing steadily beginning from mid 1962. As expected, the booming stock market spawned new entrepreneurs trying to make quick gains by going public with their businesses. In the late 1960s, ambitious employees were leaving IBM in droves. Jesse Aweida had left to start Storage Technology Inc.

I, too, was caught up in the spirit and wished to be my own boss. I contacted a former IBM colleague who had just left the company to set up a computer service company as a subsidiary of Mauchly Associates, a firm founded by John Mauchly, the legendary computer designer who created the famous Univac machine during the Second World War. The company, located in Montgomeryville, Pennsylvania, about an hour's drive north of Philadelphia, supplied software services to commercial clients.

The business venture I had in mind was to launch a programming service that would use programmers in Taiwan at a fraction of the cost to write the same program in the United

States. In those days, the term "outsourcing" had not yet been invented. It is probably safe to say that I was one of the first people to come up with such an idea. I thought the concept was feasible because I had managed projects at IBM in which design and specifications were done in one place – Mohansic, New York – and programming in another – San Jose, California. I had some ideas about how programs needed to be specified if the programmers were not sitting in the next room.

Luckily, I was introduced to Bob Stern, who became the owner of the company after Mr. Mauchly retired. I had written Bob a proposal about the business venture I had in mind. Surprisingly, he agreed to meet me to discuss my proposal in person. I drove to New York and met Stern in his suite at the Waldorf Astoria Hotel. A short man with penetrating eyes and a paunch, Bob smoked cigars incessantly. He was impatient and, as I would learn later, made decisions quickly and without much deliberation. This was the first time I went to someone seeking funding.

My sales pitch was that my innovative software development approach would help lower Mauchly's programming costs. It wasn't a long meeting. To my surprise and elation, Stern bought the idea. Later, I worked out the financing needs and decided to capitalize the new venture at US$500,000. I put in US$10,000 of my own money, and incorporated a new company, International Data Applications Inc. (INDA). I owned 80 percent of the company while Mauchly Associates owned the other 20 percent. Included in the deal was a provision that I would work in their office complex, and that Mauchly would charge my company a nominal fee for rent and secretarial support.

This was early 1968. The time was ripe for me to move on. At the age of 32, I resigned from IBM and became an entrepreneur.

4

Father's Forgotten Legacy

My line of work as an engineer seemed entirely different from my father's journalistic and legal careers. But our interests and skills had a rare chance to come together in collaboration during the time I was still working at IBM.

An introduction to my father's intellectual bent is helpful. I believe much of this trait is inherited from his forefathers. His scholarly interest had been recognized already when he launched a periodical in Shanghai called the *China Critic* in the late 1920s. It was the first English weekly in China, that published political views and analysis. Then, during the Second World War, he expressed his dismay living under Japanese occupation by choosing to retire from his work as a lawyer and a journalist. For four years, he spent his time reading and writing a series of poems. Later, after he escaped to Hong Kong as a refugee, he found work as an editor-in-chief, a position that permitted him to publish his views every day.

Father had a great mind and was a well-respected scholar in both Chinese and English. More importantly, he was a pioneer. This applied to the *China Critic*, as well as his invention developed in the early 1950s at Yale University, where he was hired as a China specialist. While at Yale and in the years that followed, Father focused much of his energy on creating a new and more efficient way of searching for and locating Chinese words in a dictionary and speeding up printing of Chinese words in books and newspapers.

The Chinese language is not alphabetic but comprised of more than 6,000 unique words. However, each word has one or more strokes that can be viewed as components. Some of these components are common among different words. Father's innovation was to come up with 53 unique Chinese components (or "elements" as he called them) that, in different combinations, would constitute the words in the entire Chinese language.

In his system, each Chinese word contained one to four of these "elements." He came up with a scheme that delineated the relationship of these elements with each other within the character. Another important principle of his system was that each element could be distinguished by its unique sound. He thought the phonetic character of these elements would make it easier for a student to remember the elements themselves. Each phonetic sound was represented by a combination of English letters. The user only needed to memorize 53 elements whose sounds were represented by English letters. Father had come to believe that he had developed a revolutionary system to help locate Chinese words more efficiently than ever before. Because the elements were represented by English letters, his system would permit Chinese characters to be transmitted via telex much like English alphabets. Finally, he recognized that the system could be adapted to make it possible for a computer to work with the Chinese language.

Father wrote a dictionary using his system. In the book, he explained that his own father, my grandfather, was a serious scholar who required him to read a difficult classical text daily and provide full explanation of it by the following morning. Father then had to constantly resort to looking up the meaning of unknown words in the traditional dictionary. He labored so hard that he thought there must be a better way of looking up a word. His early experience gave him the motivation but his interest didn't materialize until he had the time to pursue it at Yale.

He believed his system to be truly unique and it had great commercial value. He was always concerned that someone would steal his idea and publicize it before he was ready to announce it to the world. His major concern was not only to claim credit for his work but also to make a business out of it. This caution impeded his progress. In his view, the system was something that could not be protected by a patent unless it could be incorporated into a machine, such as a printer.

In 1960, Father accepted an offer to teach law at a university in Taipei. So, my parents left New York and moved to Taiwan. His move was motivated by the need to seek funding to build a Chinese printer that could use his system. However, father was not a good salesman and he failed to find any financial support. This failure, however, did not dissuade him from continuing his search for sponsorship. Indeed, I remember he was always full of confidence that his project would succeed and it would be an earth-shaking event.

Two years later, Father decided to move to Tokyo. He was already 68. He wrote me that he had a number of potential investors there who would back his project. Soon after he arrived in Tokyo, he solicited my help to design a machine that would facilitate encoding and decoding the Chinese characters, using the elements he had defined. Although I did not truly understand his system, I agreed to design and produce his machine. I could see that a system that effectively "romanized" the Chinese language could be used to transmit Chinese text more efficiently than the standard telegraph method. The latter was cumbersome, extremely labor intensive, and prone to errors.

In agreeing to work for him, I was stirred by his absolute conviction that his system would be a landmark invention. While I had my doubts, I was swept along with a sense of filial devotion and a desire to work on a project that could challenge my engineering skills. This project would be a diversion from working in a big, bureaucratic organization and it would give me an opportunity to lead its development. I know Father was very appreciative of my help.

For many months after working in the office, I spent every evening working on the engineering design to build this contraption. I had an IBM machinist do the machine work. Rain or shine, I would drive to his home to work with him on machining parts, assembling the components and so on. The fact Father was in Asia made communication between us difficult. In those days, long-distance telecommunication was not only inconvenient but also very expensive. I would send him pictures of the prototype by air mail in different stages of completion and ask for his comment. By and large, I had to improvise as I progressed. The machinist who helped me also volunteered his service for reasons that were not clear to me.

The basic system I came up with consisted of a big vertical and hollow metallic cylinder that could be moved up or down and swiveled on its central axis. Mounted on the face of the cylinder were two very large sheets of Kodak paper with about 6,000 words each. One sheet was mounted on the front side of the cylinder facing the operator. Another sheet was mounted on the opposite side of the cylinder. A camera with a film roll was fixed on the opposite side of the cylinder facing the second sheet. The idea was that when the operator located the word, its replica on the other side of the machine would be photographed by the camera. To capture the word on film, the operator simply pushed a button in front of him.

After about a year's work, I thought we had developed a workable prototype. I was very proud to have helped Father in what he considered to be his lifetime accomplishment. He had high hopes that this would be a big commercial success. I shipped the unit to Father, who had returned to Hong Kong by then, having found no financial support in Japan.

Father used the machine to demonstrate his system to the press and to some people who appeared interested in this new approach to Chinese character retrieval and transmission. He had apparently convinced the Chinese University of Hong Kong to help him publish a book containing a dictionary using his system. He also hired an assistant, a young woman, to learn to use his system by memorizing the 53 elements and the ways to use these elements in combination. Pretty soon, he thought he was ready for a public demonstration.

The press was invited to see the demonstration – Father later mailed me some of the reviews from local newspapers. Unfortunately, the reception, contrary to his expectation, was muted. After many more months of fruitless pursuits among scholars, newspaper editors in Hong Kong and potential investors – including a U.S. maker of printing press, Mergenthaler – Father finally gave up on the entire project. He was around 70 by then. Although the failure must have been a big blow to his ego and his conviction of the merits of his invention, Father never revealed any bitterness. In this, he showed remarkable resilience and an endearing sense of optimism that things would work out in the end.

After he abandoned his dictionary project, Father turned his interest to newspaper work. In this, his interest in politics and global affairs was a reflection of the family tradition. After all, his great-grandfather was an important minister in Hubei and was involved in a number of critical political developments in China during the Qing Dynasty.

Unlike some of my family's ancestors, Father never entered politics. Nevertheless, he was very interested in commenting on current political affairs. He was very good at writing opinion pieces about events around the world that caught his attention. It is too bad that he never had an opportunity to be in a position to carry out his ideas.

Father enjoyed his work right up to the day he died in April 1987. This too reflected the tradition of the family. I now know that my great-great-grandfather never retired even though his friends had urged him to do so. I don't know about my grandfather's case, as my father never spoke about him. I suspect that, if facts could be dug up, they would show he never retired either. As I write this book, I realize that it should not be of any surprise to my family that I have no intention of retiring from my work.

PART II

New Careers and a Family

5

My First Venture

Mauchly Associates was located in a nondescript industrial park occupied by a number of small industrial enterprises. The company had its own one-story building with a very large computer machine room in the middle of the premises. A number of disparate startups recently funded by Stern were located inside the building.

Coming from IBM, where there was a protocol for everything, including ordering pencils, I found the new environment quite disorganized. Stern was swamped by the needs of these incubator projects. Still, he continued to spend time looking for new ideas.

For the first few months in 1968, I tried offering my services of "outsourcing" computer programming to Taiwan to the colleagues working in the same building. Although the idea of achieving substantial cost savings through this should have been very attractive, my proposal met continual resistance. The concept was revolutionary in that it had not been done by others in the industry. On top of all the skepticisms typically levied at any startup projects, I faced the reality that each of my sister companies was building its own business "empire" and, therefore, had no interest to subcontract programming work to me.

While I focused on organizing my own little company, Stern would often ask me to meet with his other startups as his informal advisor. We frequently held evening meetings after dinner. In fact, I found myself working basically seven days a week, at least 12 hours a day. My workaholic habit must have been developed in this period of my career.

Shortly after I joined the group, Mauchly Associates became a subsidiary of a New York Stock Exchange–listed company named Scientific Resources Inc. (SRI). SRI was located in Philadelphia and run by Tom Fleming, a boisterous real estate developer. SRI had been developing real estate projects in Florida, which, of course, had nothing to do with computing. It was the mark of the time that computing was deemed to be the ticket to enormous profits and relentless growth with no end in sight. I don't know why Stern decided to have his company acquired by SRI. My guess is that he thought an NYSE company might give him better access to capital. At SRI, Fleming probably thought that, with Mauchly, its stock would attract a much higher valuation than that of a mundane real estate company. This was 1969, when technology was the biggest craze on Wall Street. Unfortunately, Fleming's timing could not have been worse. The computer industry was actually heading into the tail end of a speculative boom. The good times would prove to be short-lived.

Before I resigned from IBM, I had found a partner named Charles Wan, who was working as a programmer in Boston. He was born in Taiwan and his family had good business connections there. Charles was an optimistic person and he was interested in my business concept. He readily agreed to set up an office for my company in Taipei, the main commercial city on the island. Soon after he arrived in Taiwan, he persuaded the China Data Processing Center (CDPC), a government-owned computing center, to enter into a joint venture with us.

In the Taiwan deal, CDPC would provide 50 percent of the capital in exchange for 50 percent of the venture. This was a sound arrangement because it gave us access to CDPC's company facilities at a discount to commercial rates. Wan had also screened a number of candidates for programming work and he wanted me to make the final decision. So, in the fall of 1968, I went to Taipei to formalize the joint venture and to agree on staffing needs. Even though I had no success in lining up contracts at Mauchly, I was optimistic we would obtain work elsewhere and decided to go ahead to commit to the joint venture in Taiwan.

Taiwan had a poor economy at that time, but the government had the foresight to set up a special export-processing zone in Kaohsiung, a port in the south, to serve as a magnet for foreign investment and trade. During my visits to Taipei, I stayed at the Ambassador Hotel, which was among the best in town but would not rate more than three stars in the United States.

Most Taiwanese were still riding bicycles. Taxis were filthy and foul and the air hung heavy with pollution. Businessmen entertained each other lavishly with banquets of many courses, and whiskey flowed freely. Most dinners ended up with guests half or wholly drunk. Howell Chou, head of CDPC, took me out almost every night and I had to endure the drinking sessions as a matter of course.

I interviewed the candidates and looked for a suitable office space with Wan. Eventually, Wan found a floor in a residential building and we hired three programmers and a secretary. It was a bold move since the company had no actual business. It was clear both Wan and Chou expected me to quickly get a few customers or they would lose face with their colleagues and in social circles. Chou told me: "We are not looking for too much business and I am sure you will find it in the United States. After all, it is a big country." I knew I had much work to do.

Some of my friends in Boston had by now returned to Taipei. One was working for RCA. Another had joined a law firm. Over the years, both would help me navigate my way through Taiwan's business maze. The impression I had then was that the state of computing in Taiwan was very primitive and leagues behind what comparable businesses had accomplished in the

States. More importantly, it was evident that offering third-party programming services to Taiwanese enterprises was going to be a real uphill battle.

Back in Montgomeryville, after a three week stay in Asia, I decided I needed a new strategy if I were to provide work for the joint venture in Taiwan and to inject INDA with some momentum. I came up with the idea of developing a proprietary software package for a specific application that could be sold to many users. This was a gutsy move because the concept of using a pre-programmed software package was not well accepted then. In those days, hardware vendors like IBM were offering standard application packages for things like payroll and accounts receivables made a new business plan and strategy and presented it to Stern and Fleming, who quickly accepted it. As it turned out, the stock market was entering a bear phase. SRC's stock price soon slumped and most of Stern's startups were unprofitable. Real estate in Florida was overbuilt. Sales were slow. The strategy of diversification into computing didn't pay off because Stern kept seeding incubators that, collectively, were major cash drainers.

In mid-1969, Stern hired an executive from GE Computer Services, who claimed that he could land significant new contracts from General Electric. Soon, the Montgomeryville office was teeming with GE people, who were very different in chemistry and culture from the startup gang. If things had been chaotic before this move, the new people made the scene even worse. Business plans were drawn and thrown out in a matter of days. Often, preserving an executive's ego was more important than making a rational decision. While the ship was sinking, the focus became one of fighting for turf rather than looking for outside business. Barring a miracle, things were going downhill.

To follow through with my business plan, I hired Tom Malone, a big, tall Irishman, who was known to Charles Wan. I gave him 20 percent of the company in the form of options and profit sharing and set up an office for him on Route 128 in

Reading, Massachusetts. In his previous job, Tom had been in charge of developing a gift processing system for colleges and universities. I hired him because I thought he could develop another one for us and we could sell the package to colleges and universities. There was only one competitor in this niche market. We thought it would not be difficult to get a slice of the market by pricing our services cheaper than our competition. Since our package was being programmed in Taiwan, we definitely had the cost advantage.

While Tom went about developing the new software, I started writing to and calling schools, making countless trips to sell our new software product. Some potential customers turned me down flat. Others kept me in a limbo for months. Meanwhile, software development in Taiwan progressed smoothly and the package was more or less finished in about six months. In countless marketing meetings around the United States, I woke up to the unpleasant reality that clients were wary of using software that was not programmed in the States. Outsourcing wasn't known in those days. The marketplace was simply not ready for this novel concept.

Eventually, I got one order from George Washington University. In late 1969, I sent our programming manager from Taiwan to the client's site to install the system in our first customer site. The installation worked well and the university was happy with the result. The contract boosted my spirits and I doubled efforts to land a second client. The closest potential second customer was Fairleigh Dickinson University in New Jersey.

By the following year, both Howell and Charles were getting anxious about the lack of new business, so I made another trip to Taiwan. I had already asked Charles to solicit possible programming work among companies in the city. Unfortunately, the market was not ready for outsourcing. During my trips to Taipei, I had been introduced to an American businessman named Joe Bersten, who ran a software company in Tokyo. Hitachi was his main customer. He was intrigued by the idea of outsourcing. I thought he might ask us to work on some projects for his clients.

Despite the stresses of my work life, in April 1970 I decided to marry Teresa Wong, a graduate student in landscape architecture at Harvard University. We had met a year earlier in a typical Chinese student party. In those days, young Chinese from universities often organized dances on weekends and invited friends and their friends to spend the evenings together. This was a very popular way for a boy to meet a girl.

We were married in a chapel within the vast St. Patrick's Cathedral on Fifth Avenue in midtown Manhattan, New York. Afterwards, we had a garden reception with a small group of friends in Katharine Hepburn's home on the East Side. The entire affair on that sunny day was simple and elegant. The next day we boarded the then revolutionary Boeing 747 jet plane on a flight to Tokyo for our honeymoon.

After a few days in Tokyo, we flew to Taiwan to attend meetings and sightseeing. I brought my wife to a few meetings and was pleasantly surprised to hear her pitching the merits of our services. I should have recognized her business acumen then but didn't. We then took off a few days to visit Tao Yuan and its surrounding mountain area before returning to the States.

With no new contract and cash running low, I tried to get "second round" financing from outside sources. Through my limited contacts in the financial world, largely introduced by brokers I had used in stock market investments, I met a few investment bankers. Unfortunately, my attempt to raise new capital was ill-timed. The U.S. economy was going through a recession. In fact, the stock market crashed in 1969 and the technology bubble had burst.

SRC was hurting – not just because Mauchly was bleeding cash but also because real estate sales in Florida continued to decline. SRC went into bankruptcy proceedings in late 1970. This had an immediate and disastrous effect on my business. I had already found, when we were working on the George

Washington University contract, that banks were not interested in financing software receivables. Without Mauchly's financing, my company's working capital instantly dried up. In bankruptcy court, I bought back the INDA shares held by Mauchly for one dollar.

I knew I had to come up with Plan B quickly as the prospect of turning INDA to profitability was distinctly unpromising. I started looking for a job in earnest, and began perusing employment ads. My wife had transferred her studies from Harvard to the University of Pennsylvania. I closed the office in Reading and let Tom Malone go. Even as my cash flow situation was very tight, I supported the Taiwan office out of my savings, but the situation was clearly not sustainable.

It was hard finding a job. At 35, my experience in the computing industry had been in planning and marketing rather than on the technical side. There was a recession going on and small software companies were folding. A lot of people in our business were out of work and looking for jobs. When it rains, it pours, so goes the old saying. I must have sent close to 100 letters in a span of four months.

Suddenly, Bersten, the fellow from Tokyo, showed some interest in our software package that could be adapted to a variety of applications, including accounts receivable. We negotiated through the rest of 1970 and into the summer of 1971. Eventually, I sold him my company for a nominal sum, while he assumed some of my debts in Taiwan. The most positive thing I could say about my venture was that INDA didn't go into bankruptcy when I turned the reins over to another investor.

So my first experience as an entrepreneur came to an unsuccessful end. I blamed the failure on a combination of flawed strategy and a backer who did not deliver on our original agreement. In the beginning, I was so eager to run my own business I ignored messages from potential customers that the concept of outsourcing did not appeal to them. Even so, three years of building a new business and living on the edge of imminent failure had given me important insights into the business world and especially into the minds of investors.

I learned that, outside the structured environment of a major corporation like IBM, the business world is typically chaotic, opportunistic, and full of unknown risks for an entrepreneur. The most important lesson I learned was about myself - I began to know myself better than ever before.

I knew I was a risk taker and I could take failure in stride. I knew the entrepreneurial world was exciting and well suited to my way of thinking and my aspirations. I knew I would, one day, try my luck again.

I should add that my corporate failure was not unique. The biggest names in the computing world in the 1960s are now forgotten – companies such as Sperry Rand, which sold the original Univac computers, NCR, Burroughs, Honeywell, DEC, and CDC. The only company that still exists is Honeywell, without its computer business.

The 1960s saw a number of successful Chinese entrepreneurs in the computing field. A few years before I launched my company, Charles Wang started Computer Associates, now a global software company. An Wang started Wang Laboratories, which became a leader in the remote computing world. David Lee, who developed the daisy wheel printer, was able to attract venture capital money out of Silicon Valley and made a fortune. Outside the computing world, Peter Huang, chief executive of City Investing, was an exceptional talent. He made a good fortune by restructuring the company, spinning off assets, and eventually winding it down and returning money to its shareholders.

After months of job search, I finally got an offer from RCA in the fall of 1970. RCA was the largest consumer electronics company in the world at that time and had its own computer division. Back in the mid-1960s, Bob Sarnoff, its chief executive officer, had decided to set up a computer business to challenge IBM. By the time I was recruited, the computer business had been struggling for some years. At RCA, I worked for a senior officer in the Corporate Staff unit located in the upper reaches of the famed Rockefeller Center in New York. Our office occupied half of an entire floor and I had an office and the title of vice president. The work consisted of conducting research studies for my boss, Al Johnson, mainly in analyzing performance figures from the RCA Computer Division.

RCA's computer business was hemorrhaging cash and making losses. No matter what management tried to do, the division did not have the scale and the financial commitment to compete against IBM on a broad front. It was unable to come up with either a technological breakthrough or a niche strategy that would challenge the market leader. The only solution, in the eyes of the top management, was to change the division head. But in the eyes of the staff executives at Rockefeller Center, the only solution was to cut costs. As one could readily surmise, battles were fought between the two groups, with little progress to show for the efforts.

I soon found that I was not cut out to be a staff person. In the United States, the line personnel of major corporations make decisions and implement them. Staff personnel make recommendations and act as an advisory body to the line executive who is in charge of the unit. Staff members are instinctively distrusted by line personnel. At RCA, the line managers in the computer division were understandably defensive if not downright hostile to our staff group. Even worse, I found our group of five highly paid professionals added little value to the problem-solving process. We spent hours working with one another to improve the level of analysis or presentation format. We spent more hours making elaborate presentations to top management. The approach was expensive. While we debated, analyzed, and nitpicked, the computing division's prospects were dimming by the day.

While at RCA, I managed to save enough money to make a down payment on a house in New Rochelle, a suburb of New York City. New Rochelle was not the most desirable suburb but it had roomy old houses that we liked. Teresa found an old, elegant stucco house on a quiet street with a big backyard, and with a large apple tree in front. The house had two stories with three bedrooms upstairs, and a living room, dining room, and a big kitchen on the ground floor. It also had a big attic and an even bigger basement. We bought the house in May 1971 and I became a commuter, taking a bus to the train station every day, while my wife picked me up at the station every evening.

Life in the suburb had its distinct flavor. Of course, being married carried its own pleasures and responsibilities. We made friends with all the neighbors who were in a similar age group and career positions. All of them, in fact, had young children. I learned that keeping up with the little problems in a big old house drained almost all of my spare time on weekends. Nevertheless, I was proud to be a homeowner. Soon after we settled down, my wife became pregnant. We were very excited about the prospect of becoming parents and spent a lot of time preparing for the birth of our first baby.

Just when it seemed like we'd be raising a family in New York's leafy suburbs, an offer from Citibank came along. I had had discussions with the bank while looking for funding for INDA. Nothing came out of the funding project but the person I met there appeared interested in my computing background. Now, the bank thought I could play a role in their data processing plan for Asia.

In the fall of 1971, Dick Gooden, a young Citibanker, was transferred to Hong Kong to head up Citibank's new strategy of expanding its data processing services in the Asian region. He needed someone with a background in computing and with some business experience. According to Dick, Citibank's data processing service subsidiary was losing money in Hong Kong. My marching order was to turn the business into a profit-making one and explore other opportunities in the Asian region.

My wife and I discussed the offer, and initially, we were reluctant to accept it. We had made friends with our neighbors and liked them a lot. Additionally, we had put a lot of effort into making a number of home improvements. Moving to Hong Kong meant we had to abandon our new lifestyle, rent out the house, and move before the baby was born. Gooden was set to leave for Hong Kong in early 1972 and needed an answer before then. He seemed to have no other candidate in mind, which was not surprising because the financial package was not very attractive.

I am not sure what tipped the scale in favor of the move. Perhaps because both my wife and I had spent early teenage years in Hong Kong, we were intrigued by the idea of living there as adults. Perhaps, it was because I wanted to live near my parents. I wanted to have a line job again and it was obvious that it would not happen at RCA. In March 1972, I resigned from the company. We had to move quickly because the baby was due in May.

What I did not foresee was that the move from New York to Hong Kong would lead to a decade during which I became a modern nomad, traveling around the world and living on several continents. To me, this would be an exciting time, a time of discovery and challenges. For my family, it was a time of stress, uncertainty, and unsettledness. We led the life of neither a typical American family nor a typical Chinese family. The consequences are still working their way through our lives today.

6

On the Road to Banking

Citibank was a highly successful global bank headquartered in a gleaming Park Avenue skyscraper. It had branches in all the major cities around the world and was one of the earliest foreign banks to have a presence in Hong Kong. Tom McQueeney, a pleasant, ambitious, and articulate banker in his mid-thirties, was the branch manager there.

McQueeney had embraced the bank's prevailing corporate strategy of creating "synergistic" business activities. At the branch level, that meant managers were to develop businesses that generated fee income rather than net interest income and did not use the bank's balance sheet resources. As a result, Citibank in Hong Kong had a travel service business that grew out of its internal travel service department. It had an equity interest in the Far East Bank, a small local bank that did consumer mortgage business. It also had an insurance agency.

The Citibank computing center was located in Asian House, an older office building on Hennessey Road in Wanchai. Dick Gooden, the young Citibanker to whom I was to report, had a small staff, which occupied an office next to the computer center. There was plenty of space but no one had an individual cubicle. The building was old and the maintenance shoddy. Still, I was very excited. I was working and living in Hong Kong, the city that had become home to my parents since 1949.

Because our first child was due soon after our arrival, the bank quickly located a suitable apartment for us in the Mid Levels, close to Central, the main business district. The apartment had two bedrooms, a living and dining area, and a big kitchen that also served as a place for laundry. The best part of this apartment was a balcony overlooking the fabulous Victoria Harbor. Because it was right next to the Peak Tram line, I could take the tram up and down the steep hill to and from my office. My parents were delighted I had returned and could visit them often, especially with their first grandchild soon arriving.

Like many multinationals, Citibank allowed its expatriate staff, or "International Staff" (IS), certain privileges. For me, these included free housing, with a portion of my salary deducted at a steep discount of the actual housing costs in Hong Kong. Although being an assistant vice president, I did not qualify for the perks that senior managers were entitled to – free membership to social clubs, a car and a chauffeur, as well as tuition coverage for their children – I was grateful for the opportunity to stay in a very nice flat, well beyond what I could have afforded had I been hired locally.

My first task was to turn Citibank's data processing service subsidiary, named International Data Services (IDS), from loss to profit. I was also asked to develop a strategic plan to expand the business to other countries in Asia and to help Gooden roll out new software applications for the branch operations.

IDS had been offering computing services to local businesses, but it had few clients. I soon realized that its chief competitive disadvantage was its difficulty in scheduling computing time that would not conflict with the needs of the bank's own operations. Obviously, Citibank had the highest priority in its claim on computer use. In particular, the hours from midnight to 4 a.m. were used for the bank's transaction processing. Potential clients wishing to run the programs overnight would have difficulty getting any machine time. The second big issue was that the Citibank computing system did not have sufficient capacity, nor did the operating room have sufficient staff to operate 24 hours a day.

These problems led to delicate negotiations on the usage priorities between IDS and the Citibank computer department, with Gooden and me as principal negotiators on behalf of IDS. Gradually, we increased machine time available to outside clients in peak periods (i.e., between midnight and 6 a.m.). As a result, our company's client base expanded. By the end of 1972, IDS was breaking even at the operational level.

In an effort to expand the business to other parts of Asia, I made several regional trips to canvass the views of branch managers in the region. I found that only bank management in Singapore and Australia had any interest. After a few months of market research, I came to the sobering conclusion that it wouldn't be economically viable to develop the business of offering data processing services to Citibank clients across the region. In addition, few branch managers supported this idea. Gooden and others up the line were shocked when I recommended they abort the business strategy. As in every bureaucracy, it took some time for the organization to respond. Meanwhile, I was running IDS and helping Gooden in Citibank's own data processing work.

Early in the morning of May 16, 1972, my wife gave birth to our first child, a baby girl. We named her Katherine. She was healthy, weighing over seven pounds. I was thrilled to be a father for the first time. Parenthood made an awesome change to my earlier lifestyle. There was a children's playground down the slope from where we lived and we were there every weekend. Added to our weekend family activities were hikes on nearby islands or up the slope to the Peak. In the following months, I recorded the time of every feeding and just about every new development worth noting. We recorded the first day Kathy was able to sit up, when she first attempted to crawl, and when she uttered her first word: "da."

Overjoyed as we were in our personal lifestyle, things with Citibank were of a mixed nature. The same summer, Hong Kong met a great tragedy when an apartment building collapsed during a severe typhoon, trapping over 200 people and killing many. This tragedy became part of Hong Kong lore and was even included in James Clavell's novel, *Noble House*.

By fall, my job – like the building before it collapsed – was in jeopardy. Gooden told me the bank wanted me to return to New York, and suggested that I consider a position in the data processing department, then run by John Reed, who would become chairman in the 1980s. However, I had grown weary of working with computers and software. I had worked on the same sorts of computer applications for many years and there appeared no new challenges. The technology advance seemed to have reached a plateau. Indeed, third generation machines would not see a major advancement for many years to come.

I began to consider a career change. International corporate banking appealed to me as an exciting and rewarding field. I talked to Tom McQueeney a number of times about moving over to the banking side. Unfortunately, I didn't have any training nor experience in this area. At the age of 37, I was too old and too well paid to be a trainee. McQueeney would not consider my request.

Once Citibank's management made a decision, there was no turning back. Either I did what I was told or I would have to resign. So, in January 1973, we moved back to New York, ending my stint in Hong Kong in less than a year. My parents were bitterly disappointed. While it was a simple thing for my wife and me to relocate to Hong Kong, the return trip was quite a different undertaking. The good thing was we were young and not fazed by all the paraphernalia that accompanied traveling with an eight-month old baby.

Back in New York, we stayed with my wife's parents. Teresa's mother helped take care of the baby while my wife looked for housing. Because our home in New Rochelle had been rented out to a tenant, we couldn't move back there. Additionally, since my career status was uncertain, we felt that it would be more practical to live in the city than in a suburb. Eventually, we moved into a small apartment on East 81st Street, next to the Metropolitan Museum of Art, at the corner of Madison Avenue. There, we settled down to a life of a young New Yorker family.

In 1972, the stock market in the United States was on a recovery path. Its economy appeared in good shape. However, I was faced with uncertainties. My options, in the conventional sense, were limited. I was a new hire at Citibank and barely knew anyone in the organization. No one would be expected to be my advocate. Looking outside the company, I did not know what else I was qualified to do other than computing.

At the outset, my decision to step out of data processing to find a job on the banking side was met with indifference by senior management. Apparently, any career planning in the international banking group was more or less done on an *ad hoc* basis. Every time an officer completed his tour of duty in an overseas location, his file went to the personnel officer in charge of the division and a job search would begin. There was no guarantee that a job would be found. Of course, if one had done well and was well regarded, a promotion might be in the cards. During the time I was being interviewed, I was assigned a desk in a big room full of officers who were being laid off. I was made keenly aware that the bank harbored little compassion for officers not readily assignable to a new job.

By now, Ed Hoffman, who had hired me for the Hong Kong job, had become a senior officer in Colombia, or "Senof" in the Citibank slang. A Senof is the highest-ranking officer in an overseas location, generally in charge of the banking branches and subsidiaries, if any. A Senof has a lot of power and is deemed to be the first career step in the ladder to top management.

During my interview process, Hoffman was good enough to recommend that his boss, Jack Clark, the executive vice president in charge of the South America Division, meet me. Clark joined the bank from the World Bank. He was one of the few executives who hadn't worked his way up within the ranks, and as such, was not a typical Citibanker. After a brief conversation, he offered me a job as his "planning officer" for the South American division. The job entailed preparing an annual budget for the division which had branch offices in every country in South America. I would also undertake special assignments at his request. It didn't sound very exciting but the alternative was to accept a job in the data processing department. In March 1973, I accepted the new challenge.

To my surprise, the assignment turned out to be very interesting and rewarding. At the time I started in my new position, the bank had a verbal agreement to acquire an interest in a Brazilian life insurance company, then owned by General Reinsurance, a large, New York-based, international reinsurance firm. The acquisition was to be a joint venture with Chubb & Sons, a leading insurance company in New York. The Brazil Senof was too busy running the banking business to spend any time on it, and the deal was in limbo. Clark wanted me to resurrect and complete it. It was just the kind of challenge I welcomed, because it was totally different from anything I had ever done before. Besides, I would get to visit Brazil. The bank let me travel first class, and put me in a five-star Rio hotel. My traveling lifestyle took a big step up.

It turned out this deal was not a simple acquisition. It called for Citibank to enter into a joint venture with Chubb & Sons. The joint venture would then acquire General Reinsurance's interest in a Brazilian life insurance company. Since the insurance industry was a field I had no prior knowledge about, I bought a text book and learned the essentials of the business in my spare time. Over the next three months, I had to make most decisions on my own, because both the Brazil Senof and Clark were too busy to get involved with this minor deal. This freedom to act, if nothing else, significantly boosted my self-confidence.

After several months of work, the deal was signed in the office of Citibank's lawyer in Stamford, Connecticut. Clark and others in the bank were impressed with what I did, particularly since I was regarded a newcomer. After this transaction, I felt more secure in my job status and hoped I had lessened my chances of ending up in the room for laid-off bankers. Years later, to my delight, I learned that the insurance company in Brazil did well and it was one of Citibank's few successful "synergistic" investments in Latin America.

During the summer of 1973, I started to prepare the Latin America country management teams for the annual budget exercise. Although everyone knew that this was an entirely predictable event, it still represented a big headache for field officers. The exercise entailed countless requests for numbers, which I had to analyze in excruciating detail. Budget proposals were first made in the field and then moved through a series of intensive negotiations between branch managers and the division head. Needless to say, each branch, or profit center, was expected to improve its profit performance every year.

For the budget exercise, I visited most major cities in South America – Rio, Buenos Aires, Lima, Quito, and Bogotá. I experienced the Spanish-speaking society for the first time, with its distinct mannerisms, architecture, food, wine, music and culture. In each country, I would discuss the status and progress of projects initiated at the branch level. For example, the bank was trying to launch a credit card business in Colombia, sell a building in Paraguay, set up a leasing subsidiary in Argentina, and so on. As I traveled, I learned that Senofs had responsibilities well beyond that of merely being the big boss for a bank in the country. In many of these countries, Citibank was *the* dominant multinational. The local press and government would pay close attention to whatever the Senof said or did. A Senof had to be more than a banker; he had to be somewhat of a politician. I quickly coveted that kind of experience for myself.

In my travels, I found Argentina to be a most financially troubled country, although it featured beautiful European-styled cities full of smartly dressed men and women. Lima, on the western side of the Andean mountain range, held a unique beauty. The Andes, at an average altitude of 13,000 feet, seemed to scrape the sky. Looking out the window of a jet, the plane was not much higher than their snowy peaks. The colors of the snow at high altitude were fantastic – red mixed with yellow and patches of colors in different shapes and sizes.

Lima had a thriving Chinatown since the Chinese came to this part of the world as contract laborers in the 19th century, working in mines and building railroads. In the 1970s, they had become small shop owners, operating laundries and restaurants. The city was full of Indians, a race I encountered for the first time. I saw shantytowns where they lived, desperately poor, far apart from the comfortable neighborhoods of the Europeans. The country imposed many restrictions on foreign banks and Citibank did very little business there, other than sovereign credit and trade finance.

I enjoyed my one visit to Quito, Ecuador, a colorful mid-sized city located almost 9,300 feet above sea level. It, too, had cathedrals and churches, reflecting the influence of Spanish conquistadors. In Bogotá, I spent an evening in a nightclub, enjoying Spanish music and the company of some friendly locals. My visit to the historical museum was an unforgettable experience as it housed a fascinating collection of Inca relics.

Like other young bankers working for international banks, I was frequently away from my family. At home, we hired a Colombian woman to help my wife manage the household. Kathy had her first birthday party in May. My wife made it a very special occasion, inviting two other couples with small kids to join our celebration. Then, in the middle of October, our son was born.

Clarence was a healthy and happy baby, very easy to take care of. We had him in our bedroom while Kathy had her own bedroom for the first time. This was not an easy thing for her to accept, and the adjustment took more time than we had anticipated.

I had been assiduously lobbying for a position in banking. After the completion of the budgetary project in the fall, Clark suggested a new position for me, which could lead to banking work. The position, however, was in Montreal. At that time, Canada had recently put in a number of restrictions on foreign banks' presence. Clark decided on a new strategy for the bank —establish an office in Canada that would have two executives, one in corporate banking and one in real estate banking, both of whom would report to a new Senof. As I didn't have any banking background, my job was to assist the two banking executives. That was the extent of the job description. I was offered a salary increase and promise of a possible promotion.

Because we had only recently moved to New York, another relocation would pose hardships on the family. After negotiating with the management, we agreed I would start working in Canada on a temporary basis while visiting my family every weekend. Until I settled down in my new job, my family would not have to make the move.

When I met the other three members of the Canadian team in Montreal, it dawned on me they had not formulated any specific work for me. Byron Knief, the Senof, was tall, lean, immaculately dressed, and articulate. A Colombian officer was to head the commercial banking division and a German banker would head real estate lending.

Since my task was not clearly defined, I decided to identify my own niche if I were to make a contribution to the bank. I had no desire to be a staff person anymore, writing reports and keeping track of events. I came up with a proposal for a *de novo* entry into the consumer finance business in Canada. I prepared a strategic study, including a marketing survey, and began to work on an investment proposal. Since I knew nothing about consumer finance, I talked to numerous executives in the industry. To source candidates to lead the proposed project, I used a headhunter and started an interviewing process. In the few weeks that followed, I must have interviewed a dozen candidates. The questions and answers provided fodder for my market research as well as an idea of how to prepare my proposal.

Consumer finance was a fiercely competitive business in Canada, partly because Canada had a relatively small population and partly because all the major U.S. players were there. I decided on a wholesale strategy rather than a retail one, which meant that Citibank would not open shop fronts to compete head-on with the existing players. The plan was to offer credit packages through refinancing debt acquired from existing consumer finance companies. The key concept was that Citibank would carve out a complementary niche in consumer finance, leveraging its competitive advantage in the credit market – its cost of funds was much lower than local finance companies could obtain in the open market.

Another important piece of the strategy was to tie the back-office operation to Nationwide Consumer Finance, a Citibank subsidiary located in St. Louis, Missouri. The link was through a teleprocessing line established for this purpose. The beauty of this setup was it eliminated the need to establish a separate transaction processing center in Canada, thus minimizing costs and enabling a quick start-up. The remote processing idea was a very innovative one in the realm of data processing in those days.

Knowing the strength of my ideas, it didn't surprise me that the proposal was accepted without change. I was charged to head up and implement the new venture. My "star" was definitely rising in the bank. In just one year since returning to New York, I was given a chance to head up a new profit center. My wife and I discussed the opportunity and we decided to take it. So, we went ahead to pack and move, the second time in 12 months.

Soon after we moved to Toronto, my wife quickly found a wonderful house in Rosedale, next to Moore Park Ravine, a nature preserve. The neighborhood was full of small kids and young families. With two small children – Kathy, who was an active toddler and Clarence, a fast-growing baby, we fit readily into our neighborhood and the kids quickly found friends to play with.

Over the next five months, I hired two Canadian professionals to help set up the consumer finance operations. As they began to build the venture, I found myself with fewer and fewer opportunities to add value to the business. I was able to spend a lot of time with my family. Years later, I learned that the consumer finance business had continued to thrive even though the top management I hired did not stay much beyond my own premature departure.

In May 1974, Citibank sent Ed Hoffman, formerly the Senof in Bogotá, to Beirut. He was to reorganize the management structure serving the Middle East region that stretched from Iran in the east to Algeria in North Africa. In the aftermath of the Israeli-Arab war in 1973, the oil-producing countries had raised the price of oil from US$2 per barrel to US$12 per barrel. The six-fold increase effectively transferred tremendous wealth from industrialized countries to oil producers. It also triggered years of high inflation in the global economy coupled with low growth, or stagflation. Countries in the Persian Gulf found themselves awash with untold amount of "petrodollars." Citibank, ever on the prowl for new profit opportunities, decided to send one of its brightest young bankers to capitalize on this new emerging opportunity.

Citibank had a very competitive culture within its officer rank. Unlike IBM, which took pride in its depth of management – which meant that every management position would have at least two candidates to provide spare capacity to the system, Citibank's human resources strategy was lean and mean. At IBM, lifetime employment was a company commitment. With Citibank, most people were treated like commodities, with an up-or-out philosophy. There were no positions where people could be parked if they were unable to move up. The only exception was for select officers on a fast track, or young managers who were judged to be potential material for top management. Both Ed Hoffman and John Reed were on the fast track. When Hoffman moved to Beirut in 1974 to head the entire Middle East region, he was under 30 years old.

One day in May, Knief summoned me to his office and told me that Hoffman had a job for me in Dubai, part of the United Arab Emirates. After years of my lobbying for a banking job, the bank had now come through with an opportunity. The job was to be the branch manager for Dubai, reporting to a regional officer covering the Gulf, from Kuwait to Qatar and Saudi Arabia. I was asked to fly to Dubai to discuss the new position.

And so I did, despite misgivings as to whether my family would fit into a totally alien society. On my first trip to Dubai, while waiting in a crowded Beirut airport lounge, I was approached by a stranger in a white robe. He had a scar on his cheek and looked at me with piercing eyes. He spoke fluent English, a sign he was highly educated. In a friendly conversation between us, I soon learned he was from Sudan. This man was the first Arab I had ever met and his friendliness calmed my nerves and gave me a positive attitude toward the prospect of living in a part of the world totally unknown to me. As the plane was landing in the early morning sun, I saw from the window the pristine clear blue water of the Gulf and the vast stretches of its sandy shores.

Not surprisingly, Dubai was extremely hot most of the time, with an average daytime temperature over 40 degrees Celsius. The sun was bright with no clouds in the sky. In the small airport, people seemed to be milling aimlessly. The immigration authorities had the unusual practice of retaining all passports while visitors were in-country, no matter how long they stayed. The first impression I had was that the city was literally built on sand, interrupted only by stretches of paved roads and houses.

The heat, the sun, and the ever-present fine, sandy dust covering everything were the dominant features of the city-state.

At the Citibank building in the Deira section of Dubai, I met Henri Derkx and Steve Venter, Senof in charge of the Gulf and senior credit officer respectively. Derkx, from Holland, was a banker cut from the old banking traditions. Venter was from South Africa with a strong credit background. Both had worked in the Middle East for a long time. They had some obvious concerns about my posting. This was not surprising. I had absolutely no experience in banking, had never attended a banking course, and had never been involved in any management issues related to commercial banking or foreign exchange. Approaching the age of thirty-nine, I was already too old for a typical Citibank branch manager in a foreign country. Fortunately, both were good "soldiers" in carrying out upper management decisions and told me all about the attractions of living and working in Dubai.

One of these attractions was a Chinese store, called Wong & Sons, on the main street of Dubai. The proprietor was a young man from Hong Kong. To my surprise, his family was from Shanghai, my birthplace. Before the departure of the British after the Second World War, Wong's father exported shark fin, a delicacy for the Chinese, from Yemen to Hong Kong. After Yemen became independent and turned Marxist, his father had to leave and move his family and business to Dubai. The store seemed to be doing well. It was full of Chinese products – silk, linens, canned goods, and even bottled water. I was delighted to meet someone with a common background. However, there were no Chinese restaurants in Dubai. The closest one, operated by Wong's brother, was in Bahrain, another sheikdom along the Persian Gulf.

As an inducement for me to accept the posting, I was promoted to the rank of "resident vice president" with a 15 percent salary increase. Within Citibank, Dubai was considered a "hardship" post, and those assigned there received a 25 percent premium over their salary. The package included two annual vacation breaks, called "R & R's" for rest and recreation. As branch manager, I was entitled to a car and driver and tuition coverage for my children's' education. I also received a housing allowance, making it possible to live in a large house in one of Dubai's best neighborhoods.

I took photographs of the city, its street scenes, and people, so that my wife would have some idea of what she would encounter if we agreed to go. What I could not capture were the sounds, particularly the call to prayers that came through public loudspeakers five times a day, the swarm of flies, the intense heat, and the unique odors.

I found Arab people different in many ways from people in the West or in Asia. Their language had a totally different tonal quality from Chinese or English. The men in Dubai universally wore mustaches as a symbol of manhood. They did not wear socks or shoes, preferring leather sandals. Many held in their hands strings of beads, which they would finger continuously. They wore white robes and the kefiah, a traditional form of headgear. The advantage of this kind of dress code was you were unable to spot any class distinctions when you looked at the people on the streets. Of course, on closer inspection, you would find a few men whose robes were embellished with golden edges.

Women were clothed in black, in contrast with the white color worn by men. Since their faces were covered, it was not possible to observe their facial expressions. Traditional Arab men in the Gulf were known to be allowed to have up to four wives. As a result, a typical successful businessman had a very large family.

In Dubai, although Arab women wore long veils and gowns that touched the ground, non-Arab women were allowed to adopt their international style of clothing. Unlike elsewhere in the Gulf, women were allowed to drive, wear open shirts and skirts, shop by themselves, and swim or sunbathe on public beaches. They were also allowed to smoke and drink in public, except during religious occasions. Partly because of its liberal atmosphere, the city-state was an R&R center for Citibankers working in Saudi Arabia and other Arabian countries.

Dubai was, together with Bahrain, the Gulf's most progressive sheikdom. It did not follow the more draconian features of Islamic conservatism. Sheik Rashid, the ruler, was well liked by his people. Although his territory was part of the United Arab Emirates dominated by Abu Dhabi with its vast oil reserves, Sheik Rashid appeared to have total freedom to do what he wished in his domain. Over the years, the sheikdom had emerged from a sleepy backwater trading port to become the commercial center in the region with a reputation for entrepreneurship. By the time I flew there, it was also the banking center in the Middle East, with major U.S. and European banks along with Arab banks from as far as Egypt.

My wife supported my desire to become a banker, and agreed to make the move. My appointment surprised some in the head office. Later, I would learn that assigning someone without banking experience to be a branch manager was a most exceptional practice. For me, this was an unexpected, although much hoped for, chance to switch careers and become part of Citibank's core management.

We left Toronto that summer and checked into a Manhattan hotel to wait for my work visa. To me, this was a swim-or-sink assignment, but I was extremely excited by the opportunity.

7

Second Career in a Desert City

Dubai is part of the United Arab Emirates, a loose federation of seven sheikdoms dominated by Abu Dhabi, which is rich in oil reserves. Dubai is a thriving commercial city where law and order prevail. A low crime rate is maintained as a result of severe punishments.

During my time there, Dubai had fewer than 200,000 residents. Foreigners were welcomed, although citizenship for non-natives was almost impossible. The local people known as Bedouins were once nomads. The poor ones among them lived in concrete huts and kept camels and goats. The wealthy Bedouins lived in big mansions or villas. There were virtually no in-betweens – no middle class – other than imported professionals like myself.

The country's oil wealth ensured that even the poor of cosmopolitan Dubai did not have to stoop to menial labor. Most unskilled labor was taken care of by Indians and Pakistanis. There were Filipina nurses in the hospitals. White-collar workers in banks, offices, and government offices were mostly Lebanese, Palestinians, Egyptians, Indians, and Pakistanis.

A small city, Dubai is divided into two parts by a narrow creek. The eastern side of the creek is Dubai proper, while the area to the west is called Deira. The Dubai side was older and more established. The airport was on the Dubai side, along with the banks, mostly located along the creek. On a typical day, the creek was crowded with *dhows*, wooden boats that carried people and cargo around the Gulf and the Indian Ocean. Normally, a *dhow* could carry three automobiles and a dozen passengers. Unlike the other multinational banks, Citibank had a plot of land on the Deira side facing the Arabian Gulf with a long stretch of very fine beach. It was on the Deira side where you would find spacious homes of wealthy locals and expatriates.

In early September 1974, my wife and I brought our two small children to Dubai, stopping in Geneva to catch our breath. The children never ate well when we traveled. Either the trips upset them or they were too excited to pay attention to food. From Geneva, we passed through Beirut. As parents of small children, we had a heavy load of carry-on items including bottles, diapers, extra clothing for the kids, baby strollers, and so on. The change of time zones was stressful for the little ones. We took the same late night flight as I had on my first visit and landed in Dubai early in the morning the next day.

Citibank found a big house for us in the Jumeira Beach area, which featured large residential homes occupied by rich locals and expatriate managers in the banking and oil businesses. When we arrived in the city, our rented house was just being finished and it wasn't yet ready for occupancy. We stayed in the Ambassador Hotel near the bank, a three-star hotel if one were generous in assigning a ranking.

On the first evening, after dinner, while my wife was fussing with Clarence, I took Kathy for a walk. The sidewalks were full of local people. Streets were coated in sand and dust. Kathy refused to walk, so I had to carry her. I could see in her eyes an expression of intense anxiety I had never noticed before. The adjustment was difficult as we were far away from any friends or family. The children ate badly and my wife had trouble sleeping. Things didn't settle down until we moved into our new home, more than a month later.

In the Middle East, work schedule is different from the rest of the world. A typical week begins on Saturday and ends on Thursday. There is no business on Friday. In the morning, work would begin at 8 a.m. and end at 1:30 p.m. During the long lunch break, people would actually go home and take a nap, returning to the office at 5 p.m. to resume working till 7:30 p.m. Although the workday was long, the long lunch break meant that I could go home and see the children, put them to bed for their afternoon nap, and have some relaxation. The routine suited me fine.

Organizationally, I had three managers reporting to me. One was the corporate banking head, with several account officers reporting to him. The unit was responsible for the lending side of the business. Another was the treasury head, in charge of foreign exchange, funding the branch's balance sheet and dealing in the inter-bank market. The third was the head of operations. We had a sub-branch in the Dubai section of the city, with its own manager reporting to the operations head. One staff member was in charge of personnel. Finally, an Arabic translator who was a respected person in the community reported to Derkx, but also assisted me in my dealings with the Dubai government.

I worked in Dubai for about three years, during which I learned everything about banking and more. It was an exhilarating period in my career. The Dubai branch had a multicultural mix of personnel. The corporate banking head was American. The treasury head and the operations head were Indian. A senior lending officer was an Egyptian. There were also a British and a German. The branch's staff consisted of various nationalities: Lebanese, Pakistani, Indian, Iranian, Sudanese, Yemeni, and Palestinian. Interestingly, of the 65 people working at the branch, we had no Dubai natives at all, other than the guards.

I had a big office with a big desk on the ground floor. On the wall behind my desk was a picture of Sheik Rashid, the ruler of Dubai. I had a wonderful Indian secretary, who was enormously helpful in explaining the details of the branch operation, from when telexes were scheduled to arrive to the regular meetings I had to chair and the habits and personalities of the men reporting to me. Under her care, files were so well organized that access to information was never more than a few moments away.

My assignment, however, began with a mild shock. The corporate banking head welcomed me in one breath and, with the next, told me that he was beginning his annual leave the next day. He handed me a credit proposal for an important client that had to be approved as soon as possible. I had never seen a credit proposal before. Fortunately, the senior credit officer, Steve Venter, gave me a hand. Still, I had to make my own decision and couldn't do it without thoroughly understanding the details of the loan proposal. My next challenge came in the following week, when the operations manager informed me that a key client, an oilfield service company, had failed to make a loan payment as scheduled. I was advised to meet with its Lebanese financial officer.

At the meeting, we learned that the company was facing short-term cash flow problems. Again, I consulted with Venter and we sat down together with the client. The solution was for the bank to monitor the client's daily cash flow. No check payment would be permitted without my approval. From that moment on, I became involved intimately with this company's financial condition and was in the hot seat for several months. Fortunately, the cash flow problem was temporary, and the company flourished on the back of high oil prices and the booming Dubai economy. Looking back, it was a blessing in disguise that my first lesson in banking was grounded in solving a credit problem.

Under strict Islamic law, interest payments were illegal. The branch's biggest client was the Ruler of Dubai. Sheik Rashid kept large U.S. dollar deposits in several current accounts with the bank and the deposits were interest free. The level of deposits, however, varied with the sheik's cash requirements. I soon learned that, no matter what other business successes we developed, the size of the ruler's deposits determined the profits we made in any given month. If the sheik withdrew some of his many millions of interest free dollars, the branch's performance would suffer. Although the ruler rejected any interest earnings on his deposits, he often demanded special services. For example, at least twice a year, he and his entourage would go to Pakistan on hunting trips. For those trips, he needed substantial amounts of cash and travelers' checks. On those occasions, the entire cash department personnel would work feverishly to assemble them all in half a day and pack them away to the sheik in an armored vehicle.

As the top officer of Citibank in Dubai, I visited the sheik once a month, in his palace, to pay my respects, exchange views, and negotiate any matter that might need his attention. He was, to my knowledge, well liked by his people and highly accessible. In the tradition of the Bedouin society, the sheik was obliged to meet with any citizen who might wish to see him for a problem or a request. His audience chamber was a large rectangular hall covered with colorful and ornate carpets and with big armchairs lined up against the walls. Every day, in the afternoon, he sat in the corner of the large hall, talking to the visitors, one at a time. People waiting for their turn sat against the walls, chatting, drinking tea, or just passing the time of day. It was a very informal atmosphere, totally different from behavior before a head of state in a non-Arab society.

My interpreter and I didn't have to wait to see the sheik and would be ushered in as soon as we arrived. Sheik Rashid was of medium height, slim, and had a beard and piercing, intelligent, witty eyes. Like most Arab men, he fiddled with his worry bead while talking. He liked to scratch his feet. When I first met him, he told my interpreter I didn't look like an American. I told him that Americans come in all colors, shades, and sizes. This seemed to please him. In the ensuing visits, I never had any difficulty with him. Our visits were usually short. I would review highlights of the month's events, limiting the briefing to non-confidential matters. He, in turn, would sometimes make requests or suggestions.

Sheik Rashid frequently hosted banquets in the palace. A typical occasion might be to welcome some visiting bankers or statesmen from the West or from South Asia. Some of the longtime British residents fondly recalled the days when the palace fare was served in traditional style as finger food, without utensils. My Arab friends told me that their traditional practice was better because, in their view, fingers were cleaner than any tableware. They washed their hands before and after meals. Years ago, everyone had to sit on the ground rather than on chairs.

By the time I lived in Dubai, the palace had shifted to Western-style table settings. At a typical banquet, there would be hundreds of guests, at three long rows of tables, with no assigned seats. No women were ever invited. I usually sat with American bankers from Chase Manhattan Bank and First National Bank of Chicago. The tables were set with big bowls and plates filled with meat and Indian rice. There were no waiters to serve the food; instead, guests were expected to help themselves. There was always plenty of leftovers. After the guests were done, guards and helpers would come to the tables to eat, with an informality that was surprising to the uninitiated.

A month after our arrival in Dubai, my family settled into a two-story villa, located in an expatriate neighborhood. It was a large house with a large backyard, a small front yard, and a separate garage. Because of the booming economy, houses for expatriates were slapped together quickly and there were a lot of construction flaws. Even though there were four bathrooms in our house, only one or two toilets would be working at any given time.

The house was close to the famous Jumeira Beach, facing the Persian Gulf. The beach, with its fine, white sand, stretched for miles and miles. Unfortunately, it was usually littered with beer bottles, soda cans, and other refuse. The good thing, though, was it was never crowded and the water was very clear. In the neighborhood, the roads were always covered in sand and there was no sidewalk. Cars, goats, camels, and people freely shared these roads. Potholes were everywhere. Garbage was strewn around the area at all times. The only thing that saved us from health problems was the scorching sun, which destroyed most bacteria.

With outside air temperature nearly always over 40 degrees Celsius, we seldom walked on the beach. Not only was the heat intense, but also the air was usually dotted with flies. Our air conditioners worked 24 hours a day. My wife bought a swing set for the backyard. She also bought a big spherical climbing dome for the kids and placed it in Clarence's bedroom. The children loved to climb on it.

Every weekend, we took driving trips. We enjoyed driving to the east coast bordering Oman, passing old British forts along the way, as well as camels and Bedouin tents in the desert. I spent a lot of weekends with the kids in playgrounds and swimming pools. One day, I decided to plant a lemon tree in the sand. The wonderful thing was that, in no time at all, the tree grew as high as the second floor of the house.

We had an Indian cook and a maid. The house had screens installed on every window but flies easily penetrated them. Dust storms were a constant problem. Everything in the house was always covered with sand dust. My job, before every meal, was to kill flies so that we could eat without exasperation. The wings of the flies were so coated with sand dust that they flew very slowly, which made my job easy. We never managed to exterminate household cockroaches, a constant menace. There were occasional sightings of lizards, called house *chichaks*, on the wall and on the ceiling. These were benign creatures that helped to get rid of the flies and other insects. Fortunately, in our household, we never saw any rats. It was also important to keep the gate closed in front of our small garden. On several occasions, when it was left open by accident, we found goats from the neighboring village eating our plants and anything else at ground level.

I bought a Chrysler Imperial for business. I felt a Cadillac was too flashy and buying a foreign (non-U.S.) car wouldn't be patriotic. The regional office approved the purchase. Then I bought a much less expensive Dodge Dart for personal use. One day, I took the two kids to the beach in the Dodge and managed to miss the road and drive the car into the sand. The car was stuck, but within minutes, another car pulled up, stopped, and all the passengers came out. Although they didn't speak English, it was obvious that they were going to help. All four of them pushed the car while I sat in it and pumped the gas pedal. Together, we were able to get the car quickly onto the road. The Arabs laughed and drove off. I wondererd, if my car were stuck on a highway in the States, would I find such quick and generous assistance.

Shortly after we settled down, we placed Kathy in a nursery school run by several English women. In the second year, we put Clarence in another nursery school. By then, Kathy was going to the Dubai Kindergarten. Every morning, I took them in the big Imperial and dropped them off at school, and then continued on to my office. Our life slowly stabilized and our social activities were organized around bankers from other countries and Citibank officers.

We kept a busy social calendar. Foreign bankers and some of our clients took turns hosting dinners, and so did we. Traditionally, Arab women were not invited to social events. However, our clients included Indians, Iranians, and Pakistanis and they were quite Westernized. As a result, our social dinners weren't different from what you would expect in the West. We joined a local country club and took our children to swim there almost every weekend. I played an occasional game of squash at the club. The heat made any activity outdoors unbearable.

The first Christmas in Dubai, we visited a Catholic church. It was packed with Filipina maids and a few other foreigners.

The desert sky was unusually clear and the stars sparkled brightly. As we drove away from the church and gazed at stately palm trees against the rolling white sand, it occurred to me that this must have been the scene around Bethlehem at the time of Jesus' birth. Although Christmas in a snow-capped landscape is beautiful, the desert scene I witnessed was stunning and I felt more keeping in the real Christmas scene. It definitely inspired me spiritually in a very special way.

Because the summer months were so very hot, my wife, the children and I would use our annual leave to escape the heat. We would take an around-the-world tour every summer, stopping in Hong Kong to visit my parents and then traveling to New York to stay with my wife's parents. I would then return to Dubai by myself while the family stayed behind until just before school started. The summer months were difficult for me because the family was away. Also, as many officers took their holidays away from Dubai, work seemed to be more intense than during the rest of the year.

Citibank had among its clients all the major merchant families in Dubai. They were owners of hotels and real estate, but mostly traders of all kinds of equipment, cars, and household appliances. Trade was flourishing between the Gulf kingdoms and surrounding economies, including Iran, the Levant, and all the way to Pakistan, India, and beyond. The oil business was controlled by the state and owned by the sheik. Yet, most of the oil service companies were owned and run by expatriate Americans. Nowadays, the name of bin Laden has a tragic association with terrorism. But, back in 1976, the bin Laden Trading Company was a well-respected business in the Gulf.

One of the bank's most colorful clients was the Galadari family, originally from Iran. The family had made a fortune smuggling gold into India. The elder brother told me that, stretching back to the early 1970s, they regularly purchased gold in London and shipped it to Dubai. From Dubai, gold was loaded into *dhows* that sailed to a secret destination on the coast of India. There, the gold would be sold to agents illegally because gold import was strictly regulated. As a financial intermediary, Citibank financed the shipment from London to Dubai because this part was the legitimate side of the trade.

As a young man, the elder Galadari brother worked in India where smugglers bought the gold from him. He said this was the hard part of the business because the smugglers were criminals. Occasionally, boats had to be scuttled if they happened to encounter an Indian Navy patrol boat. The economics of the trade were incredibly lucrative. In those days, one could buy gold in London for a fixed US$12 an ounce and sell it in India for US$200. However, following the Bretton Wood agreement, the price of gold was floated and its price in London shot up to true market value. As a result, the lucrative arbitrage disappeared and the family abandoned the smuggling business.

When I met the Galadari brothers, they had long been legitimate businessmen, engaged in trading, real estate, and hotels. They talked about the smuggling days as if folklore. One of the very first projects I worked on for the branch was financing the Intercontinental Hotel, which was developed by the family. The branch also financed the Galadaris' trading business. One day, Abdul Galadari, one of the brothers, came to the branch and asked if we could reduce the bank's commission on a letter of credit issuance. I recall that the bank's standard charge was 0.5 percent. The family already had a preferred rate of three-eighths of one percent. However, Abdul asked if we could manage to charge one-eighth of a percent. He parked himself at the officer's desk for two hours, haggling and chatting. When I tried to resolve the issue, Abdul said his father had told him that being patient with bankers usually would pay off well. After one more hour, he finally saw that we weren't going to budge and relented. We drank some coffee and I made sure that he was not personally offended.

Another significant deal was the financing of the first Dubai dry dock, an ambitious and well-thought-out project that was being pushed by Sheik Rashid. The loan amount was US$250 million, an enormous sum by the standards of the day. All the major banks were competing fiercely for the deal. I had ample support from the bank's syndicated loan specialists in London. Such was the power of Citibank we could draw expertise from anywhere in the world to complete a transaction. I also had the support of credit officers in the region and the head office. The project had the attention of the bank's senior management and its success was viewed as important.

In Dubai, as in many parts of the developing world, there was usually a "fixer" who could stop or expedite approvals in government circles. In exchange for his favor, the fixer would receive a success fee. However, as a U.S. bank, Citibank was forbidden to offer payments to such intermediaries so as not to violate the Foreign Corrupt Practices Act. For weeks after our proposal was submitted, we collectively held our breath, not knowing whether our proposal would succeed without the expected bribe.

Meanwhile, I received several visits from a representative of the "fixer" who made it very clear to me that it would be entirely wrong to go down the slippery slope of playing his game. In the end, I believe Sheik Rashid decided in favor of Citibank because we had the best proposal. The project turned out to be a tremendous commercial success. I was long gone by the time the project came to fruition. The "fixer," a high government official in Dubai, went on to become a ranking official in the United Arab Emirates in later years.

With a significant amount of treasury activity, Citibank was the largest foreign bank in Dubai. Our treasury department was headed by a young Indian, Pradeep Kashyap, who had strong trading instincts, especially in proprietary operations using the bank's own capital and funds from inter-bank lines. Because of its size and reputation, Citibank Dubai had, at its disposal, a large number of international banks willing to provide funding facilities for inter-bank trading. By 1976, the bank had such an important influence on the exchange trading of UAE Dirham that it would become known as a maker of dollar-to-dirham trades. Treasury profits were a key source of income for our branch, next to the spread earned from Sheik Rashid's interest-free deposits.

In mid-1975, I received a pleasant surprise from Hoffman. I was promoted to vice president and assumed responsibility for all the branches in the UAE. I was now a Senof. The Gulf management office was moved out of the branch and I moved into Derkx's office on the second floor. In addition to Dubai, branches in Sharjah and, more importantly, Abu Dhabi, would start reporting to me. Being a Senof was a significant accomplishment as there were not more than 100 Senofs around the world. The UAE had become an important profit center for Citibank. In terms of profit generation, the UAE, Saudi Arabia, and Iran were the top three players in Citibank's Middle East region. My office was much larger than before and I now had a view of the famous Dubai creek.

Over the next year or so, I opened new mini-branches in Ras Al Khaimah, Al Ain, and Fujairah on the east coast, south of Oman. Citibank would have a presence in five of the seven sheikdoms that made up the UAE. To open the Ras Al Khaimah branch, Hoffman came to preside over the occasion. The ruler there was nearly blind but did not wear glasses. He showed up in the front seat beside the driver in a Jeep, with armed guards sitting in the back seat. After the signing ceremony, we had a typical Bedouin banquet, with far too much food for everyone present. I sat next to the son of the ruler while Hoffman sat next to the ruler. The son spoke fluent English and was an undergraduate at the University of Michigan. We had a great conversation and I found him highly intelligent, serious, and thoughtful. I got the idea that when in due course he succeeded his father, he would surely be a progressive ruler.

Al Ain was a small village, located about two hours' drive east of Abu Dhabi, where the ruler had his vacation home.

Otherwise, it was a very sleepy place. The importance of Abu Dhabi was made clear when the vice chairman of Citibank, Al Costanzo, decided to come out to open the branch. The day turned out to be exceptionally hot. What made things almost unbearable was that the air conditioning in the branch broke down during the ceremony. The hot lights of the cameras for the photo shoot made the condition even worse. We were all sweating profusely as the ceremony pressed on.

In addition to visits by Costanzo, we enjoyed the visit of Walt Wriston, who was the chairman and CEO of Citibank in 1995. Also, George Voitja, executive vice president and head of the international division, visited Dubai with his wife. Rubbing shoulders with the top executives definitely had its advantages. Competition for high-level jobs was intense and exposure to decision makers was a necessity. Although I left Citibank only three years later, in 1978, I learned the basics of how to effectively present one's views about business issues to the highest level of management.

Managing a commercial bank was definitely a challenge. It took me about a year before I felt comfortable in the job. My day was full of meetings with virtually all decisions ended up on my desk. Issues regarding personnel, operations, trading, credit, and marketing came up every day. I had to read credit proposals and other memos during the long lunch breaks. I had to respond to constant requests by the regional and head offices. Everything was urgent. I had a great secretary but I could have employed two. Fortunately, my typing speed was outstanding and this saved a lot of time. By the time I left the position in 1977, assets of the UAE branches had reached over US$100 million, a tidy sum in those days.

I found the Arabs reasonable to deal with in business. They usually kept their word. Of course, as I would find out later, most businessmen keep their word when times are good. It is only during difficult conditions that you can separate the wheat from the chaff. In Dubai in the mid-1970s, after the first oil shock and with energy prices rising, times were good and businesses were growing. The Persian Gulf states were friendly to the United States. The only major issue was the Israeli and Palestinian conflict. The Ayatollah Khomeini's Iranian Revolution was still a few years away.

Religion was never far from the Muslim mind and was an integral part of daily life. The Arabs prayed five times a day. Most people I knew appeared to live simple lives. They neither drank nor gambled, at least when they were in the region. Men typically supported four wives, which was allowed under Islamic law and was a sign that they were in the conservative mainstream. If a man tired of one of his wives, he could divorce her and marry another. The government took care of the divorcées. Muslims, like Chinese, valued having many children, and women would generally have at least four. Thus, the men might support a dozen or more children along with their many wives.

For business, I used to make regular trips to Beirut. On one visit, I witnessed Israeli fighter jets bombard a Palestinian refugee camp just outside the city. The regional office was located on the top floor of a Holiday Inn. We were in a meeting when we heard a thundering noise that shook the walls. The sound eruptions seemed to come from all around us. After a moment of shock, we raced to the window to see what was happening. Missiles were streaking down from the planes. Fire and smoke ballooned from an area not more than 10 miles away. Hoffman was just about to send everyone out when the thundering sound ceased. The strike was over in five minutes. This was the first direct strike by the Israelis on Beirut and marked not only the escalation of the Palestinian conflict but also the outbreak of tensions within Lebanon between Christians and Muslims. Less than a year later, Hoffman moved the regional office from Beirut to Athens.

The typical tenure for a Citibank officer in a hardship country was three years. The policy was, in my view, a very costly one because it resulted in a great deal of management inefficiency. In my case, it took me a year to have a good handle on the job and to have my family settled into a new routine. However, at the end of the second year, in late 1976, I was informed that I would be transferred to Athens the following spring.

The assignment in Dubai had opened my eyes to a part of the world I had previously paid little heed. There, my kids entered the first schools in their educational development. One notable event was my wife authored a book about the plants and flowers in the desert, called *Plants in the United Arab Emirates*, a project that grew out of her landscape consulting work. It was sold in shops in Dubai and orders came in from overseas buyers as well. In the three years we lived there, we collected a number of "treasures" including Iranian rugs and local furniture and handicrafts. More importantly, I had the privilege of living and working in a distinctly different culture at a time when the Arabs began to claim their share of the world's wealth.

I admired the way the Arabs valued family ties, much like the Chinese. I also admired the amount of time they devoted to their religion. However, their progress in the material world was handicapped by the fact female members of their society were disenfranchised. Social development was unbalanced. Traditional Arab values were, more than any time in history, being challenged by the world outside of their region. In my view, having so much oil under the ground distorted their political and economic development. There is no free lunch in the world.

8

Height of My Banking Career – From Europe to Asia

After Dubai, my next career stop was Athens. Thus, within five years after leaving New York, my family and I found ourselves moving to a third continent.

We moved in early 1977. As a farewell token, the bank staff in Dubai gave me a wonderful gift – an Arabian sword with inlaid filigree and semi-precious stones, which, unfortunately, was lost when shipped to Athens.

Athens was a fabled city, ancient but with modern features. Everything about the city revolved around tourism. Yet, I did not find the Greeks particularly friendly. Traffic was usually in a snarl, English was rarely understood, and pollution ranked among the worst in all of Europe. The Citibank office was located in a nondescript building in Kolonaki Square. The bank found us an apartment in an exclusive neighborhood on St. George's Avenue. From the living room window, we had the fantastic and dramatic view of the Acropolis and the Parthenon.

What was more dramatic though, was the bomb threat at the Citibank office on the very first day of my job. I still remember seeing people throng in front of the building as I approached it, with police cars everywhere. It took more than an hour for a bomb squad to clear the building. In the end, it was a false alarm.

Office hours in Athens were much like those in the Gulf. Because of the intense heat, there was a long siesta break after lunch and work would resume at 5 p.m. and end at 7 p.m. The job, which was to oversee the operations of the bank's Middle East balance sheet, was a staff function. As such, there were few deadlines. Coming from a line job, the workload was much lighter and mostly under control. As my work involved the regional treasury operations in Bahrain, I made regular trips to the city. At that time, Citibank's U.S. dollar loans to Middle East borrowers were all booked on the bank's balance sheet in Bahrain, which was experiencing rapid growth in its loan assets. As the balance sheet was expanding in size and complexity, I was asked to review the branch's operations and recommend improvements.

At that time, my daughter was almost five and my son had turned three. I felt the constant moves were no longer good for the family. While some Citibankers thrived on moving every three years to see the world, we were different. I know my wife didn't like the nomadic existence and I believed my kids would be better off if they could have a more stable life to form meaningful friendships.

I also became increasingly concerned about my parents, who were now quickly approaching old age and living by themselves in Hong Kong. They were living virtually alone inasmuch as they had lost many of their friends. I began to think of moving there in part to take care of them. I began to lobby the personnel office in the Citibank head office to look for an assignment in Hong Kong. What I found was that inter-regional transfers at my level were difficult. Although I had risen in the ranks fairly quickly, I was an unknown in much of the bank, and even more so in Asia.

During this period, several Citibankers were lured away to join other multinational banks. Iran's Senof, Jan Kruthoffer, went to American Express Bank. In summer 1977, while on home leave, Kruthoffer introduced me to several top-level executives in the bank. American Express Bank was much smaller than Citibank but growing fast. I met Ting Roxas, a well-known and highly respected banker from the Philippines, who was vice chairman at that time. In various meetings, I had the impression they were interested in hiring me to work in Hong Kong at a senior level.

Negotiations with American Express Bank dragged on for months. I had a good idea about what I wanted and would not make a move unless my terms were met. Meanwhile, at Citibank in Athens, even though I liked my colleagues, the staff work did not particularly interest me. One of my colleagues, Shaukat Aziz, who was in charge of the regional training center, became the prime minister of Pakistan in 2004 under President Musharraf. I got to know Aziz since one of my jobs was to give seminars at the training center to new recruits. I found him to be intelligent and always polite and pleasant. He cultivated friendships at all levels of management and was politically very astute. In the years ahead, Aziz moved up to the highest executive rank within Citibank.

As events turned out, I stayed in Athens for barely a year. During that time, our family saw much of Greece, including the islands nearby. By April 1978, I had finally concluded my negotiations with American Express Bank. I would be considered for the position of regional head in charge of the bank's operations in Japan, South Korea, Taiwan, and Hong Kong. The only condition was that I had to spend a year in the head office in New York to get acquainted with the bank's management staff and its systems and procedures. As the assignment would be based in Hong Kong, I didn't hesitate to accept the offer. In particular, I was delighted to be able to live close to my parents again and take care of their needs.

Citibank's personnel office made several counteroffers after I resigned, but not for any position in Hong Kong, where I wanted to live. The Kwei family was about to face yet another relocation in less than 18 months.

I think of my years at Citibank as one big learning curve. It was extraordinary the bank took the risk to allow me to become a banker. The bank was full of bright young men and women with plenty of ambition. Competition was fierce, but it served as a catalyst to push people to do more and be better. In leaving, it was hard not to have a few regrets. Although I only worked in the bank for approximately six years, I had formed some good friendships with several fellow officers. Over the years, I realized that being an International Staff officer put me in a small and select group of bright bankers. It was a real privilege. There is a bond of mutual trust and camaraderie between us, even as many of us left Citibank and joined other organizations in subsequent years.

Back in New York in 1978 after being abroad for four years, I found the city in a recession. Real estate was particularly hard hit. Several prestigious apartment buildings were virtually empty on Park Avenue. Having accumulated some savings, my wife and I decided to acquire another home in addition to the one in New Rochelle. Finding a suitable home is no easy task and it took considerable time. Meanwhile, we rented an apartment on Fifth Avenue on the Upper East Side. Much to our delight, we found out we shared the building with the quintessential New York neighbor – Woody Allen, who lived on the top floor.

We were thrilled when, in September, Kathy was admitted to the Chapin School, one of the top girls' elementary schools in the city. Clarence went to a kindergarten on Park Avenue.

American Express Bank (AEB) was located in downtown Manhattan, in the financial district. The bank was one of the subsidiaries of the parent company, which is the worldwide leader in the credit card and travelers' checks businesses. Unlike other banks in the United States, AEB's charter did not permit it to operate a domestic U.S. bank. It was strictly an international bank with branches in Asia, including Japan, the United Kingdom, Switzerland, Germany and a few other countries in the developing world. The bank was headed by Dick Bliss, chairman, and Jim Greene, president. Ting Roxas was the vice chairman and was in charge of building an investment bank. Bill Beam ran the bank's international network while Bob Savage headed the treasury operation. Under Beam, my contact from Citibank, Jan Kruthoffer, headed Latin America; Larry Greenberg headed Asia, and Bob Mason headed Europe and the Middle East.

In New York, my job assignment was not initially well-defined. Fortunately, Ting Roxas gave me the challenging task of helping him draft a new business plan for AEB's investment banking operation. Coming from Citibank, where I spent three years in the commercial banking business, I didn't know much about investment banking, which earns its profits by making deals such as mergers and acquisitions, arranging loan syndications, and issuing papers in capital markets. The assignment gave me an opportunity to learn something about a very different aspect of the banking world and I welcomed it.

Roxas had recently joined the bank. He had achieved considerable fame in the Philippines as the father of investment banking for having started Bancom, the first investment bank there, in the 1960s. Later, he met Dick Bliss, who was then in charge of international banking at Bankers Trust, and turned Bancom into a joint venture with the U.S. bank. Apparently, Bancom had become a leader in the Philippines and he and Bliss had maintained good relations ever since.

When I joined AEB, it had an equity holding in Bancom, having taken over the shares from Bankers Trust. I found Roxas very intelligent, articulate, hard working, and a real gentleman. The plan I came up with was well received. It was actually very broad but primarily dealt with expanding the investment banking subsidiary in London and setting up a new unit in Hong Kong to develop the then-budding syndicated loan market.

Soon after, the board approved the plan and asked Roxas to put it into action.

In the months that followed, Roxas asked me to go to London to help organize the expansion program. He had recently recruited a new CEO in London. He also recruited a trader in Hong Kong and a Philippine banker named Manny Pangilinan to head up investment banking. Part of my job was to persuade the commercial bankers in the bank to support the new initiatives.

Soon after the two senior investment bankers were recruited and settled into their new roles, my work with Roxas was completed. I was then assigned to work in the personnel department to develop an executive development program. The bank had grown rapidly and Bliss thought it should have a process to recognize promising officers and develop them. By putting me to work on this project, I had an opportunity to know all the officers in the bank and assess their development potential. It was a challenging assignment and, once again, I had the good fortune of working on a project that required a different discipline.

The executive development project turned out to be far more interesting than I had anticipated. I conducted many interviews with mid- to upper-level managers. In these sessions, I was able to glean the aspirations and frustrations of officers who had been with the bank for some time, as well as those who had recently joined the bank. I noticed that what made certain officers move up faster than others had much less to do with qualifications than with many intangible factors. These intangible factors reflected chemistry between the manager and the managed, and among peers at the same level. Luck played an important part as well because each new head, whatever the level, always wanted to bring people he liked and discard people he did not like.

In December 1978, my family moved upstate to Scarsdale, an hour's drive from the city. The decision didn't come easily as our kids were going to very fine schools in the city. However, living in the city was very expensive and I thought a suburban life with open space would be better in the long run for the children. When we moved into our new, two-story house with half an acre of land attached to it, the kids, now five and six, were not particularly happy. Kathy had made good friends at Chapin and disliked leaving them. I realized that our nomadic lifestyle had to change, but I also knew that we would have one more move to make in the not-too-distant future.

The summer of 1979 went quickly. The kids grew to love their new home and made friends with the neighbors. We all settled into our new suburban lifestyle quite comfortably, except that I always disliked the daily three-hour commute.

Working on organizational issues, I came away with one significant lesson: how reorganizations designed at the top often inadvertently caused great hardships for lower-rank workers. When people were treated like cards on the table while an organization was constantly being redesigned, a lot of inefficiencies and productivity losses ensued. Morale would suffer and turnover would increase. A service business needs to keep and develop top-flight employees, so it was disheartening that, in several instances, experienced officers were treated like commodities. Rapid turnover was a continual phenomenon. While top management recognized all these issues, their priorities appeared to be determined by political self-interests.

The marching order to move to Hong Kong came in September 1979. I received a promotion with the title of senior vice president. Along with the promotion came a big salary raise as well as a meaningful chunk of American Express stock options. The bank had decided to split the Asian region into two parts. I would be responsible for operations in Japan, South Korea, Taiwan, and Hong Kong, while John Magee would be in charge of operations in the Philippines, Singapore and Indonesia. Greenberg, unhappy with the change, decided to leave instead of taking a management role in the newly expanded investment bank in London.

I was excited about this opportunity to assume the top management position in Asia, far away from the Middle East, where I first learned about banking. As far as I could tell, no Chinese-American had ever held such a senior line job in the U.S. banking industry. For someone who didn't know anything about banking less than five years earlier, I appreciated the confidence Bliss and Beam showed in my ability to do the job. My wife, of course, had already consented to the relocation since she also looked forward to living in Hong Kong. Our kids, however, complained loudly and preferred not to move. By then, their opinions had to be taken seriously in many family activities. I had to promise them that we would stay in Hong Kong for many years and I would not contemplate another move unless I had the consent of the entire family.

Hong Kong is a small territory, only half the size of New York City. It was the home of all the international banks doing business in Asia. Having been a British colony for over 100 years, its law and order was recognized as the best in Asia, and it boasted the best and most modern infrastructure. English was widely used in business circles and, most importantly, skilled labor was of the highest quality.

My wife headed to Hong Kong first to look for an apartment and she ended up choosing a big penthouse at Number One, Magazine Road. At that time, rents in Hong Kong were exorbitant because the land supply was controlled by the government and because the economy was strong. The apartment rented for HK$65,000 (US$8,333) per month, an incredibly high sum by any standards in the world. But in the scheme of things, such an accommodation was not unusual for a regional banking head. In addition to accommodation, the bank also provided a car and a chauffeur.

Our family moved to Hong Kong in February 1980. As typical American expat kids, Kathy and Clarence went to the Hong Kong International School, the only American school in the colony. Fortunately, they liked the school and appeared to have adjusted quickly to the new environment. We also joined the American Club, where Kathy celebrated her eighth birthday with her new friends.

My office was located in Alexandra House in the Central District of Hong Kong. The organization was entirely traditional. The country heads of Japan, South Korea, Taiwan and Hong Kong reported directly to me. The regional office also had several key staff officers, the most important one being the credit officer. Together with him, we had the authority to approve credit limits of up to US$10 million, a very large number in those days. I also had an operational officer who would assist and monitor branch operations, and a personnel officer to deal with nearly 400 employees. We also had an investment banking unit, headed by Manny Pangilinan.

Once again, my daily routine was completely swamped by matters that required my attention or approval. There were constant internal and client meetings. I had to make sure all kinds of reports went to the head office on time and correctly. As the bank was a global organization, there were lots of regional and head office meetings. I traveled a lot. I had to balance my priorities between urgent requests by the bureaucracy in New York on the one hand, and the need for decisions on matters from the branches on the other. As I didn't want to just sit in the office and deal with papers, I tried to spend as much time as possible meeting clients and visiting their operations, including manufacturing facilities. Needless to say, I was a busy man, working flat out every day. But in the three years that followed, I reached the apogee of my banking career. Let me just summarize my major accomplishments during my tenure as the regional head:

Japan was the largest profit center in my region. AEB had been there for many years. In addition to the branch in Tokyo, the bank had an operation in Okinawa that served the U.S. servicemen based there. By the time I was on the scene, commercial banking had become intensely competitive, and the traditional wholesale loans had a wafer-thin net interest margin. It was imperative the bank seek a profitable lending niche. Another key issue was the long-term employment tradition enjoyed by workers in the country. The bank's driver, for example, was making US$45,000 per year in 1980, a fact that shocked me. But still, the bank staff held lunchtime demonstrations annually, protesting the lack of wage increases.

In time, the bank positioned itself as a major lender to consumer finance companies, such as Promise and Takefuji. This was an interesting niche because ordinary consumers wanting to take out loans were not generally served by banks in Japan. Many young and not-so-affluent families borrowed money from consumer finance companies. The lending rates were about 50 percent per annum while the cost of funds to the finance companies was not even 10% per annum. The spread for these companies was unbelievable. In extending short-term credit facilities to the major players in the industry, we realized a spread of over 3 percent. I met several of the key executives in the years we did business with them and found them rough and tough, cut from a totally different cloth. Still, we never had any bad credit problems, as their businesses were all enjoying healthy growth.

For years, the Okinawa branches did not make any profits. This was due to a number of problems, but over-staffing, along with a high salary base, was the key issue. Employees there had worked for the bank since 1945 when it took over the branches from the U.S. Military. The bank's New York management had always wanted to close the branches but never seemed to be able to make the move. This was because the severance cost would be very large and its impact on the rest of the bank's Japan operation could not be totally anticipated. We consulted with labor lawyers in the States and Japan but did not receive any definitive advice. In 1982, the country head and I decided to make a move. It was a good time to do this because our Tokyo branches were finally making a handsome profit, which could cover losses to be incurred in the branch-closing effort.

We decided on a severance package that allowed staff to accept transfers from Okinawa to Tokyo, betting that most would not move in their old age. This proved to be true. I remember the day in 1982 when I went to Okinawa to sign all the papers and formalize the procedure. On the eve of the formal branch closing, I and three other senior officers were treated to a most elaborate Japanese dinner with entertainment by traditional singers and dancers. We drank many toasts with good wishes for a happy future to all the staff members who were going to lose their jobs the very next morning. It was, I thought, a very graceful way to handle a most unpleasant and difficult occasion. Something like this could only happen in Japan.

Taiwan in the early 1980s was still largely run by an authoritarian regime. The rule of law was questionable at best. Taipei was an old city and modernization efforts lagged behind its needs. Streets were jam-packed with bicycles and motorbikes. Taxis were small and smelly. The traffic was chaotic and the streets extremely noisy. Air pollution was awful. Still, many U.S. multinationals had plants and offices there, as Taiwan was regarded as an "emerging tiger," growing rapidly by virtue of foreign investments and rising exports. Foreign banks' ability to compete against local banks was, however, restricted, as they were not allowed to accept or lend in local currency. Competition was tough and profitability was hard to come by. Fortunately, AEB's branch there had been doing business for years and was well regarded in town. Therefore, we had many of the leading businesses as clients. The bank's focus was in extending trade financing along with short-term credits.

There were a number of longstanding, nonperforming loans that were mired in courts. I consulted with a couple of lawyer friends from my Boston days to help resolve these seemingly intractable matters. Foreign lenders had little recourse to securities pledged to support credit facilities. This was a rude awakening for me. The other problem was that the branch was over-staffed. We had a headcount of over 90. Working with the country head, we decided to downsize the manpower. Although Taiwan did not have the same union issues as in Japan, in practice, such an exercise was almost unthinkable. Chinese people value "face" and laid off staff would be subject to loss of face in their social circle. .

After many dialogues with senior management and our legal counsel in the city, we finally came up with a plan that was approved in New York. This time, it fell upon me to make the announcement. I did this with great reluctance. Overnight, in the summer of 1981, the branch's headcount was reduced to 50. I think we were very generous in our offer of severance, but obviously my standing among the local bankers took a hit. As events later turned out, other foreign banks, particularly Citibank, followed our lead and gradually restructured their operations as well.

South Korea was a different story. In the early 1980s, it was a developing economy. The country, ruled by military leaders, was slowly recovering from the Korean War of the early 1950s. The government had given great support to so-called *chaebols*, or conglomerates, such as Samsung, Daewoo, and Hyundai, to pursue its own industrial policies. The development model mirrored the early success story in Japan.

AEB's branch was located in the Daewoo Building, close to the downtown train station. It was one of the few modern buildings in the city at that time. Other foreign banks also had offices in the same building. The bank counted some of the largest *chaebols* as its clients. Foreign banks generally stuck to these corporations because they were deemed to be good credit risks (since they had government backing). Over the years, these large *chaebols* had become highly leveraged but none of the banks appeared to be worried. In fact, foreign banks made little effort to try to go beyond the *chaebols* to find clients, except for government-related entities. Our strategies were pretty much in the mainstream. The business was very profitable as South Koreans were willing to pay to get the required funding. The economy was growing fast as long as easy credit was readily available. But this happened against a worrying undercurrent – rising debts in the economic system.

South Korea was then a dictatorship that encouraged nationalism. One interesting phenomenon was the martial music piped into elevators in the morning while workers went to their offices. As in Japan in the early days of industrialization, there were periodic street demonstrations for democracy and the rule of law. Foreign banks did not notice this at first. Neither did I. My priority was to continue to grow the business by increasing loans to clients.

At the time I assumed the regional management position, political tensions were steadily rising, stemming from student demonstrations against President Chun Doo Hwan's regime. I happened to be in Seoul in 1982 when I witnessed a confrontation between the police and students. That morning, I had an appointment to visit the Korea Development Bank. The country head, Mark Black, and I were in the company car when suddenly we saw a huge crowd of protestors shouting and throwing stones at a distance in a major street, marching toward where we were. On the other end of the long street, lines of helmeted police or army officers marched toward the protesters. Evidently, a terrible clash was about to occur. The driver stopped the car on the curb, said something to Mark, and disappeared, leaving us in the car. Mark said that the KDB building was only one block away. We decided to get there on foot. We chose a street running parallel to the one that would soon see a major confrontation. As we hurried to our appointment, we could hear tremendous shouting and clashing sounds nearby. Tear gas blanketed the area. We quickly reached the KDB and went inside.

Throughout the day, students marched in many parts of the city. Late in the afternoon, from our office in the Daewoo Building, we could see the palace ground. In front, tanks guarded the entrance. Waves of marchers threw stones and the police used tear gas and water to keep them from advancing. Emotion was running high and our young officers obviously sympathized with the marchers. Work was totally disrupted as the staff engaged in heated discussions.

I spent some time composing a telex to inform the head office management about the riots. I had to come up with an assessment as to whether the protests would develop into a national crisis. Events such as these that reflected social turmoil would cause foreign bankers to take caution and rethink their lending policies. Credit rating agencies might lower the country's sovereign risk rating. In the worst case, banks might reduce their loan exposure and cause an inevitable credit crunch. Having discussed these issues with AEB's outside lawyer, Mark and I recommended that we hold our commitments in the country. This turned out to be a wise decision as there were no defaults arising from the social unrest. South Korea would continue to be an important profit center for the bank.

The political and social structure in South Korea moved slowly toward democracy in the ensuing years. The student demonstrations in 1982 were the result of President Chun's brutal suppression of anti-government demonstrations in Kwangju in May 1980. As has happened so many times in history, it was the students and the youngsters who had the courage to risk their lives and bring about change. In 1987, President Chun decided not to seek re-election and the country had its first free election in history, electing President Roh Tae Woo. Yet, the country's tradition of supporting *chaebols* did not change.

The major break came in late 1997 when Asia fell into its worst financial crisis. South Korea was dragged along into insolvency and needed a bailout from the International Monetary Fund (IMF) to recover. To the country's immense credit, its economy recovered quickly from the crisis and repaid the IMF loans within three years. Since then, South Korea has become a true democracy. It broke up the *chaebols*, reorganized the banking system, improved corporate governance and opened its economy to the global marketplace.

In Hong Kong, the bank was doing very well. The American Express brand was well recognized and respected. The bank had several branches on the island and in Kowloon to take deposits and serve clients. The largest companies in Hong Kong were not our real targets, as they were well sought after by major international banks. Our real target was the niche market of the robust and fast-growing manufacturing sector and several real estate groups that would agree to provide properties as loan collateral.

Because Hong Kong was dominated by medium-sized, family-owned companies, the comparatively smaller size of the bank was not an issue. Interest margins were attractive because the government at that time fixed deposit rates. I supported the investment-banking unit to expand its manpower. In particular, I supported Manny Pangilinan in his quest for a large loan syndication project. Through his persistence and hard work, we eventually received a mandate to raise a US$200 million syndicated loan for a large cement project in Indonesia. In the year that the Indocement syndication project was completed, AEB achieved the fourth ranking in the investment banking league table in Asia.

In private banking, I tried to leverage the AE brand name to launch the so-called "high net worth banking" concept, or what is now known as private banking or wealth management services. We targeted the wealthiest families in Hong Kong and offered deposit and lending services. We had a senior officer servicing these special accounts. Although we did not offer investment services, we were cross-selling AE cards and traveler's checks. This new initiative turned out to be a very profitable one.

Between 1980 and 1982, at the height of my career, assets under my management grew to over US$1 billion and profits reached over US$10 million. During that almost three-year period, my life was exciting, challenging, and rich in variety. I traveled extensively as I supervised the branches in my region. In an internal management meeting in Mexico during the summer of 1981, I gave a speech telling why Asia would one day be the most important region in the world. Looking back, it wasn't without foresight that I made the statement. In the region, traveling with senior management from New York, I met many important government officials and business leaders, including the chairman of a top Japanese bank and the premier of Taiwan. My region's performance had been exceptional as I met budgets every year. And, best of all, under my very cautious supervision, loan credits were excellent with very few nonperforming problems. Assets grew and the initiatives I described earlier were bearing fruit.

My family stayed in the first apartment for only a year. In early 1991, we moved to a house in a compound known as Strawberry Hill. It was located in an exclusive area on the Peak. There were some 40 attached units, surrounded by a tennis court, a large swimming pool and an entertainment hall. Living there was a joy. On many Sunday mornings, I rolled out of bed and walked to the tennis court to have my regular game. The kids could splash in the pool and safely biked in the compound. The supermarket was just a five-minute walk away. At times, I walked to the Peak tram station and took the tram down the hill to Central. Frequently, I got the kids to jog with me around the Peak. Since I traveled so often for work, I relished my rare weekends with them.

When I did get to spend the weekends with my kids, I usually took them to a bookstore in the morning and let them pick out books that interested them. In the afternoon, the three of us would go to visit my parents. There, we would play mahjong with my mother while my father sat on a sofa and watched us. We talked and played and had a wonderful time. It was a real blessing that, late in their years, we could share our lives with them.

At home, I made sure that music played an important part in our lives. In my study, I had an advanced hi-fi system installed. In the alcove next to the dining room, we had a piano for Kathy and me. We tried to keep the kids occupied with activities like ballet, Chinese lessons, painting, and pottery for Kathy, and judo, drawing and Chinese lessons for Clarence.

Now that the kids were old enough to travel, we took them to visit at least one new country a year. In 1980, we took the kids to Singapore and Malaysia. In 1981, we took them to Japan. And in 1982, we went to a dude ranch in Wyoming.

Because of the relatively little time I got to spend with my family, I particularly welcomed the local custom of combining business with family outings. Many of the leaders with whom I did business would entertain me and my family on their yachts and take us to the beautiful outlying islands. As a matter of fact, boating, even more than golf, was a social custom for the rich in Hong Kong. Besides the boating trips, we were often invited to cocktails and dinner parties.

Compared with the majority of the local population, we were leading a highly privileged life. Unfortunately, the good times did not last. In 1981, word spread in the bank that AE was attempting to sell the bank. This sudden turn of events was caused by the acquisition by the parent company of Shearson Loeb Rhoades Inc., the second largest securities firm in the United States, headed by Sandy Weill.

After Weill became the president of the much larger AE, he made it known that international banking would not fit into his grand scheme of things. He thought lending to various businesses with a thin spread didn't justify the associated risk. To him, a bank's business is to take money from others, not to extend money. His philosophy was very close to the *modus operandi* of a Swiss private bank.

Being a traditional international banker, Bliss didn't agree with Weill's ideas. He abruptly resigned in August 1981. His departure from the bank led to a series of changes at the top. Somehow, Al Smith, a GE financial controller, was hired to be the president, even though he had no background in banking, let alone international banking. Along with Bliss, Greene also left. The rest of the management team was left untouched. Life went on as before. With Smith being the president, Jim Robinson, chairman of AE, assumed the chairmanship of the bank. For the next 12 months, no other organizational changes were made. In Hong Kong, we had one of the best years in business in 1982.

The axe fell in the spring of 1982, when all the senior managers around the world were asked to attend a crucial meeting in New York. Each of us, when checking into our hotel during the weekend, was given an envelope. Mine specified that I should meet Smith at 10 a.m. on Monday. Curiously, the meeting appeared to be a private one. By the time I got to the executive floor, I knew that something was amiss. No one was working. Everyone was talking to everyone else. I quickly found that almost all the senior executives were fired. This included Beam, who was my boss, and two very capable executives named Al Beadleston and Guy Krug, along with Magee, the regional head for South Asia. The wholesale reorganization was certainly the most dramatic event I had witnessed in my entire corporate career.

I went to the meeting and was greeted courteously by Smith. Also present was Runny Sarda, a Philippine banker who headed the global leasing business. Smith sketched out the rationale for the reorganization, which was designed to streamline the management layer and reduce costs and cut down unprofitable activities. He said I was doing a very good job and he would like me to stay in Hong Kong. He even added the Philippines to my portfolio of responsibilities. In addition, he said that I would take over the job of running the Hong Kong operations. Finally, he said I would now report to Sarda.

By the end of the day, I found that I was the only regional head that didn't get fired. This fact gave me no joy nor relief. I was sad that so many careers had been ruined in one stroke. In the ensuing years, Magee left banking, disappearing from the radar screen, and was last known to be in Thailand. Beadleston joined Bliss in the latter's new investment banking venture that started in late 1982. Krug headed a family-based investment bank in Geneva. Beam was the worst hit. He drank heavily in spite of his doctor's advice. He retired and died a few years later.

My relationship with Sarda was rocky. I was then 47, soon to be 48. Something in me changed. I found myself less willing to listen to management instructions that didn't make sense to me. Perhaps the fact that I had received a lot of support from Bliss and Beam had spoiled my attitude. Perhaps, I was becoming somewhat arrogant and less accommodating as I entered middle age. More importantly, now that I had been able to acquire some material gains, my entrepreneurial spirit resurfaced. I was itchy to be on my own and I began to think of finding investment projects that would interest me. After all, I now knew a number of very wealthy families in Asia. In my wishful thinking, I thought it possible for me to tap their support to acquire a business I would run.

I was also getting tired of the long meetings and long hours and constant need to respond to requests by New York from every side, ranging from credit to marketing, treasury, operations, and personnel. I knew I should cater to Sarda's whims, but found the lack of chemistry between us a big problem. I also harbored the resentment that my old colleagues had all gone by the wayside just because someone, Smith, wanted to have a team of his own people. In many ways, my morale had reached a low.

At this uneasy juncture, Sarda called me one day in October 1983, and said that I would be recalled back to the headquarters.

My new job would be to work for George Carmony in corporate planning. His call didn't surprise me, as I had been warned by another colleague in New York earlier. I didn't have a choice but to move back to New York at that time. But when I said goodbye to my many friends and clients around the region, I knew that, one day, I would be back in Asia, where I now felt I belonged.

9

The Big Transition

Looking back, my work in Hong Kong as regional banking head for American Express Bank (AEB) represented the apogee of my banking career. During this exciting period, I had the opportunity to travel to all corners of the world, and my wife and children enjoyed living in different countries and experiencing different cultures.

I met and worked with many interesting people, including business leaders who went on to greater heights, such as Li Ka-Shing of Cheung Kong, Raymond Kwok of Sun Hung Kai, and Gordon Wu of Hopewell. Others, however, through excessive greed and miscalculations, ended up in jail or on the run. One headline-making character in the latter category was Willie Yu, head of Dollar Credit, a hard-drinking financier who enriched himself at the expense of everyone else and escaped Hong Kong while his business collapsed.

My years in Hong Kong, between 1980 and late 1982, coincided with a period during which Asian economies did well relative to the rest of the world. China was still a closed economy and foreign banks were not allowed to do business there. However, Hong Kong industrialists had already set up factories in Southern China to capture lower labor costs. The process of hollowing out Hong Kong's manufacturing base had begun. In 1983, China's then paramount leader Deng Xiaoping announced the establishment of a Special Economic Zone in Shenzhen, just north of Hong Kong. Permitting private enterprises to establish factories in the special zone with tax benefits and convenient export and import procedures was a revolutionary idea. This zone would become a turning point in China's economic development in modern times.

As a conservative banker, I had approved good credit proposals and turned down many bad ones. I believe targeting aggressive loan growth had to be placed within the context of the economic condition in which the business operated. Growth had to be measured against the risk involved. Far too often, a loan officer would aggressively build up his portfolio with no regard for future consequence, knowing that he might not be around when something imploded. Meanwhile, he might be awarded a bonus for booking the new business.

In one instance, an expert from our London office recommended a ship construction loan that offered more than 100 percent of the actual construction cost for the ship. In effect, the client didn't have to put up a cent to build the ship. Under the bank's matrix management system, I got to have a vote on this credit because the loan was to be extended to a Hong Kong shipbuilder. I strongly voted against the credit but it went through anyway, eventually turning sour only a year later when the company verged on bankruptcy.

To really understand business beyond financial numbers, I found it worthwhile to visit our client's factories. Meeting middle-level managers often gave me insights that I wouldn't obtain from discussions with the owners. These efforts were important in forming my judgment as to how credit should be made available and how much security was needed. Even though I was trained in the Citibank system where cash flow lending (i.e., no collateral) was the new paradigm, my instinct told me that cash flow projection for a manufacturing or trading business had to discount lots of uncertainties.

We moved back to New York in January 1983. My previous life in Scarsdale had taught me I wasn't a fan of commuting. We decided to live in the city this time around. Fortunately we were able to move into an apartment that we had purchased five years earlier when the city's real estate market was depressed. My wife had presciently grabbed the place as it turned into a co-op in 1978. The three-bedroom, two-bath apartment at 111 East 85th Street was much smaller than what we had become accustomed to in Hong Kong. Still we were able to all fit in.

We enjoyed the neighborhood because it had just about everything a family would need. I didn't mind taking a long bus ride to work, as it was still much shorter than a train ride from suburbia. Of course, living in the city was expensive, but this was the price one paid for the privilege of living in the most vibrant city in the United States. Soon, Kathy was admitted to the Hewitt School, a private girls' school off Park Avenue. Clarence went to St. Bernard, a boys' private school on the Upper East Side. Both offered a fine education.

In the American Express Bank's head office, I was given the assignment of completing the acquisition of Trade Development Bank, a private bank based in Geneva and owned by the billionaire Edmund Safra. This acquisition fit into the bank's new strategy of becoming transformed into a deposit-taking and wealth-management institution, and away from making loans as its main focus.

Trade Development Bank was primarily a bank for wealthy clients who placed large deposits in numbered accounts. American Express (AE) paid US$800 million for the bank, a very significant amount in the 1980s. My job was to lead a small team to perform due diligence to make sure there were no hidden skeletons in the closet. Thanks to bank secrecy laws in Switzerland, the bank's management refused to disclose any client records to us.

In the ensuing years, Safra found the AE culture and management style incompatible and decided to sell his stake in its shares. In the process, the AE shares dropped from above US$40 per share to the low US$20s. As a result, Safra did not receive anywhere close to the value of the deal at the time it was done. Worse, he was prevented from competing against Trade Development Bank for a number of years. In time, however, he did set up another private bank and named it Safra Bank.

I was assigned to explore other acquisition candidates – an exciting task as I had a chance to meet some interesting executives in other industries. Once, when I was assigned to look into possible joint projects with the Republic National Bank of New York, I had an opportunity to visit the bank's gold vault in the basement of its head office in lower Manhattan. The room was made of steel and lined with large cages, each of which contained numerous gold bars – a sight not easily forgotten.

In early 1984, I realized that my career at AEB was going nowhere. I really didn't enjoy office politics and didn't like being away from real action in Asia. I found that the adage about executives living in ivory towers was true. Even though the pay was great, I wanted to be in a position closer to the customers. I contacted my headhunter friends in Hong Kong, hoping to land a job there once again to continue my banking career and look after my aging parents. In no time at all, Andy Choa, an old friend from Citibank and now head of the Hong Kong office of Russell Reynolds, a global executive search firm based in New York, found an interesting opportunity. It was to head up a small merchant bank for a well-respected Indonesian family.

The Soeryadjaya family, a very prominent name in Indonesia, owned Summa International Finance. Back in Indonesia, the family controlled the Astra group of companies, a conglomerate that included the largest auto assembler and distributor in the country. The offer was to head up Summa International Finance Ltd (SIFL), the finance unit in a larger group that spanned several businesses in Asia. SIFL primarily served the trade finance needs of small- to medium-size companies in Indonesia. I apparently fit the type of CEO they were looking for: someone with considerable banking experience, a strong reputation, and the ability to improve the profitability of the small but important entity in the family's international businesses.

The opportunity to head up a small finance company was very interesting even though my responsibilities as the regional head for AEB had been a lot weightier than the Summa's state of play. That this job would allow me to travel to Southeast Asia and to meet business leaders there was enticing. Andy's advice was that if I was interested in returning to Asia, this would be as good a starting opportunity as I was likely to receive. Encouraged by the prospect, I discussed the offer with my family.

By then, our kids had an equal weight in terms of our family's decision-making process. After some candid discussions, they said that they would support my move if this was what I really wanted to do. So I told them, "Yes, what I want is to leave the corporate ivory tower."

By the end of May, Summa agreed to my terms, including a binding five-year contract. With this in hand, I decided to leave American Express. Once again, our family got ready to pack and move. The hectic but exciting life in New York came to a premature end.

At the time, the macro environment in Hong Kong wasn't good. Shortly after I returned to the United States in late 1982, Hong Kong suffered one of its worst economic setbacks in many years, thanks to the austerity measure instituted by President Reagan to stem inflation in the States. Short-term interest rates soared to double digits in the States. Because the Hong Kong dollar was pegged to the U.S. dollar, Hong Kong, too, had to raise its interest rates substantially. As a result, its stock market took a big dive, reminiscent of the crash in 1973. While I was in New York, the Hong Kong dollar was re-pegged from 5.6 to 7.8 to one U.S. dollar.

By the time I returned to Hong Kong in early August 1984, the property market had just hit the bottom. Investors' sentiment was fragile and business confidence was subdued. There was talk about a Sino-British agreement to return Hong Kong to China. Some observers believed that Hong Kong's special capitalist system would be preserved for some time while skeptics thought the best years of Hong Kong would soon be over.

Summa's unique advantage was that the owner's family in Indonesia had a vast network of business contacts and was thus able to make judgments on the integrity of potential borrowers. Because foreign bankers were eager to do business with Astra, they considered Summa favorably when it came to extending credit to the finance company. Finally, Summa had few competitors with Indonesian roots in Hong Kong to serve the trade finance needs of small- to medium-size Southeast Asian businesses.

My family resettled into Strawberry Hill again, attracted by its many amenities. This time, we lived in a house that had a small garden overlooking the south side of the Hong Kong Island. The kids slipped right back into their lives at the Hong Kong International School. They were, by now, old enough to want to spend their weekends with friends instead of always with their parents. So, on Saturdays, I visited my parents mostly by myself. Every Sunday morning, I went back to playing tennis, now mostly with my old friend Andy Choa.

I made many trips to Jakarta and Surabaya, Indonesia, in search of new clients. This effort was greatly facilitated by the shareholders' network in their home country. Still, it was tough because the firm's funding costs were relatively high and, in many cases, our offers were not competitive enough. One success I had was in recruiting a foreign exchange trader who was able to generate fee income through currency trades in the interbank market. I also shortened the maturity of the loans to more closely match the short maturity of the firm's funding sources. As things turned out, this one step probably saved the company from serious troubles ahead.

There were two startling events that I didn't anticipate when I joined Summa in mid-1984. First, the Indonesian economy was suffering from high interest rates. Second, in 1985 in Hong Kong, the Overseas Trust Bank with roots in Malaysia went belly up. The bank was a well-respected and longstanding financial institution so its quick demise was all the more disturbing. The knee-jerk reaction of foreign banks was to cut banking lines to all the Southeast Asian–based financial institutions including Summa. While we used to have facilities from regional U.S. banks, they now politely informed us that the lines were not going to be renewed. The liquidity crunch became a serious issue.

Fortunately, HSBC was an exception, because it has had a very long relationship with Astra. In the months following the Overseas Trust Bank crisis, I regularly met with John Bond, a mid-level executive who oversaw the Summa credit. Bond, being groomed in those days in the mid-1980s, was already on the fast track to upper management. He later became the chairman of the HSBC Corp. Since my management style was super-cautious, Bond had no problem in keeping the lines open. In addition, branches of several Indonesian banks in Hong Kong extended credit to replace funding resources withdrawn by Western banks.

In 1985, British Prime Minister Margaret Thatcher went to Beijing to negotiate the end of the colonial rule of Hong Kong. The result was a Sino-British Declaration that would turn over the sovereignty of Hong Kong to China under the "one country, two systems" concept first espoused by Premier Deng Xiaoping. Under that system, Hong Kong would preserve its capitalist framework for 50 years.

In this macro environment full of uncertainties and with the company's assets shrinking, it was obvious that the potential for growth was limited. In several meetings with the Soeryadjaya family, I suggested we should explore the possibility of entering into fund management activities. The firm needed another source of revenue, namely, revenue from fee income to be generated out of the proposed new strategy. The family was not keen to pursue my idea, mostly because I had no background in fund management. These discussions continued through the first half of 1986 with no progress.

One day in the summer of 1986, I was having lunch in the Bankers' Club when I ran into Peter Woo, Chairman of Wharf Holdings, a large publicly listed property-based conglomerate. Peter is the son-in-law of Sir Y.K. Pao, one of the most prominent and successful shipping tycoons in Asia. Pao had just acquired a 13 percent interest in Standard Chartered Bank in the United Kingdom in a dramatic effort to prevent the bank from falling into the hands of another English bank, Lloyds. I had known Peter for some time. He was from Shanghai and we had met on several social occasions. I casually asked Peter what his plans were following the very large investment. I left the impression I would like to be of some help, if it were appropriate. To me, it was just a friendly gesture. Unexpectedly, I later received a call from his office, asking me to meet with him.

My original idea was to obtain an advisory assignment from either Woo or Pao to help them sort out typical issues involving a bank investment. With years of bank management experience, I believed I was one of the best professionals to do this.

After I was served tea in the executive suite of Wharf on top of the Wheelock House in Central, Sir Y.K. and Peter entered. The meeting was short and direct. It was clear Peter had no intention of using my services as an advisor from Summa. Peter's offer was to hire me to work with him directly on matters that would come out of the board of the bank for his attention.

This was the first time I met Sir Pao, whose reputation was global in extent. He had started with one ship using borrowed money after he and his family left Shanghai and moved to Hong Kong in the late 1940s. He shrewdly proceeded to expand his fleet to one of the largest worldwide shipping empires through good and bad times. Pao was cautious and his conservative way of running his business ensured that he would survive the cyclical downturn suffered by the industry in the 1980s. Furthermore, he was astute and lucky enough to gain control of Wharf, one of the top real estate based conglomerates in Hong Kong.

Working on banking issues at the board level would allow me to be involved in decision making at the highest management level – an opportunity I welcomed. In addition, I would probably work on other assignments for Peter. At the end of the meeting, I felt I had received a new lease on my career even though I didn't know any details of the offer, particularly those related to compensation. In any event, I was ready to jump ship, not just because of the nature of the assignment, but also because I was interested in gaining some insights into how the Pao family maintained control of its vast network of investments.

Though I had a five-year contract with Summa, I resigned after just two. I thought the departure was mutually welcomed as the Indonesian shareholders realized I could add little value under the prevailing conditions. Despite difficulties during my time at Summa, I have maintained a very good relationship with the Soeryadjaya family in subsequent years.

My brief tenure at the top of a family-owned finance company, on balance, added much to my experience, particularly in getting to know the people in Southeast Asia. When I resigned, market forces were quickly driving smaller institutions out of business. Summa Int'l Finance was eventually merged with European-based Indover Bank. Many small finance companies in Hong Kong simply ceased to exist.

With the exit from SIFL, my banking career officially came to an end.

◆

I joined Wharf Holdings in mid-September, right after I left Summa. My role was to go over all materials sent from Standard Chartered Bank and advise Peter Woo of my views. In addition, Peter asked me to look after various share and bond investments related to the company's pension funds. While I'm not at liberty to discuss much of my work on the family's investment in Standard Chartered Bank, I will briefly describe my experience as a first-time portfolio manager.

Before I joined Wharf, its pension investments were managed by outside investment managers. In early 1987, Peter believed that under his supervision, I could manage the funds in-house to save management fees payable to the external managers. This decision fitted neatly with my personal long-range plan to work in fund management. It didn't take me a second to accept the challenge. I recommended to Peter we should permit outside managers to run 50 percent of the funds so we could compare our performance against that of the real professionals. He agreed.

To get going, I got in touch with several major multinational brokerages such as Kidder Peabody (now extinct), Goldman Sachs, and several others. Since the funds were to be invested globally, Peter and I set up an investment committee with the Wharf treasury personnel. The committee would decide how to allocate funds between asset classes and which regions of the world they would be exposed to. Although Peter would make the final decisions, in practice, he left it pretty much up to me to make the stock selections. I started becoming a professional stock picker, poring over materials to find companies that would deliver long-range earnings growth.

At this time, our kids were old enough to begin thinking about college. As parents, we had long thought about sending them to the States. After talking with friends and educators, we decided it would be best to send them to a U.S. preparatory school so they would have an easier transition to an American college. Even though I knew we would miss the kids greatly if they left home, we suggested the idea to them. Surprisingly, they loved it and agreed to put in the work to make it happen.

In the spring, the Taft School in Waterbury, Connecticut, accepted our kids – Kathy to the 11th grade and Clarence to the 10th grade. In early September 1987, we took them there with a lot of mixed emotions. The good thing was they appeared to enjoy the change of their lifestyle and being independent of their parents. But, suddenly, our home was quiet. Like all parents before us, Teresa and I had to adjust to a new life in an empty nest.

Our family has been fortunate in that all of us have been healthy. Rarely did we need to visit a doctor and this applied to my parents as well. So, it was a jolt that, one day in April 1987, my father passed away unexpectedly. Father had seemed perfectly normal when I talked to him that afternoon about some trivial matters. There was no sign of ill health. Just eight hours later, at about midnight, mother phoned with the news he had passed away while sitting in his favorite chair in the dining room. He was 91.

My father had accomplished a great deal in his long life. His work ethic had certainly passed onto me. His integrity, honesty, and stubbornness were traits I have also inherited. I know he was happy our family was close to him after so many years of living oceans apart. My only regret was there were no parting words and I didn't have a chance to comfort him in his final moments.

That same year, the world was shaken by the biggest stock market crash since the Great Crash of 1929. October 19, 1987 was dubbed "Black Monday." The crash didn't just happen unexpectedly. There were plenty of warning signs along the way.

Since 1985, global stock markets had been rising steadily. By March 1987, there was some talk about a bubble forming, particularly in Japan. Still, the New York stock market had been going up steadily as if on autopilot. The dollar was, however, weak, in spite of heavy intervention by the Central Bank of Japan. I noted that Brazil had just announced it would not pay interest on their sovereign debt and wanted creditors to cut a new deal. Of more interest, the U.S. Congress worked out a mild version of an import restriction bill President Reagan signed into law. Then, the United States decided to retaliate against Japan on its semiconductor exports and trade tension reached a very high level.

By May, the U.S. long-dated bonds were yielding 8.75 percent and prime rate was 8.5 percent. Inflation was creeping up. In the exchange market, the dollar continued to be weak. Then, Citibank shocked the financial world by announcing that it would reserve US$3 billion against third world loans. Markets took a dive but they recovered shortly. Investors were already nervous but they hadn't given up on the booming stock markets. Sensing that the warning signs were onerous, I grew increasingly cautious, anticipating it would be only a matter of time before the burst would hit the equity markets.

In June, stock markets continued to gain ground. In Hong Kong, even though the prime rate was raised to 7 percent, the Hang Seng Index was breaking new highs. My pool of equities was under-performing the outside managers because I started to take profit and moved more of the assets into cash-equivalent, short-term investments.

In late September, the first sign of trouble was seen when the U.S. market began to slide, dropping 200 points in the last three weeks of the month. The dollar was weak as the U.S. trade deficit reached US$16 billion in August. Still, market speculation was strong, especially in Hong Kong. Then, on October 7, Wall Street saw a major fall of 91 points. The U.S. long bonds were now yielding 9.8 percent as inflation continued to rise. The U.S. prime rate was raised by another 0.5 percent, following increases in Japan and Germany.

On Friday, October 16, right before Black Monday, the Dow Jones Industrial Average plunged 108 points on the highest turnover in its history. The Average had already dived more than 10 percent in a week and over 17 percent since mid-August. I had been steadily selling the fund's equity exposure while I noticed the outside fund managers had kept their equity exposure at 80 percent of the total funds under their management. We had a number of discussions on this point but the professionals were adamant that stock markets would head higher.

October 19 was a historical day in the global financial markets. The selling started in Tokyo. Prices plunged because of what had happened in New York the previous Friday. U.S. Secretary of State James Baker added fuel to the fire by suggesting the United States would let the dollar fall if surplus countries (meaning Japan) did not cooperate to support the dollar. In Hong Kong, the Hang Seng Index lost a record-breaking 420 points. Worse, the futures market quickly fell to the daily limit. Investors could not hedge their positions after the first two hours. Then, European markets opened and were sold off.

I had put in all my sale orders for the U.S. market during the day and went to Peabody's office that evening to see how the market would open. It started the day 67 points down. Many big-cap stocks such as General Motors did not open for several minutes. Those were some seriously unnerving moments.

By the end of the day, double-digit drops were common among the blue chips. IBM fell 30 points to close at US$103 per share. The Dow Jones Industrial Average fell 508 points, or a whopping 22.5 percentage drop. The combined falls on the preceding Friday and on that Black Monday were greater than the losses sustained in the first two days of the crash in 1929. It was estimated that US$1 trillion of wealth was wiped out in the US alone. To stave off total disaster, banks began cutting interest rates, but the dollar sank to all-time lows against the German mark and other currencies.

In Hong Kong, regulators decided to close the market, an unprecedented move heavily criticized by just about every analyst and expert. When it re-opened on October 26, the market dropped 1,120 points, or 33 percent! The Hong Kong futures markets opened with the support of a HK$2 billion safety net provided by the government, and the bailout money soon doubled in size. Many futures brokers were instantly wiped out. Untold thousands of small speculators and investors in Hong Kong lost their fortunes as they failed to meet margin calls.

Everyone was shell-shocked. At Wharf, although we had suffered losses in our equity exposure, they were nowhere near the losses sustained by the company's outside managers. Peter promptly fired all of them. In fact, he decided to keep all the money in cash.

The crash changed a lot of people's mind-set regarding risks and equity investments. Although it appeared a recession would surely follow such a huge market crash, I believed stocks were trading at a bargain level and they should be bought. This was a contrarian call. Peter didn't buy the idea.

The weeks following the crash were full of doomsday sentiments. I had to cancel attending my first Parents' Weekend at Taft. I re-read the history of the market crash in 1929 and found many differences. The most important difference was that, unlike in the earlier debacle, the Federal Reserve pumped money into the monetary system and lowered the cost of funds to borrowers. This softened the blow dealt by the stock market crash. At the same time, the entire global financial system was now much more flexible and could better adjust to exigencies such as this recent event. Nevertheless, it was an unnerving experience. Many businesses went under and many personal bankruptcies were reported. I thought this was a once-in-a-lifetime crisis. Little did I know I would face another one closer to home just a decade later.

Among the people I knew, many had lost most of their savings. For example, my accountant told me that his margin account was liquidated by his broker and he was now deeply in debt. He cried: "What can I do now? What can I do now?" To cheer him up, I replied: "I am sure you will make it back sooner or later." True to my prediction, he did just that barely a year later. This is but one example of Hong Kong people's resilience in the face of adversity. The "never-say-die" attitude has made the city a beehive of entrepreneurs.

When all Wharf's pension fund assets were turned into cash, Peter moved their management to the treasury office. This left me with little work other than the Standard Chartered assignment. Several investment projects on the front burner were now set aside. Peter's attitude turned decidedly more cautious as banks worldwide took big hits. Banks' collateral values sank in the wake of the financial meltdown while their less creditworthy borrowers were unable to repay their obligations.

While business conditions couldn't be worse, I had two work opportunities beckoning. First, Bank Indosuez in Hong Kong approached me about an assignment to reshape their business strategies. Second, I was approached by Dick Bliss, ex-chairman of American Express Bank, who had earlier formed a small merchant bank in Hong Kong named Asian Oceanic Group. He asked me to join his bank. In November, when most investors were just barely recovering from the market crash, Dick was in Hong Kong to look for someone to head his company's new investment management function. Clearly, he specifically had me in mind when he brought up the subject.

During the New Year holidays, my wife and I talked about my various career options. We decided I should leave Wharf Holdings to take up the Indosuez assignment and then join Bliss afterwards. The former was a lucrative contract and it would give me an opportunity to act like a management consultant. The latter was also exciting as my discussions with Bliss had progressed to a point where I was getting comfortable about his organization and his executives. Once again, I changed employment, the second time in two years.

By the end of 1987, the world had taken a massive financial hit. Hostilities between the United States and Iran erupted when, in October, the US hit three Iranian oil storage targets in the Gulf. Still, there were some bright spots. In July, President Chun Doo Hwan of South Korea, under popular pressure, decided to permit direct election of the next president. The decision took place after two weeks of street demonstrations. It was one of the most important developments in the modern political history of Asia.

Even in Russia, Mikhail Gorbachev was leading liberalization initiatives that would eventually lead to a fundamental change in the Soviet political structure. At the end of the year, I was once again optimistic about the world and my own future.

In the years that followed, I remained interested in the banking world. As an investor, I have invested in several Asian banks. Much has changed in the banking industry since my days as a banker. Bigger banks are getting bigger and their reach has expanded globally through mergers and acquisitions. More importantly, in seeking to grow their earnings beyond the organic rates determined by economic conditions, banks had been allowed to become financial supermarkets offering everything from securities to insurance to wealth management.

Few remember such a conglomeration of services with totally different risk-to-reward ratios led to the financial collapse of 1929. Today, the rapid expansion of all types of banking services has led to a world awash with debts, both private and public. Not satisfied with the wide range of playing fields, banks and other financial institutions have been allowed to use so-called derivative instruments to further improve earning prospects. The highly complex derivative transactions conceal the true leverage and prevent easy calculation. No one knows how much risk has been built up in the off-balance commitments banks have made to each other.

When I was in banking, I was amazed to see how inter-bank lending with the goal of making a tiny spread was allowed to escalate, virtually unchecked by regulators. If a bank was perceived to be sound, there was no limit to how much short-term money market transactions it could conduct with counterparties. The entire system was a house of cards held together only as long as no player would pull out his card. Today, the risks are much, much greater than some 20 years ago. Therefore, the risk of a financial misstep in this global card game is far greater than what most people are willing to admit.

I believe we are approaching the extreme end of a pendulum swinging between tight regulation to the left and total market freedom to the right. This pendulum swing to the right has been stretched repeatedly by financial engineers of all kinds and patched up repeatedly by central banks too afraid to halt the excess. The day will no doubt come when the pendulum will swing back. It is impossible to surmise how the financial landscape will look like after the current excesses are wrung out. It would not surprise me to witness a tremendous transfer of power from debtor countries to a new group of creditors.

The above words, written in 2006, read as prescience now that the world has suffered an unprecedented financial crisis since mid 2008. While it was triggered by subprime mortgage loans in the United States, the crisis has been materially aggravated by off-balance risks. These risks have been driven by derivatives abated by rating agencies, poorly understood by market makers, and overlooked by financial regulators. I will have more to say about this in a later chapter.

10

My Private Equity Years

When I joined Asian Oceanic Group (AOG) in March 1988, the company had been in business for more than six years. Founded by Dick Bliss, AOG was backed by capital from Cigna Insurance Co., ORIX Financial and Nissho Iwai in Japan, and Kuwait Foreign Trading, Contracting and Investment Corporation (KFTCIC), an investment bank from Kuwait. Its corporate mission was to help growing private enterprises in Asia raise capital and then to take them public when appropriate. Investment banking was a key part of the business strategies. Over the years, it had completed several notable deals, financing in Hong Kong such businessmen as Y. S. Lo of the Century City group and Allan Wong of Vtech Holdings.

My main responsibility as chief investment officer was to head a new activity for the company, namely investment management. My job entailed reviewing and advising Dick Bliss on all investment proposals. I had the authority to veto a potential deal. Only Dick could override my decisions. I believe Bliss felt my presence would take some pressure off him for rejecting many of the proposals generated by the organization.

Another objective was to develop a new revenue source for AOG that was independent of investment banking fees and treasury trading gains and losses. Unlike the latter two activities which, by nature, had volatile revenue generation, investment management would provide a steady revenue stream because it received regular management fees. This was the main attraction for me to be part of AOG.

I had two choices on starting the investment management business. One was to raise a fund to invest in public equities in Asia. Another was to raise a fund to invest in private firms likely to go public within three years. I made the decision to raise a private equity fund after I had spent some time reviewing the company's track record. What I found was the firm had, since its founding in 1982, successfully invested in several companies and I could use these transactions as the firm's track record. However, because the company's track record in investing its own capital was not extensive and because I could not personally claim any experience in this business, I knew raising money for this project was not going to be easy.

The private equity industry in Asia was still in its infancy. Two former Citibank officers I knew, Lou Bowen and Anil Thadani, were considered pioneers when they launched their Asian regional fund in 1983. Bank Indosuez had started one that was headed by Tony Lo. CEF, an organization associated with Li Ka-Shing's Cheung Kong, had a small fund run by Alan Ho and Ed Ahnert. Another early pioneer in private equity funds was Bob Thaleen, who had organized Chinavest. Because they were in the process of investing their first fund's capital, none of these firms had a long track record. The nascent stage of the industry provided the kind of challenge I welcomed.

After consulting with colleagues, I named the to-be-launched fund "Asian Special Situation Equity Trust" (ASSET). The fund would invest in established companies experiencing high growth and requiring outside capital to expand. The key exit strategy for the fund was to take the investee companies public and sell the fund's holdings over time.

The fund would have a term of seven years and would be limited to investing capital in the first three years. Further, the fund could not re-invest any returns from the exits so that any realization would be returned to investors. The management fee was 2.5 percent per year and there was a performance incentive of 20 percent of profits payable after the investors received their principal and had an annual return of 9.5 percent.

My plan was to raise US$25 million – a reasonable sum in those days for a first-time fund – with 50 percent coming from AOG's shareholders. Through the spring of 1988, I worked on the prospectus and began talking to the institutional investors of AOG. Initially, all of them turned me down – a surprising blow. Further, I didn't have much luck attracting professional third-party marketing firms to help raise capital.

During the second half of the year, I made numerous trips abroad to meet potential investors – San Francisco, Houston, Atlanta, New York, Chicago, Boston, Dallas, London, Milan, Madrid, and Geneva. I met investment managers in private banks, intermediaries, private investors, and corporate pension fund managers. It didn't take long before I knew all the questions and had ready answers for them. It was then I learned a typical fundraising period could last as long as three years. The early negative response to my approaches didn't discourage me. In fact, I assumed the attitude that "when the going gets tough, the tough get going." I completed the fund's placement memorandum at the end of July.

1989 turned out to be another tumultuous year. It started with the world in relative peace. George H. W. Bush was now President of the United States. The Palestinian Liberation Organization had just renounced violence and the United States began to work with Yasser Arafat to reach a peace deal with Israel. Russians were pulling out of Afghanistan, a defeat that would have profound consequences in later years. North and South Korea appeared to be eyeing each other for a better relationship.

In financial markets, equities were doing well. Leveraged buyouts, or LBO deals, were in the hot seat. These deals were pioneered by Drexel Burnham to facilitate acquisition of presumably undervalued assets by issuing less than investment grade bonds, so-called junk bonds, at very high interest rates. Institutional investors were buying them as quickly as they were issued. By 1989, all the major investment banks such as Morgan Stanley and Goldman Sachs were in that business. They raised huge amounts of money for increasingly questionable deals. Michael Milken, the head of Drexel, was regarded as a genius and a hero. I was often visited by investment bankers who invited me to join their game. I never did because I thought it was highly imprudent to buy bonds of issuers that were running negative cash flow and appeared to have no ability to turn their cash flow positive anytime soon.

By the end of January, I had the assurance from AOG's investors that they would each put in US$2 million for ASSET as seed money. More importantly, Bliss assured me AOG would invest a total of US$4 million. I needed this vote of confidence if I were to have any chance of attracting outside investors.

With shareholders' assurances, I began to look for potential investments. My target was to seek successful private companies looking for expansion capital in the range of US$5 million to US$10 million. Even though AOG had a corporate finance arm, I was looking for deals mostly through my own network. My advantage was that I had been working in finance in Hong Kong since 1980 and I already had many good contacts.

In looking for viable deals, it is always a challenge to sift through the chaff to find the wheat. When investors like me encounter businessmen seeking private capital, they are obviously already successful; having overcome God knows how many obstacles and difficulties. Yet, this is not a guarantee that they will succeed in the future.

In Asia, family and friends traditionally funded most private businesses when they started. Management typically came from family members as well. Outsiders were not welcomed because either they were perceived as untrustworthy or the family members didn't wish to disclose certain situations to those outside the family. There was nothing wrong about this way of doing business as long as the family members were professional, competent, and didn't play around with unethical transactions.

However, when a successful business grows beyond a certain size, outside professionals have to be hired and responsibilities delegated and proper management controls installed to keep growth momentum intact. The willingness of the entrepreneur and his family to develop a proper organization to meet increasingly complicated challenges is a crucial factor in how far the owner can take the business forward. This human factor is not always easily discernible. I view this as the single biggest risk factor when investing in private equity transactions.

In spring 1989, I undertook another marketing tour, this time to Munich, Geneva, London, Toronto, Boston, Portland, New York, Atlanta, Los Angeles, and San Francisco. I never stayed in any place longer than four days. I also made a lot of cold calls based on contacts sent to me by various parties.

While there was a general interest in my presentation and the support by AOG's shareholders was valuable, I couldn't satisfactorily assuage investors' concern about the credibility of AOG and my ability to make the fund successful. I came to realize I was not a strong marketing person. I simply did not have the aggressiveness, charisma, and mannerisms to attract investors to believe in my claims.

Meanwhile, Bliss and Francis Estrada, President of AOG, decided to invest in a Hong Kong company called SemiTech Holdings, headed by James Ting. SemiTech was a small company with a manufacturing facility in Shenzhen. AOG had taken this company public earlier. Now the company was seeking acquisitions for growth. With a stake in the company, Estrada thought AOG was in a strong position to act as the exclusive investment banker for Ting. Bliss was excited about the new arrangement.

In February 1989, Ting made a deal to acquire the sewing machine division of the Singer Group in the United States. Singer, in recent years, had diversified into the aerospace business and decided to jettison the sewing machine group that had originally been the basis of the company. The sewing machine business had become loss making. Ting thought he could make the business profitable by shutting down the expensive factories in the United States and Europe and moving the manufacturing to China. The only issue was how to finance the deal. From newspaper reports, Singer hoped to sell the group for at least US$300 million.

Not surprisingly, AOG was appointed as SemiTech's investment banker in this transaction. After the company won the bid to buy the Singer Sewing Machine Company for US$38 per share, AOG proceeded to underwrite an equity issue to take out the bridge financing Ting had arranged for the transaction. The total size of the transaction turned out to be US$270 million, the largest acquisition in history made by any Asian company in the United States. AOG had hit a home run, while taking enormous risks at the same time.

In early May, upon the death of former Premier Hu Yaobang in late April, about 10,000 students marched in Beijing to mourn this liberal leader who had been ousted by Deng Xiaoping two years earlier. Initially, the Chinese authorities did not use any force and there were no casualties. However, beginning May 4, there were massive student demonstrations in Beijing and other cities demanding democratic reforms. These demonstrations turned into mass sit-ins in Tiananmen Square. Sympathetic support for the students poured in from around the world.

On that fateful day of June 4, I was in New York, having just flown in from a visit with my daughter, who was in a special study program on the coast of Maine. I first heard of the news in a call with one of my investors. When I turned on the TV in my hotel room, I saw tanks and troops mowing down unarmed people in the square at night. Chaos, bloodshed, and sheer violence ruled the day. Later, I read an estimated one million people in Hong Kong had gathered at least three times to protest the massacre.

One Sunday in early July, there was another demonstration in Hong Kong to protest the Tiananmen massacre. By then, my kids had come back from the States. I took them to march with a very large crowd. It was a peaceful march with lots of singing and slogan shouting. It wasn't too often I felt compelled to express my feelings in a public demonstration. For several years afterwards, I would continue to go to annual gatherings in Victoria Park, commemorating the June 4 tragedy.

The massacre shook the world at large and took the wind out of my fundraising activities. Investors turned negative on Asia because of perceived heightened political risks. I decided to close the fund and stopped seeking additional capital. The total commitment turned out to be US$12 million from AOG and its shareholders, and another US$500,000 from two U.S. families. ASSET achieved only 50 percent of its targeted size. Nevertheless, I was eager to begin making investments.

In the ensuing three years, I made 11 investments for ASSET, creating a portfolio that was diversified in terms of industries and countries. The investments were made in the telecommunications industry, contract manufacturing, semiconductor packaging and assembly, computing systems reselling and service, synthetic fabric production, injection molding equipment manufacturing, travel services, and consumer appliance production. These businesses were located in Hong Kong, the Philippines, Singapore, Thailand, and Indonesia.

I sourced many of the deals from my old contacts in the financial industry and banking clients. All of these deals required a great deal of work, checking out industry sources, visiting plants, interviewing mid-level managers, and, in some cases, sending third-party accountants to audit the accounts.

By early 1990, markets began to head south because of interest rate and inflation fears. The LBO market, which had been in vogue for the past two years, was now in trouble. In early February, a major Canadian real estate developer filed for Chapter 11 bankruptcy. Barely 10 days later, Drexel, which pioneered the LBO business and had been touted as the most innovative investment-banking house on the street, resorted to Chapter 11. In no time at all, the entire house of cards collapsed. Indeed, in the summer of 1990, of the 10 core holdings recommended by Morgan Stanley in the midst of the junk bond craze the previous year, all but two would go into bankruptcy in the next 12 months.

In late May, Kathy graduated from the Taft School. The whole family was there to celebrate. We were very pleased and proud Kathy won two awards, one for her painting and another for her Independent Study Project, for which she created a very large and outstanding batik piece. We were also pleased Kathy had been admitted to Cornell University, her first choice. Then, in mid-August, I took Clarence to visit college campuses, as I had done with Kathy a year ago.

In August, Saddam Hussein invaded Kuwait, a move that was quickly followed by the U.S. deployment of troops into Saudi Arabia. Tensions over an imminent war ran high and escalated in succeeding months. One consequence of the Iraqi invasion was that KFTCIC, one of the AOG shareholders, moved all its senior executives to London. The bank basically ceased to operate in Kuwait and many of their loans went sour. The increasing fears of war took a toll on financial markets. In late September, stock markets around the world were falling and oil prices began to move up.

The year 1990 ended with the world waiting for Hussein to agree to a U.N. resolution to retreat from Kuwait. If he failed to do so by January 15, 1991, the United States had the authority to go to war to enforce the resolution. Meanwhile, a major economic downturn appeared imminent with high oil prices and high interest rates acting as strong headwinds against economic growth. Bliss called me late one day in December to talk about reorganizing the entire AOG group by downsizing corporate finance and building up investment activities. I thought such a move would make sense but was probably a little too late.

The U.N. deadline came and went. The inevitable war began soon after and lasted less than a month. However, the devastation in Kuwait was severe and the loss of Iraqi lives was horrendous. President Bush decided not to go after Hussein personally and permitted him to remain in power. Thus, although the United States won the war, it did not lead to any lasting peace in the region.

While I was happily doing my deals and building credibility in the market, AOG's fate turned uncertain. This was largely due to a real estate deal it had sponsored two years earlier in Boston. The project, which involved the construction of a residential building on the site of a former shipyard, had now been completed. The timing couldn't have been worse as the completion occurred in the midst of a real estate slump. AOG had to repay the construction loan, but it could not find any bank to provide mortgage financing to take out the previous borrowing. To add insult to injury, home buyers interested in acquiring individual apartments in the building could not find mortgage loans. As a result, finished apartments sat unsold. This crisis led to a desperate search for new shareholders as the existing ones didn't wish to subscribe to any new shares of AOG.

Sometime in the spring of 1991, Cigna, AOG's largest shareholder, found a potential new partner in a finance company called MBF Finance. MBF was one of the fast-growing finance companies in Malaysia. Its founder, Tan Sri Loy, was a hard-charging and aggressive entrepreneur. Loy had an advisor named Leslie Merszei, who was nominated to be the COO of AOG, even before the financing deal was finalized. He took over the helm in Hong Kong and, immediately, Estrada and most of his corporate finance team were dismissed. So, in the Hong Kong office, only my group and a few staff members remained. In New York, the headcount had shrunk to the bare minimum, with Bliss still at the helm.

Several months passed before MBF claimed that it was unable to obtain Malaysian Central Bank's approval to remit funds it had committed to AOG shareholders. In this very uncertain time, I decided to raise a second fund because ASSET's capital was almost totally invested. My idea was to identify strategic investors around the region who would inject parts of their businesses to the new fund in exchange for shares in the fund.

In the second half of 1991, I was encouraged when several major industrial groups agreed in principle to participate. Still, the AOG crisis began to require me to work with Merszei in fashioning a new business plan. As 1991 ended, AOG's future was very much in doubt.

In this fateful year, Clarence graduated from Taft, making us extremely proud. Now a very fine young man, Clarence decided to attend Tufts University outside of Cambridge, Massachusetts and major in economics.

As 1992 began, the world was in recession and the U.S. dollar was weak. On the other hand, interest rates were low and stock markets were doing well. The Soviet Union by now had disintegrated. In the United States, election fever was building. There was a general expectation that President Bush would be re-elected in the fall. My spirit was high even though AOG was in dire straits. A rising stock market was good because portfolio investments could only be realized profitably when market conditions were favorable. I was quite successful in selling investments in the ASSET portfolio. By the end of June, I had returned over US$3 million to investors.

The AOG demise began in late March when MBF decided to pull out of the deal. The only hope was with AOG's Kuwait shareholder, KFTCIC, which began to take a serious look at bailing out the sinking ship and hopefully protect their investment.

Unfortunately, KFTCIC was itself in a liquidity bind because it had a lot of nonperforming loans from clients whose businesses were ruined by the Iraqi occupation. This was not surprising. I witnessed firsthand the devastation of Kuwait City, littered with bombed-out buildings. Black smoke was still rising from nearby oilfields.

In mid-April, we learned that the Kuwaitis declined to step up to the plate. This decision meant the end of AOG. KPMG was immediately appointed to handle a so-called voluntary liquidation. The fact that AOG was not forced into bankruptcy was a godsend to me, as according to Hong Kong laws, a director of a company forced into bankruptcy would be involuntarily barred from serving as a director for three years. More importantly, my standing in the community would take a hit for sure.

In the following months, much of my time was spent in helping KPMG, which pored over every document to determine if there was any fraud or hidden losses. The nasty thing about liquidation was that the liquidator treats every director as guilty until proven innocent. By now, I was the only executive left in Hong Kong. Everyone else had been fired. Only a few clerical staff remained to help the liquidators. The atmosphere was incredibly strained.

I spent much of my time talking to potential investors in Asia about taking over AOG's investment management unit. I thought the demise of AOG could be a blessing in disguise as it afforded me an opportunity to begin my own investment business.

With this in mind, I organized a new company named Pacific Capital Management Limited (PCML). One of my contacts at Baker Mackenzie helped me, pro-bono, to apply for an investment adviser's license with the Securities and Futures Commission, the regulatory body in Hong Kong.

In mid-July, all the ASSET investors met in Hong Kong to hear about the status of the fund and my plan. Their principal concern was whether the fund would be dragged down by AOG's demise since AOG was one of the investors in ASSET. During the meeting, KPMG assured the investors they had no intention of pulling the plug on ASSET and viewed the fund as well-run and profitable. KPMG said they hoped to find the highest bidder for the fund's management contract. Implicit in their statement was their intention not to keep me as the manager, if they could find a better alternative.

I was determined not to see my efforts with ASSET derailed. I recalled that, about 11 years ago, I had to jettison my firm, International Data Applications. I wasn't going to have a similar experience the second time around. In my search for a white knight, I identified two serious interests, one in Jakarta and one in the States. Meanwhile, several firms appeared interested in hiring me to expand their private equity businesses. So, my prospects began to look promising.

Late in July, I was asked to surrender my office keys to KPMG. Luckily, KPMG appointed me to continue managing ASSET through my new company, PCML. This was indeed a most welcomed decision as that was my sole source of income. KPMG no longer viewed me as one of the directors of a defunct company but one of their "partners." I had earned their trust.

In the second half of 1992, I sold another US$4.6 million of the portfolio investments. I continued the process until the selldown was completed in mid-1996. The fund realized an average internal rate of return (IRR) of 35 percent per annum over a lifespan of seven years. This made ASSET one of the very rare funds that was organized in the late 1980's that had its entire portfolio investments realized without any leftovers. It was one of the top performing private equity funds in Asia.

Looking back, the most exciting aspect of my work in managing a private equity fund was finding candidates for investments. There are basically two deal types. One is sourced from investment banks. This type of deal is likely to be expensive because it is basically a bidding contest. The other type is what the manager originates himself, the so-called proprietary deal flow. The latter requires arduous work. A successful investment manager needs to have a great deal of fortitude, persistence, and continually draw on a deep well of optimism. To get a deal signed up, he has to find the right candidate, complete detailed due diligence, negotiate favorable terms, and hope no other investor makes a better offer. A lot of things can go wrong in the process, and they often do.

While managing ASSET, I made several noteworthy investments that were good examples of what went into the work of a private equity investment manager. Let me share my experiences with the reader below.

My first significant transaction for the fund was a buyout in 1990 of a contract manufacturing business in Singapore from its parent in the United States. The U.S. company, Flex Holdings, had contract manufacturing plants in California as well as one in Singapore and another in Hong Kong. Flex was on the verge of defaulting on its debt when its creditors forced the company to spin off its Asian operations to pay off its debt.

A U.S. investment bank handling the sale approached us, along with all the other private equity firms in Asia, to assess this opportunity. At the very outset, Ed Ahnert of CEF and I agreed to work on the deal together as neither of us had sufficient capital to make a solo bid. We went to Singapore in March to meet the management and gained a firsthand view of the operation.

At that time, contract manufacturing had a great future as U.S. multinational companies had begun outsourcing their production to third-party service providers, particularly in Asia, in order to lower their production cost and to avoid making major investments in plants and equipment. The Singapore plant specialized in assembling printed circuit boards for the US electronics industries. Flex Holdings had a good array of clients, but margins were thin even though sales were growing. Controlling production and engineering cost and maintaining a high yield rate were keys to making a profit on each production run.

Before we made the bid, Ahnert and I brought two other private equity investors into our group. The first was HSBC Private Equity and the second was the private equity arm of the Security Pacific Bank. The transaction was complex and it was the first MBO (management buyout) deal in Asia. We divided the due diligence work among the four. Negotiation of key issues was handled in the same way.

As events unfolded, our group was able to establish a good rapport with the Singapore management team. We grasped the essence of their business issues quickly, and our plan to move forward after acquisition satisfied the current management. By late April, all the issues were resolved except valuation. Price negotiation took a couple more weeks before the parties came to an agreement in May 1990. We agreed to value the business at US$50 million, the equivalent of paying five times the profits of 1989.

A new company, called Flextronics, was set up to acquire the assets and the business of Flex. The new company would have sales of around US$100 million and profit before tax of US$10 million. The buyout was financed with a US$25 million loan from Security Pacific Bank's Singapore branch. The bank also took a position in the equity part of the deal. After the handshake, it took another month of hard work to complete all the legal agreements. Meanwhile, HSBC dropped out and I persuaded Asian Oceanic Group to warehouse their commitment for a period of six months. Eventually, I sold that piece of equity to Jardine Fleming's Private Equity with a small profit.

Because the U.S. was in recession from 1991, the company's revenue and profit slid for two consecutive years. Meanwhile, to lower production costs, we set up a plant in Johor Bahru in Malaysia, just across the border from Singapore. We closed the Hong Kong facility and set up a pilot plant in Shenzhen, just north of Hong Kong.

In my role as a director, I visited Flextronics' key customers in the States and played a part in closing down its office in Massachusetts and its pilot plant in California. We beefed up and reorganized the U.S. sales force. By emphasizing quality operations and customer service, the company expanded its customer base to many of the world's largest companies, including Hewlett Packard, IBM, Siemens, Lifescan, and more.

In 1993, we made a number of senior management changes. We recruited Mike Marks to head the company. He had been a plant manager in California. Mark brought in new investors to contribute urgently needed additional capital. Marks' presence made a huge difference and the company went public in 1994 at US$14 per share on NASDAQ. ASSET exited its investment in the company during the first half of 1995, realizing a compound annual return of 17 percent per year. In the years that followed, Marks built up Flextronics to be one of the major players in the contract manufacturing industry, with billions of dollars of sales in 2005.

The second investment deal I want to mention is the one with ODSSPI, a leading IBM equipment reseller in Hong Kong. It was founded by Roger King, husband of Alice Tung, daughter of shipping magnate Tung Chee Hwa, who would become the first Chief Executive of the Hong Kong Special Administrative Region. After King returned from the States, where he had worked at Bell Labs, he chose to start his own company instead of working for the Tung family business.

Having recently acquired a competitor, King thought it was time for him to find a strategic investor to help him grow the business with the addition of extra working capital. He was comfortable having me as that investor.

Each private equity deal has its own rhythm, and one cannot push it too fast or allow it to slide. King and I took our time in negotiations. We explored different structures before settling on an innovative approach. It was an "increasing rate convertible note," which offered the holder an increasing rate of interest that would approach the kind of return I would expect for a straight equity deal in three years. Additionally, I had an option to convert the note to equity at a predetermined price at the end of the term. After months of negotiations, we finally cut the deal in early November 1990.

During the period ASSET held the investment, ODSSPI became by far the largest reseller of IBM PCs and computer systems in Hong Kong. Its profit grew 2.5 times between 1991 and 1993. While business was growing every year, King tried to accelerate its development by exploring merger and acquisition possibilities with another comparable vendor. We also explored the IPO option on NASDAQ. In early 1995, Jardine Matheson, the venerable old British trading company, acquired ODSSPI. Jardine Matheson had a small subsidiary in the same business so the purchase made a lot of sense. After months of negotiation, King was able to extract a decent price for the exit. In November 1995, the entire stake was sold, yielding the fund a return of 57 percent per annum.

In 1991, I completed two more significant transactions. One was a proprietary investment in Bangkok-based Hana Microelectronics, a low-cost subcontractor for Swiss watchmakers founded in 1984 by a Hong Kong Chinese surnamed Han. When I met Mr. Han's son, Richard, back in 1990, he was in the early stage of diversifying the company business in watch assembly into the packaging and assembly of semiconductor chips. As the new venture was very capital intensive, Richard thought a strategic investor would add capital to and lower the family's risk exposure in their investment.

In my visits to the plant close to the Bangkok International Airport, I found the labor skills required for the packaging and assembly of electronics were basically the same as those needed to put together watches. Although the company was still losing money, I thought the management was experienced. The production manager had been recruited from National Semiconductor's plant in Thailand and had the right kind of track record. Richard had keen business acumen and his father appeared to be a cautious person. What the business required was some patient capital to sustain cash flow needs while multinational clients took their time to qualify Hana's production.

The due diligence took some time and the deal was concluded months later. Like the Flex deal, we brought together a group of four investors, raising 137 million baht in new shares. Over the next few years, Richard and I worked to add value to the business, first by setting up another plant in northern Thailand, where labor costs were lower, and then by acquiring a competitor in Hong Kong. The company's shares were listed on the SET (the Stock Exchange of Thailand) in February 1993. The IPO raised another 280 million baht for expansion. By late 1993, the stock traded up to 220 baht per share. At this point, ASSET exited its investment. Our investment realized an annual return of 68 percent per annum for a holding period of almost three years. I would continue to serve on the Hana board for two more years before resigning.

Many people do not realize that a private equity investment manager typically spends a huge amount of time screening deals and working on what will eventually be aborted. Many factors cause deals to fall apart. One of the most important is valuation, that is, the value one assigns to the ongoing business. The buyer, i.e., the investment firm, obviously tries to invest at the lowest possible price while the seller, i.e., the entrepreneur, tries to obtain the highest price.

Another reason for a failed transaction is related to hidden issues not disclosed during the initial screening process. This is not unusual because the typical Asian entrepreneur has not previously encountered a professional investment firm and often has skeletons in the closet that are eventually discovered.

The third common reason for an eventual aborted transaction is simply a change of strategy on the part of the owner, who may be tempted to take the company public, especially when the public market is robust, instead of selling a stake to a strategic investor as a first step to public listing at a later date.

Finally, when there is a good deal, you can almost always expect fierce competition among investment firms.

Let me give you two examples of deals that were not concluded. Both were proprietary transactions, at least when the deals started.

The first example concerned a Taiwan manufacturer of tennis rackets. When I met the CEO of the company, he was willing to look into the possibility of having an outside investor. In the following months, I spent a considerable amount of time and effort to make him understand the process of working with institutional investors. For example, due diligence required us to review the financial accounts in substantial detail. We also needed to contact the company's key customers, including Wilson Sports in Chicago. There were a number of talks about valuation methodology. Discussions dragged on for months while the Taiwan stock market kept sinking. Still, the owner was reluctant to make total disclosure.

One day, the owner disclosed that he was in a joint venture with an American firm based in Seattle. Since the Taiwan firm was an expert in production, the Seattle affiliate was created to market a line of rackets with its own brand name. The idea seemed quite exciting. This affiliate already had an offer from a small investment bank to take it public in the States. Since the negotiation with the Taiwan deal was not going anywhere any time soon, I was invited to take an equity stake in the Seattle company.

While working on this transaction, I met tennis greats such as Jimmy Connors, John Lloyd, and Boris Becker who eventually endorsed the new line of rackets being sold worldwide. Still, we could not close the valuation gap between what I was willing to pay and what he was ready to offer. I had to walk away from the deal. The footnote to this project was that the Taiwan company remained private and the Seattle company, after two years of contract with Becker, was closed down.

Another transaction, aborted for a different reason, had to do with a company that made an automobile accessory in Shenzhen, located just north of Hong Kong. The owner was a typical entrepreneur from mainland China, strong, jovial, and successful in his own right. When I met him in 1991, he had a big house in Repulse Bay, Hong Kong, and owned a large yacht, which he showed me in great style.

I visited his two factories in Shenzhen and found that they were basically large machine shops, doing everything from making the smallest pieces such as screws to performing the final assembly of the accessory. During my visit, the owner quoted costs of everything to impress me. Later, I sent Julien, my associate at AOG, and an outside advisor to look into his company's books, and found them totally inadequate. It was evident he had no way of knowing the true cost of all the parts and pieces he was making. I suggested he should engage a professional financial controller. This he promptly did, but I found that the new controller wasn't really qualified.

I was having serious doubts about this situation when I learned that another private equity fund was also looking at this business. The straw that broke the back of the deal was when he offered me a sizable number of shares in the company if our fund would complete the deal.

This company went public two years later and I was sure the private equity fund made a good return. The epilogue of this project was that the company went bankrupt a few years after its public listing. The entrepreneur expanded into a totally unrelated field of business and the rapid expansion dragged down his entire enterprise.

While I enjoyed my work in private equity investing, building up a very good track record for ASSET, I could not turn my success with ASSET into a winning formula. Nevertheless, the return I generated in ASSET turned out to be an exceptional case as Asian private equity funds that were started in the late 1980s had generally produced losses due to inexperience of managers.

Over time, the Asian private equity industry evolved to be increasingly dominated by major investment banks, and independents slowly disappeared. As more money is concentrated in fewer and bigger players, smaller deals are now often neglected. The kind of deals I used to make with ASSET are now few and far between.

In the future, when good results are produced, independent players will return. I hope the industry in Hong Kong and, more particularly, in China, will develop in a way it has in Taiwan. There, the private equity and venture capital industry is big and robust, supporting startups and late-stage development in technology and non-technology fields.

11

Starting My Investment Advisory Business

While working with Summa back in 1985, I had been exploring the idea of starting my own investment management business. This was not an off-the-wall idea. I had done considerable research about what it would take to be a successful investment manager and found that there are three very important qualities. First, one has to think for himself and not necessarily follow the crowd. He has to be calm and take a lot of pressure without being overly stressed out. Second, a successful investor has to have great self-confidence and the ability to act decisively, even when, as is inevitably the case, not all the information for a decision is available. Third, one has to be intellectually curious about the world around him. He is usually someone who knows some things about everything but not a lot about anything. I was convinced I possessed exactly all these traits.

Another important factor in my decision to pursue this career was, unlike many other businesses, an investment manager's success can be clearly quantified. Like athletes, his score determines whether he wins or not. A winning personality may help, but, over time, it is the measurable element of his work that will determine his future success.

There is something concrete and solid about investment work. Further, I believe creating wealth, not by speculation or unsavory means, is a great profession because material progress cannot be made without it. Unlike owning a bank, which would require great amounts of capital, starting an investment management business needs almost no capital. Equally important, this is a profession that has no retirement age. Warren Buffet has continued to work well into his 70s, and I have heard of a few managers over 80. All these factors were great attractions to me.

There are downsides as well. Who would trust me enough to give me their money? Where would I locate potential clients? I have seen several market bubbles and crashes and know that markets are volatile and timing is an uncontrollable factor in determining success. Does the world need one more investment manager? It is already full of managers who fit into every kind of investment style imaginable. Finally, is my age going to be an impediment? In response to these concerns, I address the last one by simply knowing I had a lot of energy and motivation and no problem working long hours. As to the other concerns, I would not know unless I plunged into the fray.

When I started my new career in 1992, I had to change my routine in order to conserve cash. Instead of driving, I started riding the bus to work. I began to fly economy rather than business class. Whenever possible, I used public transportation from airports to hotels.

I wasn't as frugal with important family events. My kids usually came home around mid December for the holidays. My wife and I would host a big party each year to celebrate the Christmas season. We ordered two turkeys from the American Club and the kids prepared some Japanese dishes. We all spent a lot of time decorating a great Christmas tree. Our living room and dining room were fairly spacious so we put up three tables and serve more than 30 guests. Kathy, with her fine artistic touch, bought small red woolen socks, stuffed them with gifts, and handed them out as party favors. This family effort was great fun and meant a lot to us.

New Year's Eve was spent at the FF Ball, which took place in the Furama Hotel, situated in a relatively quiet section of the

Central district. FF is the short name for a Chinese student fraternity that began its existence during the very early days of the Chinese going to the United States as university students. The fraternity has many "chapters" in various college towns. In Hong Kong, many of the returning students formed a local chapter. Every New Year's Eve, the fraternity would organize a dance to celebrate the coming year. The ball has become a tradition among many Chinese who had gone to the States for studies.

Although I am not an FF member, several of my good friends are. So, my wife and I join the occasion virtually every year to have fun with old friends. As usual, we were having a very good time when, shortly after midnight, a tragedy occurred in the nightlife district of Lan Kwai Fong. This trendy area in Hong Kong features small narrow streets that slope down from the hillside and are crowded with bars and restaurants. For no apparent reason, the New Year's celebration turned into a stampede. In the chaos, 18 people were trampled to death. Most were between 15 and 17 years of age. Clarence was in the area and Kathy, who had just joined us at FF after midnight, went to look for him. Fortunately, she found him and his friends in good shape but somewhat shaken by the incident.

The first half of 1993 was a transitional period for me. My first objective was to find a strategic investor for my new company to help me raise a successor fund to ASSET. I needed to do this because ASSET, similar to a typical private equity fund, had a life of seven years and would be wound up in 1996. I proceeded to prepare a business plan coupled with a financing proposal. While doing so, I began to seek potential interest in a new fund I would organize.

Managing ASSET didn't take much time because I was making no new investments. On the downside, as I sold more investments, the management fee, pegged to the net asset value of the fund, began to trend down. I had to find a quick solution as my income was slowly drying up. During the months that followed, I networked with different prospects in Hong Kong and elsewhere in Asia and the United States. Unfortunately, my search wasn't fruitful. Most people had no interest in backing a startup firm with only one entrepreneur.

To help conserve resources, I moved to another business center in the Central district in 1993. I had one small desk, a chair, and a small bookshelf in a tiny room. I liked the couple who ran the place. They were working on a unique project promoting windmills as an alternative source of energy in developing countries in Asia. Their CFO also helped me organize the accounting functions for my company. I was getting used to being the head of a company with no staff. I had to do virtually all the menial work. For example, I had to go to the bank and deposit checks and make payments myself. I was also the bookkeeper and the clerk who did all filing work.

By May 1993, after having networked for over six months, I began to conclude that forming an alliance with a third party was too difficult. In a way, the assumption that I needed a strategic investor showed a lack of self confidence in what I could do on my own. Eventually, I turned my attention to raising a new fund.

I went to the United States and made my proposal to a number of contacts. I found little encouragement. However, a few suggested they would consider providing a small amount of capital if I would set up a fund to buy public equities. They thought my work in private equity deals would be useful in sorting good stocks from bad ones in the public markets. The idea sounded interesting. I had entertained the same notion back in 1985 when I headed up Summa International Finance.

Running a public equity fund had a number of advantages. First, the investable horizon would be much wider than that for a private equity fund. Further, incentive payments would be payable annually when there were profits. Unlike the structure of a typical private equity fund, I didn't have to wait for years until the investors had their invested capital returned before payment of incentives was available. I thought raising money for a public equity fund would be easier if the fund could be redeemable on short notice. I knew there were many one-man investment advisers in the States managing equity funds, so having no staff wasn't a big issue.

I returned to Hong Kong, reasonably convinced I ought to give this idea a try.

In the next month or so, I concentrated on writing the placement memorandum for the fund and named it Asian Select Equity Investment Partnership, L.P., (ASEIP). I contacted David Lindskog, my classmate and senior partner at Curtis, Mallet-Prevost, a New York-based law firm that had several fund management companies as clients. I also contacted several banks in Hong Kong to find a custodian/administrator for the fund. This process turned out to be more difficult than I thought. Big banks were not interested in a startup fund by a one-man outfit. Fortunately, I had known the CEO of N.T. Butterfield Bank & Trust in Hong Kong for some time and he agreed to support my project. Finally, I appointed Ernst & Young, the auditor of ASSET, to be the fund's auditor.

While the fund was being organized, Mark Barth, the lawyer assigned to my project at Curtis, put together a structure that was comparable to that of a hedge fund. The new fund would be a limited partnership to be organized in Delaware. I would set up another partnership as the general partner. The management fee was pegged at 1 percent per annum on the net asset value of the fund and there was a performance fee of 15 percent on profits. Investors could participate in the fund or exit the fund quarterly. All these features made sense and I readily agreed to them. I engaged Henry Steiner, an old friend, who is arguably the best corporate image designer in Hong Kong (his work included the logo for HSBC), to design the front cover for the placement memorandum.

By the end of June 1993, I had achieved another realization of US$4.1 million for ASSET. The total distribution to investors had now reached almost US$12 million. On the books of ASSET were still investments valued at more than US$20 million. It was clear, by then, that my little private equity fund would be a great success. While this was very comforting to investors, the management fee, which was a percentage of the initial capital of the fund, was now a fraction of what I had received only a year earlier. Fortunately, out of the blue, a Hong Kong–listed company (which shall remain confidential) asked me to help them organize a real estate fund. I gladly accepted the assignment and this work helped my cash flow situation immensely. The assignment also permitted me to spend much of my time away from the little cubicle I had in the business center.

All the essential elements to launch ASEIP came together in early October. On November 6, I flew to New York on my first-ever road show for my new fund. I had with me a presentation summarizing my professional background and the main features of the fund. I checked into the Yale Club of New York, which would be my home away from home for several years.

The challenge of raising capital cannot be adequately described in words. Only people who have actually done it can appreciate the difficulty of extracting cash from investors who are understandably careful, hesitant, and skeptical. Raising a first-time fund is always difficult as there are many alternative funds with good track records already up and running. Who was to say the world needed yet another fund, especially one focusing on Asia, excluding Japan, a region considered developing, volatile, and full of risks?

As things turned out, three factors helped me kick off the project. First, the Asian markets were particularly strong and their performance was headline-making in the second half of 1993. Hong Kong would score a gain of over 100 percent for that year. With markets running hot, potential investors were willing to listen. Second, I was helped by several key people without whom the fund could not have been launched. Third, I had the energy and persistence and the never-say-die attitude that would not permit rejection to stand in the way of achieving my goal.

I spent 17 days in the States on my first road show. For the first week or so, I spent hours making calls to contacts and their referrals. Initially, this was a tough thing to do as I am not a natural salesman. However, I realized there is no other way to find investors. My experience in raising capital for ASSET in 1988 and 1989 had prepared me to face rejection without getting upset.

To increase my batting average, I started making phone calls to people who were unlikely prospects, just to rehearse my pitch and gather confidence. I practiced my presentations with a few contacts who agreed to act as critics and skeptical prospects. The rehearsals allowed me to feel confident about my story.

Keep in mind this period was pre-cell phone and pre-Internet. The fastest communication was through fax and overnight courier service. One's productivity was nowhere close to what can be achieved today. Making arrangements to meet took time and effort. I was fortunate that Peter Vlachos, who heads Austin Asset Management Inc. and whose clients invested in my ASSET fund, allowed me to use his office facilities in New York to make calls. His generosity in supporting me in this way will not be forgotten. I was a regular at the Kinko's copy center, especially on weekends. Such was the life of a "road warrior."

In my presentation, I stressed my long career in the financial industry, particularly in Asia, using the investments I had made for ASSET as examples of the type of investments I would be seeking in the new fund. My private equity investment experience was highlighted as a differentiating factor against other fund managers. My six-page presentation showed the dynamics of the Asian region and suggested its economic future was bright and promising. To my delight, the salient points in my presentation played well among early prospects.

One of my first meetings was with Lee Klingenstein, a senior partner at Neuberger & Berman, a major investment management firm in New York. I had met him previously because he was on the board of the Taft School, where my kids had studied. He agreed to arrange for me to meet a few colleagues and I ended up pitching to four very experienced and knowledgeable investment managers of exceptional quality.

Another early meeting was with Tom Chrystie, an ex-vice chairman of Merrill Lynch, who lived in Jackson Hole, Wyoming, and happened to be visiting New York. He was very encouraging and said he would pass my material to a few others in his vast circle of contacts. We had a wide-ranging discussion and I felt that he understood my investment philosophy and agreed with it. Tom would become a good friend and generous supporter over all the succeeding years.

I then went to Boston to meet Guli Arshad, who was running a boutique investment management firm with his partner, Jamie Nuland. The introduction was made by Bill Bullock, my classmate at Yale. Nuland & Arshad managed money for some wealthy families in the area. Arshad showed tentative interest and told me he would introduce me to some of his clients on my next trip. I was delighted.

Shortly before Thanksgiving, I returned to Hong Kong, knowing I would be back in the States soon to follow up on the initial discussions I made. I didn't accomplish much but I thought I might have garnered the commitment of around US$2 million. I thought I would launch the fund if I could raise around US$5 million.

After Thanksgiving, I cleared up some matters in the office and returned to the States. My travels took me to San Francisco, Portland, Chicago, Atlanta, New York and Boston. In Atlanta, Bob Varn, who ran a successful boutique investment firm, introduced me to several prominent businessmen in the city. He hosted a lunch at the City Club, where a dozen potential investors showed up. At lunch, I met Elliott Goldstein who asked me to see him privately the next day. I did and I received the distinct impression he would participate. It was the first time I had received some definite expressions of interest and now felt my effort was finally gaining traction.

Most investors asked me three questions. First, they wanted to know why they should invest in Asia. Second, they wanted to know why they should invest now. Third, they asked me why they should select ASEIP. I built the answers into my presentation. I also learned that my anecdotal comments on what I had experienced in my years in Asia were of interest to my audience. My tinges of gray hair were a big plus for people seeking an experienced manager. It worked against me, however, when investors were looking for bright young upstart managers.

It was obvious my biggest challenge was to overcome the fact I had never invested in public equity markets professionally. There was no assurance that I could deliver what I proposed to do. Another difficult issue for me was I was clearly a one-man show. A lot of potential investors told me that they wouldn't invest with my firm until it had an organization and proper succession plan. Fortunately, the United States is a big country and different investors are comfortable with one strategy or another. I soon learned my investing style and people with confidence in the future of the Asian region fit into a small niche in the world of equity investment in the States. Nevertheless, the small niche was big enough for my appetite.

The most positive thing about selling myself to tough prospects was it allowed me to know my own strengths and weaknesses. In every session, I learned something about myself. I learned to state my case clearly. I had the obvious advantage of experience that, without any conscious effort, would surface in my discussion. I was surprised I could walk into a room full of strangers and feel energized by the crowd and deliver a talk that varied according to the reaction of the audience.

In my presentation, I would never promise anything I couldn't deliver, and that included the promise of what sort of return the fund would produce. This modesty would sometimes backfire. However, I felt it was important to have investors who truly believed in my investment style and my character. So, I began to build a reputation of honesty and transparency that has continued to this very day. As things turned out, most of my investors would become very long-term supporters and good friends.

During the trip, Dick Bliss, former head of Asian Oceanic Group, introduced me to a prominent New York family. The head of the family was a very famous former banker whose identity I cannot reveal. He was already in his 80s and impressive in his demeanor. He was healthy and alert about current events. At one cocktail party, he and I were chatting for about an hour with others – standing. When the food was served, I asked him to sit down with me as I was tired. He, on the other hand, showed no sign of fatigue whatsoever. His spirit and energy were simply incredible. In a later meeting, his daughter indicated they would invest US$1 million, thereby becoming the biggest and arguably the first investor in my fund. Their support lifted my spirits to new heights. I knew then there was no way I would turn back on this road that I was traveling.

Two other likely prospects emerged in the following days. In New York, I met John Lee, a classmate at Yale. He was on the board of Yale Corporation and had received the Yale Medal, the highest honor a Yale graduate could receive from the university. Lee' support gave me another lift. I met Charlie Moore, an independent third-party marketing agent at one of the bars in the Waldorf Astoria. Over the din of bar chatter, I explained my case and he became interested. He talked to Frank Meyer, a fund manager of a fund of funds operation in Chicago, and arranged for him to see me the next morning. The meeting went well and Moore later told me he expected Meyer to participate. This was fantastic news.

I then took a well-deserved break when Kathy came down from Ithaca. It was snowing lightly and we went to the

Rockefeller Center to see the lights on the gigantic Christmas tree. The old magic still worked. My spirits were now much improved. We went to buy some books at Barnes & Noble and saw a movie together. The next evening, we went to a Christmas dinner hosted by Bliss. On the following day I flew back to Hong Kong with my daughter. As befitting a successful trip, both of us were upgraded to business class for the 21-hour journey.

The year 1993 ended on a happy note. I was making progress in my new venture. The kids were doing well at school and were noticeably maturing. My income was not great but sufficient. In the second half of the year, I realized another US$1.3 million for ASSET. By then, I had returned the entire invested capital to all the investors. On the ASSET balance sheet, three of the four core investments remained, and I knew the companies were doing well. The fund's success was virtually assured. I was working long, hard hours, but being a workaholic, I didn't mind a bit.

I was juggling a number of balls in the air, what with the important advisory assignment from my Hong Kong client, the sale of ASSET portfolios, and the role as director on the boards of three companies. At the same time, I was organizing ASEIP from soup to nuts. With all the work going on, I still managed to have some social activities with my wife on weekends. In many ways, at the age of 59, I hadn't slowed down a bit.

On January 6, 1994, I went on a critical road show in the States to nail down commitments from interested prospects. After five cities in two weeks, I managed to convince eight investors to commit US$4.5 million, just short of my $5 million target. Of my eight initial investors, three turned out to be extremely important.

Tom Chrystie, ex–vice chairman of Merrill Lynch, was among the first to commit. He has been a steadfast supporter ever since. In subsequent years, he has been generous in introducing me to people he knows – and he knows many. Through his introductions, I now manage an individual investment account for a prominent Texas family. Bob Varn in Atlanta had been another faithful supporter until his untimely death a few years ago. Through him, I found several investors, including the Atlanta Historical Center, which has participated in the fund since 1996.

Among my investors, Elliot Goldstein is one of my heroes. He graduated from Yale just before the Second World War ended and was in a tank unit at the Battle of the Bulge. After his commander was killed in the first day of the battle, which took place in a clearing in a forest, he took charge and held the Germans at bay for three days. Goldstein was one of the few to survive the battle, as most of his unit's soldiers were either killed or captured. He never wanted to tell the story until a few years ago when he published a book about the experience. After the war, he returned to Atlanta and built Powell Goldstein LLC into one of the most prominent law firms in the city.

Goldstein and his wife have been generous to a fault. For about three years, I stayed with them on my regular visits. The art collection displayed in Goldstein's home is magnificent. In October 2005, I went to his 90th birthday celebration in Atlanta and found him alert and in good spirits, as always.

Another major supporter was Dick Bliss, my old boss at American Express Bank and later at Asian Oceanic Group. His confidence in my ability to deliver results had never wavered. He introduced me to the Asian Cultural Council, which committed US$1 million early on. He also introduced me to the retired CEO of a major Wall Street investment bank, who committed US$1 million at the outset. Bliss and a couple of his colleagues who were with him at American Express Bank later participated in my fund. They have remained as participants to this day.

After I returned to Hong Kong, I began to receive capital from the investors throughout the month of February, the starting month for ASEIP. Very quickly, I set up the first broker trading account with DMT Securities, which was controlled by an Indonesian group. I had known the CEO for many years, and he allowed me to freely use the fund management unit facilities of his company. I used their research materials and often sat at a trading terminal in the company's dealing room. Since I was really new to the business, being with the professionals in trading, research, and fund management was extremely important. I was lucky to have the support of DMT's infrastructure, without which my learning curve would probably be long and full of bumps.

Looking back, the startup period was the most exciting and challenging period in my long career. I had, in the span of seven months since the summer of 1993, launched a new career that has carried me to this day.

12

Building My Business – the Early Years

In the years that followed, I became one of those road warriors piling up almost 1 million frequent travel miles. Technology now made it possible for me to work virtually anywhere in the world and do my job without missing a beat. International brokers started getting toll-free 800 numbers so I could put through trades while in the United States without incurring telecommunication costs. Using my 2.5 pound laptop computer, communicating with my office and reviewing materials from any source was made extremely simple. .

My workload was split into two different realms. In Asia, I sought the best investment ideas by attending conferences, meeting investment bankers and analysts and visiting companies and their production facilities. Reading reports and the business press kept me up to date on the latest developments. When traveling outside of Asia, I focused my time on finding investors, primarily in the States, but occasionally in Europe.

From the very beginning, my marketing efforts had never been a great part of my time and effort. I have preferred to spend the majority of my time in delivering superior performance for the investment partnership. Initially, I relied on the contacts I had in the States. Since then, I have relied mostly on word-of-mouth referrals to obtain new clients. I have continued my marketing initiatives in the States because the U.S. investors are far more willing than investors elsewhere to take a risk on using a small investment boutique.

Even though I had only been in business for several months, I was well aware of the niche I filled in the vast market of investment funds. Obviously, the interested prospect had to want to invest in Asia in the first place. It would be fruitless for me to try and convince someone about the merits of Asian investment if he were set against the idea. The investor had to want to invest with an independent investment manager, not an institutional manager. Research studies have shown independents outperform institutions in the long run. Finally, the investor had to prefer a firm on the ground in Asia, not a firm in New York or San Francisco. After applying these filters, the chance of an investor landing at my desk would be reasonably good, provided that I could get over the hurdles of being a one-man firm running a new fund and being of my ethnic background.

My investment style and strategy attract a small niche of investors – usually U.S. private families who want to get in on Asian equities in a cautious way. My investors are typically well informed and sophisticated. What distinguishes them is that, like me, they value capital preservation above all other investment criteria. In fact, they shy away from investment managers who tout top of the range performance. Through experience, my clients understand that, when it comes to investing, there is no free lunch. They know that incredibly high performance cannot be obtained without incurring an equally high level of risk.

Instead of talking about performance, I spend most of my time talking about my investment strategies, the Asian economic and political landscape, and how I select stocks for the portfolio. A few investors made their commitment without spending much time analyzing my fund's performance. While my investors have stayed with me for a long, long time, the downside is that my firm's assets under management have remained painfully modest. I have not found a way to grow my business faster than the slow pace that it has experienced since 1993.

When I started receiving my first batch of subscription money from investors in early 1994, the Asian markets were already falling. Partly, this reflected normal profit-taking from an overbought market that ended in 1993. Partly, investors were concerned about the Fed raising interest rates. So I held back and didn't make many commitments. By the end of the first quarter, my fund was down marginally while the overall Asian market was down a whopping 16 percent. It was not a bad beginning but I suspected achieving positive performance was not going to be an easy task.

In the early days, my investment focus for ASEIP was directed quite a bit at Southeast Asia, including Singapore, Malaysia, Thailand, Indonesia, and the Philippines. I did that for several reasons. First, the South Korea and Taiwan markets were not open to foreign investors in general. Special accounts had to be created to trade in those markets. Our fund was simply too small to be allowed to open a trading account in those markets. Second, China shares had just begun trading in Hong Kong. It was extremely difficult to access management of these companies and the stocks had little trading history on the exchange. In addition, it was simply convenient for me to visit companies in Southeast Asia, because, being a director on the boards of one Thai and one Indonesian company, I often traveled in the region.

It wasn't long before I figured out the reality of accessing company information. While big cap companies would send their investment relations (IR) staff to meet me and provide only information available to everyone else, I found my visits to smaller companies attended by senior management were much more productive. Perhaps, my gray hair and my experience made the conversation interesting both ways. I had acquired the ability to gain insights about businesses that might go unnoticed by more youthful analysts. In addition, I enjoyed visiting factories and chatting with supervisors, who generally provided answers that would give me a good sense of reality on the ground. These visits and the assessment I made would form the cornerstone of my investment decisions.

In some markets, I also had friends and contacts who could give me market insights that might be missing if I were to use only brokers' information. In Bangkok, I had two special relationships. One was the family of a prominent banker and the other was the head of the only re-insurance company in the country. Because they were completely plugged into the business world there, I obtained important insights about which groups were reputable and which groups were not. In Singapore, Indonesia, and Taiwan, my contacts made during the private equity years were useful sources of market hearsay and often confirmed facts and opinion.

I had another good idea for tracking down facts. One of my good friends was a journalist with a major U.S. magazine group. He knew many stringers who were traveling in the region for stories. If I needed to check out something, I would commission the work to him. He would outsource it to a stringer. Such due diligence work was generally reliable and inexpensive. In fact, I avoided buying a Malaysian stock because I obtained input from one of the stringers there. At that time, many brokers in the region were promoting this company as a great buy. Within a year, the company was caught falsifying records and eventually went bankrupt.

My workload became somewhat lighter when I found a part-time assistant to help with bookkeeping, cash management, and other clerical work. She and I sat in the tiny room I had rented in the business center. It was the first time I understood how people in Hong Kong could live in such crowded places and appear perfectly happy. I found her intelligent and efficient and we worked well together.

In May, Kathy graduated from Cornell and our family celebrated together in Ithaca. We were exceptionally proud to see

Kathy in her gown, rejoicing with her friends and classmates. She had already lined up a trainee job at an investment advisory firm in New York City.

The first half of 1994 was a difficult period for Asian markets. HSBC, a widely held blue-chip stock, had slid to HK$87 per share from HK$115 in the first six months of the year. Many hedge funds crashed because of the sudden rise in U.S. long interest rates. In fact, investors had lost so much money their risk appetite disappeared overnight. I was pleasantly surprised my next trip to New York, Boston, Atlanta, Chicago, and Portland produced good results. The best news was that Nuland & Arshad in Boston promised to put a client's capital into the fund.

During the summer of 1994, I moved my office to a space in a small building called Wilson House, located on Wyndham Street in Central. The building was on an uphill slope in the main commercial district of Hong Kong. From my office, I could see the Hong Kong Garden in the Mid Levels. For the first time since 1992, PCML had its own premises that consisted of a small conference room, a tiny meeting room, two small offices, and an area for three secretarial desks. The space was cramped but I was proud to be working out of my own office again.

Meanwhile, I continued to liquidate investments in ASSET. By year's end, I would return another US$1.3 million to my investors. My income actually plummeted because the management fee from ASSET was falling as I liquidated its investments. Besides, I had recently completed my advisory assignment with the Hong Kong client. Fortunately, just as my financial situation was deteriorating, I was approached by ORIX Investments, one of ASSET's institutional investors, to help with its private equity activities based in Singapore. Discussions were proceeding well and I was looking forward to the advisory assignment, which promised to be interesting. The new fee income would be most welcomed as the fund's small size was hardly sufficient to pay for the company's operating expenses.

ASEIP ended its first year of operation with a net asset value of US$6.4 million, down 4.6 percent, while the Asian region took a big tumble, down 13 percent. It was a disappointing year in terms of performance, but I was delighted I had launched ASEIP from a standing start in mid-1993. I was grateful to have so much help from everyone I came into contact with. With assistance from my consulting work in private equity investing, I knew I could build up the business.

The crush of work before the holidays drove me to start looking for help right after the New Year. My assistant at the time was getting ready to take maternity leave. We had too much going on to simply find a part-time replacement.

I found the perfect candidate in a young woman named Bela Chu, whom I had met in the business center where I worked before moving to Wilson House. Though she didn't speak much English, she was pleasant, earnest, motivated, and hard working. She had a positive attitude and willingness to work on a variety of assignments. She was also happy to work in a small office without the usual office politics. Neither of us knew then that she would become my longest-serving employee and confidante in all the years since 1995.

From those early days, Bela's scope of work has broadened and it now encompasses just about all the back office functions required in an investment management firm. She does all trade settlements and performs month-end reconciliation of accounts with data from the custodian. She handles bookkeeping, cash management, filing, and all other clerical tasks. She is also responsible for getting tax reporting out to investors every year. On top of all that, she has been an upbeat cheerleader on many occasions when markets in Asia were hammered and I was totally frustrated.

My negotiation with ORIX soon came to an agreement. My assignment was to seek direct investment opportunities in the region and to give advice on investment-related work requested by various regional managers. From early 1995, I often traveled to Singapore, where the senior managers worked. Like other Japanese investment firms, ORIX was a deal taker (i.e., the firm invested in deals originated by others), with a lot of deals on its books. Now, management thought it should begin to originate its own deals. I was delighted with this opportunity because, while working for ORIX, I had the flexibility of visiting investment candidates for ASEIP. And I was pleased that ORIX, which had invested in ASSET, showed its confidence in my professional abilities.

The first quarter of 1995 saw the Kobe earthquake, a major disaster, and a sarin gas attack in a Tokyo subway station that killed seven and injured hundreds. Closer to our business, Barings PLC, a respected investment bank in the United Kingdom, went under due to trading losses in its Singapore office. It turned out that US$1 billion of losses in derivative trades were piled up by one trader! Somehow, that fact didn't surprise me.

For weeks, markets reacted adversely to the U.S. bailout package for Mexico. Investors began to exit emerging markets, including markets in Southeast Asia. Thailand had been raising interest rates. So had Indonesia, Malaysia, and the Philippines in an attempt to defend their currencies as funds flowed out of their countries. The U.S. dollar was also weak, breaking all-time lows against the German mark and the Japanese yen. But the U.S. stock markets were steadily rising. In fact, the U.S. market had just begun a six-year bull run that would be one of the longest in its history. Quickly, investors' interest in emerging markets plummeted. I had a strong suspicion, going into the second quarter of 1995, that it would be difficult to raise new capital in this environment.

In mid-May, I went to the States to attend Clarence's graduation from Tufts University, and to meet investors and prospects. Clarence had majored in economics and had already found a job at the Federal Reserve Bank of New York.

During the trip, my schedule was stretched to working in two time zones. During the day, I would meet clients and prospects.

Because Asia is twelve hours ahead of New York, during the night, I would be on the phone to Asia, speaking to brokers and analysts. Evening hours in New York translate to the next day's working hours in Hong Kong. Those were the days before the Internet was developed and I had to have broker comments summarized by Bela and faxed to the hotel or the Yale Club where I stayed. Only on Friday and Saturday evenings would I be able to see a show or relax with friends.

I was certainly the oldest fund manager in the industry in Asia. Most managers were in their mid-30s. Occasionally, I would meet managers from the States and Europe who were in their late 40s. I noticed I had a different way of assessing companies than they did. Perhaps it was because I didn't have a background in fund management and didn't rise up through the professional ranks.

I found most managers were principally interested in having an update of a company's financial performance. Their interest focused on margin trend, profit outlook, capital expenditure, revenue trend, and more. There is a set of standard questions that most people ask and company representatives would have the answers ready in meetings.

My approach to assessing a company goes beyond the numbers. My line of questioning would probe into a company's operations to determine their competitive edge. In one meeting in South Korea, I recall the company executive queried whether I wished to buy the company as opposed to just its stocks. Many senior executives enjoyed my visits because most liked to tell their stories to someone actually interested in learning about their business instead of just the numbers.

Calling on companies would be a key prerequisite in my investment process. In a typical year, I would visit more than 120 companies including many of their plants.

While I am good at finding attractive and investable companies, I am not so good at cutting losses. I knew I had to learn to trade, not only on fundamentals, but also on market volatility.

In this business, fund managers would sell on the whim of bad news before any questions were asked. Another important factor was that global hedge funds had waded into Asia and were buying and selling stocks only to make short-term profits. Globalization of markets attracted a lot of foreign money into emerging markets, and that was a good thing. On the flip side, it raised market volatility because of the short-term trading strategies of hedge funds. In 1995, I cut losses too late when markets were sold down and didn't chase the markets when they turned around sharply in the last two months of the year.

For my 60th birthday I decided not to celebrate, but rather spend the day quietly, taking my mother out to dinner at the American Club. Still, I knew I had much to be thankful for and I thought my life was truly blessed. The following was what I wrote in my diary that day:

> *So, here I am, looking to build a new business, in a profession I am not familiar with. Learning every day. The challenge keeps me going, for sure. Most people at my age are thinking of retirement. But I am having too much fun to give up what I am doing. I think my life is truly blessed. So many good friends. So many interests – reading, sports, music, etc. Good health and my mind hasn't slowed down, although more forgetful.*

I have to watch myself not to talk about the past, being boring to others. Speaking about blessings, I have two wonderful kids who have grown to be good and responsible adults. They are the living evidence of my good fortune. So, I have absolutely no complaints about life. I am still so optimistic most of the time. Yesterday, I was so excited about everything that I couldn't go back to sleep, just itching to get up and go to the office. OK. I am a workaholic, but I am handling it with grace and good spirit. Don't think that is so bad.

I spent Christmas week with my family in New York. I was in good spirits as the markets turned around in November and the fund had recovered from losses in the earlier months. ASEIP would end the year at US$7.3 million. Unfortunately, it was down 2.7 percent for the year while its benchmark index showed a gain of 6.8 percent. This was the only year in which I underperformed until 2004.

Before year's end, I had sold all the holdings in my private equity fund, ASSET, and could no longer count on any fees from it. ASSET had an extraordinary performance record, realizing IRR of 36 percent per annum for its investments, and returning to investors 16.7 percent per annum for seven and a half years.

In an encouraging gesture, the Federal Reserve came through with a rate cut in early 1996 that resulted in a market boom. In Asia, all markets were up, except Taiwan, as China was reported to have prepared a military invasion plan. ASEIP had the best month in its young life, up 7.9 percent in January, leading me to think there would soon be light at the end of the tunnel.

A new technological development had recently gained traction in Asia when I had my first encounter with the Internet. I was very impressed when I viewed a demonstration by a PC dealer. I was hooked and had the Internet capability installed in my PC soon thereafter.

Several noteworthy events happened in the second quarter of 1996. First, I was approached by Cigna Investments, the controlling shareholder of AOG, to advise them on their private equity investing activities in Asia. The arrangement was similar to the one I had with ORIX. Now that two of the investors in ASSET, my private equity fund, had remained my clients, I felt I must have done something right. Second, because of the growing commitments, I began to look for a portfolio manager to help me with the ASEIP work.

In early April, I was asked by the ORIX management in Tokyo to accompany two executives to visit Yangon, capital of Myanmar. The visit was intended to be an information-gathering exercise. It was arranged by Bernard Pewin, who had good access to business groups and government authorities in the country. Pewin used to work at American Express on the travel side of the business when we knew each other, and we had played tennis on many occasions in Hong Kong. He had studied in the United Kingdom and worked in various locations in Asia for American Express. He decided to return to Myanmar, his birthplace, in 1991 and now had a number of business interests in the country.

Yangon was a city, aged and clearly out of step with the rest of Asia. Although poor, the city had few signs of dire poverty. In the downtown district, the Shreddagon Pagoda offered an extraordinary sight. Its golden spires rose high into the sky against a background of low buildings. There were no high-rise buildings in the city. I spent the weekend there to see some sights and to attend the wedding of a friend of Pewin.

After the wedding, we drove by the home of Aung San Suu Kyi, the opposition political leader who had spent many years in and out of jail. That afternoon, she was free and addressing a crowd in front of the gate of her big house. She was using a loudspeaker system so her words would reach the peaceful crowd in front. There were policemen directing traffic around the group. I saw her radiant face and a look of commitment that was the hallmark of her leadership.

During the short, two-day visit, we met the Central Bank Governor, an economic advisor to the SLORC (the ruling party), chairman of the First Private Bank, an executive of a major business group, and a foreign investment firm's senior representative. While the meetings were frank, no politics was discussed. The country had very few foreign investors, only several from Singapore, South Korea, Japan, and Germany. We learned about its very primitive banking system and tentative attempts to attract foreign investments. Overall, I recognized that the country's political risk would be too high even for the most intrepid investor.

Myanmar had enormous economic potential because it had one of the highest populations in Southeast Asia, abundant natural resources, an old culture and unique historical places that would attract a large number of tourists. Sadly, the government has, to this day, retained its oppressive policies and will not adopt the kind of changes that we have seen in China and elsewhere.

My business was beginning to acquire momentum. In Atlanta, Bob Varn and his investment committee at the Atlanta Historical Center approved an investment in ASEIP. This was the first endowment fund to become an investor. Since then, its interest has grown and it has remained an important client.

In Boston, I received a modest commitment from a prominent family. Over the years, this relationship would grow to become the most important one for my firm. The family's continuing support and referrals have helped broaden my network and eventually made a connection with the Institute of Private Investors, an organization that serves private family offices.

Two new interesting alliance opportunities emerged. I was introduced to a prominent investment management firm in San Francisco that specialized in socially responsible investing. The CEO and owner, whom I had met earlier in the year, had become interested in working with me to launch a socially responsible investment mutual fund for Asia. This kind of fund was virtually unheard of in Asia at that time, so I was extremely excited about the prospect of undertaking this pioneering project. Then, a major investment management company, Fiduciary Trust in New York, contacted me about my firm becoming a sub-advisor to a new Asian fund that they planned to launch. These two developments suggested my business might soon truly take off. In August, CIGNA signed an agreement for me to act as its advisor in its pursuit of private equity investments in China.

Just as I was having difficulty keeping all the balls in the air, Laurence Chang, a young man of 28, came to join my firm as a portfolio manager in early September. I met him through an industry contact. Having previously worked with a U.S.-based investment management firm, Laurence was bright, hardworking and, like me, passionate about finding investments. His presence required a major reshuffling of the office configuration.

Our fund did well in the third quarter. Its performance benefited from a small cap stock named Fangda Building Materials, listed as a B-share in the Shenzhen Stock Exchange in China. Fangda's principal competitive advantage was a patented construction methodology for aluminum curtain walls used in the construction of tall buildings. The owner had been a professor of engineering in Beijing but founded the company with funds from the local government in Shenzhen. Jardine Fleming had taken the company public early in 1996. Kyle Shaw, a friend who used to sit on the board of Flextronics in the early 1990s, had become a board member. Having a foreign board member was certainly a first in the development of corporate governance in listed companies in China.

The Asian markets were quite volatile in 1996. They reached a high in April, weakened for the next four months, and then climbed back to end the year with a gain of around 9 percent. It was a year when the U.S. market witnessed a strong advance. By year-end, ASEIP was up over 19 percent. Its asset size stood at US$12.8 million, $5 million greater than the beginning of the year. In three years, the fund had outperformed the benchmark by 11 percent! This was indeed very encouraging as I was told I would find a much larger pool of potential investors after the fund had been in existence for three years and had achieved superior performance.

Another positive development from a trip to the States in December was that several investors were attracted to my idea of hosting an investor conference in 1997. I was convinced, if I could persuade investors to actually visit the companies firsthand, they would have far greater confidence in my work. With advisory assignments from CIGNA and ORIX, my business was flourishing; 1997, I believed, would be my break-out year.

In early 1997, another endowment trust decided to participate in the fund. The Asian Cultural Council, a prominent and respected organization sponsoring talented artists from Asia to study in the States, notified me of its commitment. No doubt, Dick Bliss, who sat on the investment committee of the Council, must have been an important contributing factor. ASEIP's superior performance and my constant contact with the investment committee through monthly letters and semi-annual meetings were, in my view, also key factors. In addition, one of Neuberger & Berman's partners was a gatekeeper for the Council and my established relationships with several of Neuberger's partners may have helped influence their favorable decision.

Ever since September 1996, Asian markets, particularly Chinese stocks traded in Hong Kong, had become exceptionally strong, defying all expectations. For example, in the fourth quarter alone, "H" shares, stocks of Chinese companies listed in Hong Kong, went up 23 percent. The so-called red chips, Hong Kong companies that own assets and businesses in China, were up 49 percent.

ASEIP's performance did not benefit from this trend because I did not invest in any of these counters. My reasons were basic. I was concerned by their lack of transparency. I had formed this opinion after attending many meetings when these companies sought listing in Hong Kong. Like the frenzy of US junk bonds in the 1980s, investors' appetite for these two classes of stocks seemed unlimited. I remember fund managers buying the stocks with reckless abandon, with absolutely no regard to valuation or other criteria. It was a bubble that would shortly burst.

Since Laurence came on board that September, we had opened accounts in Taiwan and South Korea, where foreign investors had previously faced many restrictions. As these two countries relaxed regulations regarding foreign portfolio participation, I decided it was time to allocate a part of the fund to these markets.

Early in 1997, I informed our investors we would hold our first investors' forum in mid-May, coinciding with the annual CLSA Asia Forum in Hong Kong. My idea was to have our investors attend my meetings on the first day and obtain permission for them to attend the CLSA forum the following days. Over the years, the CLSA event had become the leading forum for corporate leaders to tell their stories to fund managers and make themselves available for personal meetings. I arranged for my group to Texwinca on another day to give them a firsthand glimpse of a medium-size, successful Chinese manufacturer.

Texwinca, then a relatively unknown textile producer, had recently acquired a brand-name of casual wear line called Baleno. It also had a division making garments for a number of U.S. fashion names. The stock was trading at a deep discount to its intrinsic value. I had visited their factories in Southern China. There, I met the owner, Poon Bun Chak, a short, middle-aged man and a real hands-on executive.

Poon had a remarkable personal history. He told me he came to Hong Kong at the age of 19 by swimming from China, having drifted in the water for two full days! He still swims every day, but now in his own swimming pool. Poon's first job in Hong Kong was as a laborer in a small garment factory. He learned his business from the bottom up and, like many immigrants from China, has become a very rich and successful businessman in Hong Kong.

After a very strong run in the final months of 1996, markets became volatile Again. To me, it was sign of an impending crisis. But being an optimist, I did not see the freight train coming soon enough. April turned out to be a pretty bad month, with most markets plunging. In particular, the Philippines market was down 17 percent. I was having a tough time figuring out what I should talk about in the Investors' Forum because Asian markets had underperformed the rising U.S. market for the last three years. In this environment, only superior stock picking would save the day. But I couldn't claim that I had a long history of doing that. In any event, the fund had only delivered a modest return since its inception in 1994.

Interested in learning more about public stocks in China, I went to Shanghai to visit a number of "B"-share companies. In China, there were two classes of shares. The so-called "A" shares were reserved for domestic investors. Foreign investors using foreign currencies such as the Hong Kong dollar or the U.S. dollar were allowed to trade the so-called "B" shares. In China, companies were allowed by the authorities to issue either "A" or "B" shares, but not both. Most of the "B"-share companies were small- to medium-size manufacturers, although some were in the service industries. My impression from the trip was that Chinese managers were mostly production-oriented, with little understanding of merchandising, marketing, financial control, or business planning functions. On a level playing field, these companies could not compete against their peers in other countries. Trading at over 50 times earnings, the shares were clearly unattractive. Yet, according to the Jardine Fleming analyst who accompanied me on these visits, liquidity would drive the stocks even higher.

An early sign of the impending Asian financial crisis emerged during the week of May 12 when speculators in the form of hedge funds mounted an attack on the Thai baht. At first, the speculators appeared to be winning the battle. All the Southeast Asian markets dropped sharply. Then, the Thai Central Bank prohibited banks from lending baht to offshore entities. On May 15, the overnight rate reached 1,000 percent, squeezing out the short sellers. Later, reports indicated that George Soros, Goldman Sachs, et al., lost US$300 million in their trades. The

Thai government won a temporary victory but had spent billions of dollars from its reserves, forcing it to keep interest rates at an exceptionally high level.

Against this backdrop of market volatility and tension, I hosted our first investors' forum on May 19. Eight investors made the trip from the States. I had booked a conference room in the American Club, located in the Exchange Square in the Central district of Hong Kong. I had prepared three sessions for the first morning. The first session addressed investing strategies in Asia and was delivered by a strategist from a regional investment bank. The second was presented by a journalist with *Time* magazine, who offered insightful remarks on the two Muslim countries in Asia, Indonesia, and Malaysia. After a short break, I took the group to the Hong Kong Stock Exchange, where Lawrence Fok, head of the Listing Division, delivered the third segment, an interesting talk on the history of the Exchange and recent developments regarding the listing of Chinese companies.

We then went back to the conference room, where Ti Sheng Young, head of UBS Equity Research in Taiwan, gave a luncheon talk about the Greater China markets. Afterwards, Laurence and I made a presentation of ASEIP and how we interpreted the recent market volatility.

Later that evening, the group had dinner at the Hong Kong Club. Invited to dine with us were three impressive guests: Vernon Moore, an executive with Citic Pacific, a large red-chip conglomerate with holdings in airline, infrastructure, and financial service businesses; Mike Kalyck, head of the Shangri-La Hotel chain in Asia; and Stuart Leckie, a well-known financial consultant to the government of Hong Kong. The discussions jumped from one topic to another and we all had a great time.

I took my guests to Texwinca the next morning, crossing the border with China amid a formidable line of trucks to and from the other side. We were accompanied by Simon Ting, Texwinca's CFO. He spoke fluent English and was good at explaining his company's various business lines while en route to the factories. We visited the textile and garment plants and then went to Guangzhou to see one of the Baleno stores. There, one of my guests bought a pair of pants for US$6, put it on, and told everyone it was great. The trip certainly gave my visitors a new understanding of the strength of Chinese enterprises.

The following day, my guests attended the CLSA Asia Forum. In that evening, we had dinner at the China Club with guests including Peter Jackson, head of AsiaSat, the biggest satellite telecommunication company in Asia; Frankie Wong, head of Shui On, a major construction and cement producer in Hong Kong and China; and Jacques Trauman, head of Paribas Bank in Hong Kong. The conversation was lively and spirited. To wrap up the week, I hosted a final dinner at the Hong Kong Country Club in Deep Water Bay, away from the hustle and bustle of the city. The entire event was very successful and I was convinced I should make it an annual event.

As I entertained my guests, the Chinese authority passed a law that forbade state-owned enterprises from stock speculation. Immediately, "A" shares traded in Shanghai plunged 15 percent. Still, speculation in red chips continued. A conglomerate named Beijing Enterprises was listed in Hong Kong and its shares were 1,000 times oversubscribed. On the first day of trading, the stock more than doubled. To lower my fund's volatility, I started unloading positions in Southeast Asia in anticipatiojn of more speculative currency attacks in the days ahead. ASEIP ended the month of May up almost 5 percent, a very commendable performance.

To my regret, the investment management firm in San Francisco that was interested in launching a socially responsible Asian Fund began backtracking. The reason was simple: the U.S. market was strong, but Asian markets continued to struggle. Other emerging markets were advancing sharply, with Brazil up 60 percent year-to-date and Europe up more than 20 percent.

A historical event was about to take place in Hong Kong: the handover of the territory by the British government to China. To celebrate the occasion, we had a five-day holiday. The Hong Kong market was strong and, according to street talk, supported by the Chinese government to make sure everyone would be in good spirits through the end of the month. On the handover date, June 30, the weather failed to cooperate as the city was covered by pouring rain and heavy wind during the ceremony. I watched the activities on TV at home. Despite the rain, the speeches, performances and fireworks all went well and were very impressive. President Jiang of China, in his remarks, said that things would be left unchanged, including Hong Kong's Basic Law, the new mini-constitution of the new "Special Administrative Region" of China. The scene of Prince Charles boarding the British yacht, leaving Hong Kong in heavy rain, was a poignant and memorable one. This was how the British rule of Hong Kong ended. Hong Kong had now begun a new chapter in its history.

ASEIP's net assets now stood at almost US$15 million. The fund was up nearly 6 percent while its regional benchmark was flat. Unfortunately, my investors' general negative sentiment about Asia would turn out to be prescient. A financial crisis that had its first salvo in Thailand in May would intensify in July and create a major political and financial disaster in Asia, which would transform the region in profound ways. During the process, my business would be hit like all other businesses in the region.

Photos

Mother in her socialite days (1930s)

Father in his Shanghai office (1930s)

Me and my twin brother (on the left) with mother (1936)

Family in 1948, brother on the right

Me and brother (on the left) just after high school, 1954

College graduation day, June 1958

Wedding day, April 1970

Opening a Citibank branch in Ras al Khaimah (1976)

Clarence (son) and Kathy (daughter) in their late teens (1991)

Making a presentation to prospects, 2003

Father's old home site, Kaixian, Sichuan, China (2004)

Brother and I at 50th reunion (brother on the left), 2008

My wife, Teresa, and kids (2006)

Trekking to Taktsang Monastery, Bhutan (2007)

In my office (March 2009)

13

The Crisis Years in Asia

In international trade, Asian countries have always pegged their currencies against the U.S. dollar. In the 1980s, when the U.S. dollar was weak and the Japanese yen was strong, Asian countries enjoyed competitive advantages because of the currency alignment with the U.S. dollar. As a result, those economies enjoyed unprecedented growth. Hong Kong, Taiwan, Singapore, and South Korea came to be known as the four Asian Tigers.

In the 1990s, the dollar strengthened and brought Asian currencies up with it. In 1994, China effectively devalued its currency from 5.85 Yuan to a dollar to 8.3 Yuan to a dollar. This move made Chinese goods more competitive against those of her neighboring countries. The move didn't raise any criticism because trade with China was insignificant at that time. Over the years, however, the stronger currencies in Asia created a distortion by hiding the inflationary pressure in their domestic markets. In fact, their currencies had become overvalued in relation to the countries' trade accounts and balance-of-payment conditions.

In spring of 1997, hedge funds, including the one managed by George Soros, began to notice these distortions. Although Southeast Asian fiscal and trade accounts were not nearly as bad as those in South America, they were vulnerable to currency speculators. These economies were small and they did not have the implicit backing of the U.S. government. More importantly, because their governments had been supporting a fixed exchange rate regime for many years, corporate borrowers had taken loans in U.S. dollars as U.S. interest rates were significantly lower than those in domestic currencies. Any devaluation of the country's currency would almost by definition place these borrowers in dire straits.

For months, the International Monetary Fund (IMF) had been urging countries such as Thailand to raise domestic interest rates to defend their currencies against speculative attacks. Any attack would immediately throw economic growth into reverse gear. The governments were obviously aware of this threat. In addition, in a devaluation scenario, many of their prominent businessmen would have to be bailed out, one way or another. They would face insolvency or worse, bankruptcy.

Despite spending US$33 billion to defend its currency, Thailand submitted to reality in July and unpegged its currency, the baht. Although Thailand's stock market shot up, the baht's value plunged 20 percent, wiping out any gains in U.S. dollar terms. The Hong Kong market dropped sharply and the red chips (stocks of companies with assets in China and traded in Hong Kong) were worse hit. The week of July 7 was an extremely turbulent period, with markets falling everywhere. Domestic interest rates were sky high. It was evident Southeast Asia was in deep trouble. Following the baht attack, traders now focused on other Southeast Asian countries. The Philippine peso was soon devalued, forcing the overnight rate to 30 percent at one point. I was most concerned about the possibility of competitive devaluation in the region. Some economists described the phenomenon as the "contagion effect." Facing the turbulence, my fund exited Indonesia and the Philippines entirely, and I positioned 70 percent of the portfolio in North Asia. I also raised cash and hedged much of the portfolio by selling futures.

To assess what was happening on the ground, I flew to Bangkok in mid-July to get a sense of the damage inflicted by the latest crisis. My talks with several contacts made it clear that companies with U.S. dollar–denominated debts would never be able to pay back their obligations. What made things worse was that foreign banks were pulling out, demanding repayments when their borrowers were down on their knees. It was a lose-lose situation. Indeed, the bankers' herd instinct meant that none of the international financial institutions would step in and help. On August 20, the IMF announced a US$17 billion support package for Thailand.

While I was traveling, currencies, as expected, were falling dramatically relative to the U.S. dollar. After two days in Thailand, I visited companies in Taiwan, which turned out not to have been hit by the regional crisis. In fact, exports were up because their principal market, the U.S. economy, remained strong. Taiwanese manufacturers, particularly in electronics, had become globally competitive and their engineering and production skills were in great demand. The only issue was that the market remained buoyant and valuation was demanding. It was difficult to find bargains.

Thankfully, my fund was up 2.3 percent for the month of July on continued strength in Taiwan and Hong Kong. My decision to reallocate investments away from Southeast Asia had worked, at least for the moment. However, a sense of gloom built up quickly as all Asian markets were hit by relentless selling in August. The Indonesian rupiah came under attack and the government decided to abandon its fixed exchange rate policy. A few months later, the country announced it would seek IMF aid. The aid was provided in the form of a $40 billion stabilization package in November.

In Malaysia, then Prime Minister Mahathir made a singularly bold decision by defying the standard IMF prescription of devaluation and raising domestic interest rates to curtail capital flight. Instead, he changed his country's trading rules and imposed capital control restrictions to prevent foreign investors from selling their holdings and taking their money out of the country. He could take these steps because the country was oil-rich and not beholden to foreign banks. In hindsight, these capital controls spared the country from the contagion that engulfed the rest of the region.

I continued selling futures to hedge the fund's long positions. Even though there were lots of bargains in the Philippines, I didn't want to catch a falling knife. By mid-August, gloom was everywhere as no market was spared. In Hong Kong, interest rates shot up to 12 percent at one point.

Sitting in front of my Bloomberg terminal, I saw red numbers (i.e., a drop in price) on the screen, day in and day out. Fund managers in London and New York were summarily liquidating their positions in Hong Kong. On August 28, Asian markets experienced a complete meltdown. Manila was down 9 percent and Jakarta down 4.5 percent. In Hong Kong, red chips and "H" shares crashed as brokers sold margin accounts aggressively, aggravating losses. My stomach churned as I watched currencies and markets fall. In just one month, the fund was down 5.8 percent. However, the regional index was down a whopping 18.6 percent. My hedging strategy and over-weight in cash helped cushion the negative performance. It was obvious there would be no new investors in October, the month when the fund would be opened.

During the tumultuous times, I kept my investors fully informed as events unfolded. For a few days, I sent them daily market commentaries as well as my tactics for managing the fund. It was remarkable that my investors stayed calm and made no plans to pull out of the fund. Since I somehow managed to limit the fund's losses as compared to the regional benchmark, a couple of investors congratulated me for my relative success.

September saw heavy selling of all China shares listed in Hong Kong, with prices dropping about 40 percent. Markets remained extremely volatile and several of my trades showed that we got whipsawed. Asian currencies continued to fall against the dollar and interest rates stayed high. I should have stayed short but my optimistic nature got in the way at times when markets had technical bounces and I bought. These false indications were known in the trade as "dead cat bounces."

Tired of worrying about the daily volatility, I flew to Shanghai to visit potential investment candidates in China. This kind of due diligence in the relentless bear market was somewhat quixotic. Clearly, stock picking was not going to make any difference in the fund's short-term performance. Still, I decided my investors were paying me to do what I could do best – to find gems among the listed companies.

In October, the Hong Kong market plunged 29 percent. Investors were fearful that the Hong Kong dollar might not hold its value and, like other Southeast Asian economies, might be unpegged from the U.S. dollar. On October 28, the Hong Kong market plummeted – it went down 1,400 points, making it a day that reminded me of the market crash in 1929. Luckily, our fund was fully hedged, so it actually went up on that day. I had sold so much that the fund had 50% of its assets in cash. Nevertheless, in the month of October, the fund was down 10 percent while the regional benchmark plunged 23.4 percent.

At this point, there were two negative developments in my business. First, Laurence Chang decided to go back to the States. He had had enough of the bear market tension and thought he could do better where markets continued to be strong (i.e., the United States). Second, I was told by ORIX my advisory contract would not be renewed at year-end. This was not a surprise. Japanese banks had almost entirely pulled out of Asia in the beginning of May. ORIX was no different. Its appetite for Asian direct investments had vanished. The only cheer would come from my assistant Bela, who reminded me: "The night is darkest before dawn."

In the final months of the year, the financial crisis inexorably spread northward toward Asia's developed economies. Like other countries in the region, South Korea soon succumbed to the inevitable, and on November 21 sought IMF support. Its foreign currency reserves were virtually depleted by massive capital outflow. On December 3, the IMF and South Korea agreed to a US$57 billion support package. Later, South Koreans elected, for the first time ever, an opposition leader, Kim Dae Jung, as the new president. This dramatic development would usher in an entirely new and positive chapter in the political and economic development of the country.

In Japan, Yamaichi, the fourth largest broker, closed down in November. This bankruptcy further exacerbated the Asian markets as the broker started unwinding its Asian stock portfolio. Selling by Yamaichi contributed much to the widespread plunge in China shares. Earlier, the tenth largest bank in Japan had folded. The Asian financial crisis now had reached the northernmost country. There was absolutely no relief in sight.

In the midst of financial chaos, I flew to Atlanta in December to brief my investors. With the U.S. markets advancing, and Asian markets falling off the cliff, it was obvious the bet on Asia a few years ago had become a disaster. I had not expected any new prospects and indeed expected redemptions. So, it was a great surprise when I actually received a warm reception from my investors. They commended me for protecting the fund from more drastic losses. They encouraged me to look beyond the prevailing bear market for the day when there would be a turnaround.

Even more surprising, I was told that the investment committee of the Atlanta Historical Center would add US$1 million to ASEIP. With this good news, I flew to Boston to give a presentation to Nuland's investors, who were clearly unnerved by the unprecedented Asian crisis. The group, fortunately, decided pulling out when stocks were virtually being given away wasn't a very smart idea. Back in New York, I met our investors to continue damage control. My overall impression was investors were totally turned off on Asia.

I flew to Jackson Hole to take a much needed break. There, Tom Chrystie took me to ski with him on the Grand Teton ski slope. Although the temperature was 35 degrees below zero on the ground level, it was sunny, the air was dry, and I worked off much of the pent-up anxiety I'd held in for months. The next morning, I gave a breakfast talk about the Asian markets to a group of 22 guests invited by Tom. The reception was favorable and I actually obtained a new investor from the breakfast group.

The year 1997 has to go down in modern history as the most serious financial crisis in Asia. My fund was down around 20 percent while the regional market benchmark lost over 45 percent! In spite of my best efforts in hedging the fund's positions, I could do no better than I did. By now, Asia had turned from a region of dynamic growth to a place where deflation, currency meltdown, and recession loomed ahead. As the year closed, regional currencies were down from 10 percent in Singapore to over 50 percent in South Korea, Indonesia, and Thailand. The latter economies were basket cases.

Bankers are known as "fair weather" friends. This was most clearly demonstrated in times of crisis. Let me cite a few examples. In this fateful year, Japanese banks' claims on developing Asia collapsed by US$39 billion, or 29 percent, from US$132 billion at the end of June 1997 to US$93 billion by the end of 1998. There is no doubt that international banks contributed to the bust of Asian economies. Further, the IMF solutions didn't help. In fact, in my view, IMF funds totaling US$125 billion were mostly used to bail out foreign lenders and precious little actually dribbled into the desperate economies. I cannot prove this statement but it was my judgment from observations at that time.

Markets continued to fall along with regional currencies as the new year of 1998 began. Indonesia's rupiah crashed through 10,000 and reached 12,800 on January 18. This was truly a disaster for the country. As late as March 1997, the rupiah had been trading at 2,500 against one U.S. dollar. What's more,

Asia's high-flying investment bank in Hong Kong, Peregrine Investments, went under. It suffered a fate similar to Asian Oceanic Group, my old employer, in that it financed a bridge loan that couldn't find an exit. In the case of Peregrine, it had organized a US$250 million dollar note to an Indonesian company before the financial crisis. Obviously, the note went into default.

In the days that followed, I explored the possibility of acquiring Peregrine's asset management business and discovered its portfolios of around US$300 million was riddled with bad positions. It was incredible how the company had maintained an impeccable reputation while its internal operations were in such a poor state of health. Before the month was over, Schroders Securities, a venerable securities firm of long standing, declared it would close down its stock trading business in Hong Kong.

Sensing the bear market wasn't going to end anytime soon, I decided to return capital that had been remitted for subscription by two new investors early in January. I felt this gesture was necessary to preserve my integrity even though I desperately wanted to build up the fund's asset base. Another development that didn't surprise me was that Cigna informed me they would no longer need my advisory service. Like most investors, they had gotten cold feet about Asian investment opportunities. DMT, the Indonesian finance company that had supported me in the early days, decided to wind down its asset management business as redemptions brought the funds under management to an insignificant level.

The month of January saw the fund drop another 10 percent. My hedges didn't work as markets started a bear market rally toward month-end. The rally gathered steam quickly, especially in South Korea, Taiwan, and Thailand. Currencies began to recover.

On a trip to South Korea, I learned that ordinary people were turning in their jewelry and even wedding rings to the government to help pay off the IMF loans. One of my South Korean friends in Hong Kong had told me that his brother lost his construction business and had to sell his house to pay off the mortgage. Yet, he was not downbeat and was looking to starting anew. One middle-aged senior executive was laid off and was found holding down a job as a waiter in a restaurant. He told a reporter he had not lost hope that things would turn better. In meetings after meetings, South Korean corporate managers were talking about improving corporate governance and transparency. This was the latest mantra designed to appeal to foreign investors and the message was getting across. The government was determined to break up the *chaebols*, conglomerates favored by previous governments to develop the South Korean industrial economy. The trip convinced me the country's recovery was only a matter of time.

In the month of February, the regional benchmark gained 24 percent while ASEIP was up 20 percent. This was the first positive month since July 1997, over 9 months ago. I was encouraged by the resilience of the Taiwan market and focused on finding suitable candidates there. In Asia, outside of South Korea, Taiwan is the one economy with globally competitive businesses that were benefiting from the US outsourcing of production of all kinds of goods. Many of the Taiwanese companies were located in Hsin Chu Science Park, just east of the international airport. If you drive in the Park, you will see tree-lined avenues full of low-rise modern buildings – not unlike Silicon Valley in California.

During February, I proposed another investors' forum in May, coupled with a trip to see the Three Gorges on the Yangtze River in the Sichuan Province of China. I hoped the sightseeing trip would attract investors to the second conference. Meanwhile, markets started heading south again in March. I was surprised when a few investors notified me they would add to their subscription in the next quarter. In fact, one investor sent another US$1 million in April. My spirit was greatly bolstered by the confidence my investors placed in me.

Even though the fund's performance had been negative, our firm's assets under management had actually grown since July 1997 when the crisis hit Asia. My workload also increased and I needed to have the support of an investment analyst. I placed an advertisement for two days and received over 200 applications. Such was the poor state of the securities industry in Hong Kong. A number of firms such as BZW Securities, Schroders, Euro Pacific Advisors, Nomura, were laying off people or closing. I wanted someone with around three years of experience and found Eugene Soo Hoo, an American Chinese. He came on board in May and helped me with research and financial modeling work.

Around that time, my discussion with Fiduciary Trust of New York took an encouraging turn. It became evident that I would be part of its investment management team. Fiduciary Trust intended to launch a new Asian equity fund, which would capitalize on the region's recovery prospects. This was a splendid idea and I was very enthusiastic about it. We would meet almost weekly to map out strategy, investment management process, and so on in the months ahead.

The second quarter of 1998 turned out to be Asia's darkest hours before dawn. The regional market plummeted 33 percent in three months. I had been far too complacent in terms of hedging the downside potential of the market. When stocks were trading on sentiment and not on company fundamentals, I should have been guided by market action to preserve capital. The technical upturn in February turned out to be a false signal. Selling accelerated in May and June. The bubble in China shares burst and they were particularly hard hit.

Our company's second investors' forum scheduled for May 18 did not draw much interest. In fact, on May 14, Indonesia was in the throes of a riot as President Suharto lost control and eventually resigned his office. The rupiah was trading at over 15,000 to one U.S. dollar. Markets, of course, responded by plunging even lower. Gloom and doom were widespread.

Tom Chrystie and his wife came to the forum. Bob Varn sent his daughter and husband on their first visit to Asia. I took our small group to visit a sports shoe production plant of a medium-size shoemaker producing merchandise for brand names in the States. We saw how it took more than 500 steps to make an athletic shoe. The production lines were clean and the workers were motivated and well-nourished. Impressed with what they saw, my visitors felt, as I did, that given such strong work ethics and competitive enterprises in China, the Asian financial crisis would one day be viewed as only a bump on the road to economic growth.

July 6 was a noteworthy day in Hong Kong's history as its new airport in Chep Lap Kok opened. Unfortunately, the day was marked by missing luggage, long delays, and canceled flights. On July 15, I tested the airport facility on a trip to Bangkok. The airport was a great achievement and, by then, all the kinks had been worked out. In a few years' time, the Hong Kong International Airport would be ranked the best in the world by business travelers.

In Thailand, I found the country still in the midst of a severe credit crunch. Banks would require a lot of new capital to be restructured. The government had decided that, in insolvencies (and there were plenty), workout plans had to be approved by the creditor, the borrower, and the court. This decision had the benefit of not causing instant bankruptcies, but it also dragged out any solutions for a long, long time. Unlike severe actions that were taking place in South Korea, Thailand had elected to ignore mainstream ideas from the States and pursue its own solution. For the time being, investors stayed away from Thailand until they could see how banks would resolve their nonperforming loans and raise new capital.

The month of August offered yet more drama. Markets kept going down early on as the new Japanese government proved disappointing. The yen was down to 246 to one U.S. dollar. There was continued fear of a devaluation of the Chinese currency. Its value in the black market was rumored to be at a discount of 12 percent to the official rate. Then, Hong Kong, the last bastion of the U.S. currency peg, saw its currency under massive attack by speculators. The three-month inter-bank rate shot up to 13 percent. It seemed everyone expected the currency to be unpegged and devalued.

However, Hong Kong's government did something unbelievable. Beginning on August 14, it started supporting the stock market by buying shares every day. The government said that it wanted to punish the speculators. It was an unprecedented gamble and it could only happen in Hong Kong because the government had huge foreign currency reserves and was running a surplus. In the following weeks, the government kept buying more shares, supporting the market while the rest of Asia kept sinking daily.

By then, my fund was more than 80 percent in cash. With hedges, ASEIP was actually, for the first time, in a net oversold position. A week later, markets worldwide collapsed because Russia defaulted on its international obligations and floated its currency.

The Hong Kong government spent upwards of US$12 billion to buy shares in the open market for 15 days. The scale of support was huge in the last two trading days of the month as everybody else was on the sell side. While buying shares, the government was selling futures to depress the September value to discourage speculators rolling their positions into the next month. As a result, futures ended the month at a massive 600 points discount to cash.

With bad news all around, those days were especially nerve-racking for me. All of Asia, except for China and Taiwan, was contracting economically. Now, South America was under siege as the financial crisis swept beyond Asia, with Venezuela being the hardest hit. Both the U.S and European markets were falling steadily. In fact, many stocks dropped about 50 percent in the two months ending in August.

Russia was in complete turmoil and Japanese stocks and currency kept going south. How could Hong Kong stem the speculative attack? No government had ever succeeded in defending its currency against market forces. The pain of keeping the Hong Kong–to–U.S. dollar peg had become virtually unbearable, as the overnight interest rates hit 25 percent at the end of the month. I was in a very negative frame of mind, expecting a huge global market meltdown in the not-too-distant future. At this juncture, ASEIP was down just less than 5 percent while the regional index had dropped almost 16 percent.

Kathy, my daughter, returned to Hong Kong in 1996 to take a break from the finance industry and life in the Big Apple. It took her some time to find her bearings but she chose to use her talent in art and her interest in fashion to guide her future career. Fortunately, she found work in the marketing unit of Louis Vuitton in Hong Kong, organizing shows and taking the company's products to China.

At about the same time, my son Clarence also decided on a career change. While in graduate school for architecture at Columbia University, he decided, in early 1998, to strike out and set up his own dot-com company in the furnishing and architectural field. This was a completely innovative idea and I supported the project fully. In the two years that followed, he not only became an entrepreneur but also did all the technical work of launching his website.

In early September, Bela, my assistant, gave birth to a healthy baby girl. The day before giving birth, Bela had, at my behest, returned to the office to help me with the usual month-end reconciliation and reporting tasks. The baby girl looked picture-perfect when my wife and I went to see her and her mother later that day. As events turned out, beginning on the date of the baby's birth, Asian markets started recovering, and as one would say, they never looked back.

The Hong Kong government action in August had raised the profile of government actions as an effective way to stave off economic disaster. The doctrine of free capital flows was being challenged globally. Hong Kong enacted many measures to prevent speculators from shorting stocks and currencies. After relentless selling for months and having been burned by the Hong Kong government's market actions, some buying interest emerged in Hong Kong and elsewhere in Asia. Still, the Asian financial crisis had spread to Latin America and, in particular, Russia, where hedge funds were seriously hurt.

Unbeknownst to most investors, the financial turmoil around the world unraveled the largest hedge fund in the business. Long Term Capital Management (LTCM) had an asset base of US$129 billion plus an off-balance sheet derivative position amounting to $1.25 trillion. When panicked investors sold Japanese and European bonds and bought U.S. Treasury bonds, LTCM sustained huge losses. On September 2, 1998, LTCM partners sought additional capital from investors and, unsurprisingly, no help was forthcoming. By September 19, the fund's capital had gone from $2.3 billion at the beginning of the month to only $600 million. The next day (Sunday), a delegation from the New York Federal Reserve and the U.S. Treasury visited the fund to assess the situation. The group concluded a rescue was needed to avert a potential global market collapse. In the following days, the Fed put together a consortium of 14 prominent banks and brokerage houses to invest $3.65 trillion of equity capital in LTCM in exchange for 90 percent of the firm's equity.

The LTCM affair and the subsequent unprecedented quick cuts in interest rates by the Fed turned investors' psychology from a doomsday mindset to one of euphoria. Interest rates around the region retreated from their extraordinary levels. After six months of horrendous losses, the Asian market was up 10 percent in September. Our fund only went up 2.5 percent, because it still had more than half of its assets in cash. Although the advance was strong, market volatility remained high. I was just glad the Fed had stepped in and saved the day for equity investors worldwide.

Two new business developments had been brewing for months. First, my work with Fiduciary Trust had been ongoing through the crisis months. The fund structure had been formalized and an action plan was formulated in October. I was hopeful that, given Fiduciary's solid standing in the marketplace, its fund-raising aspirations would be met without much trouble. Second, Kyle Shaw, with whom I had teamed up for the Flextronics buyout in 1991, had been approaching me since 1998 to organize a new Asian private equity fund. Our discussion had reached a stage where he decided to leave his work at Schroders Capital to set up a new firm with me and another partner. My role in this new venture would be in an advisory capacity and I felt that there wouldn't be any conflict with my ongoing commitments. Given my experience in private equity, I thought the two sides of equity investments had complementary aspects and my public equity investing would gain insight from potential deals sourced by Shaw.

The last months of 1998 saw markets steadily recovering. Stunned by the pace of the fast advance, I piled into the market and bought stocks of companies I thought would most benefit from the upturn. Many analysts were still negative about global economic prospects and they were probably right. On the other hand, I knew market behavior was suggesting something different. I knew that the typical funds, like mine, had too much cash and, therefore, had to be invested before year-end. After so many months of bloodbath in the market, I was happy to see stock prices moving up daily -- a sudden welcome change from the dire scenario just a couple of months ago. If the market was a true leading indicator of economic health, then we were on a path of recovery.

In the final quarter of the year, our fund had three months of positive returns amounting to almost 25 percent. Nevertheless, the risk appetite of U.S. investors remained cautious, due to the roller-coaster ride of the U.S. market, and the debacles in Russia, Brazil, and other countries. Negative sentiments regarding investments in the emerging markets did not change. I expected no new subscription and received none at the end of the year.

As 1998 ended, our fund lost 4 percent for the year while the regional benchmark lost over 7 percent. By year's end, there were signs the Asian economies were on the mend. Currencies had strengthened along with the markets. There would be many studies and papers on the causes and effects of the Asian financial crisis, but this is not a book to dwell on those topics. Nevertheless, I would like to make the following points.

First, the crisis showed that, in the globally linked financial markets, what happened in one corner of the world would spread to other parts of the world. In this context, the world is definitely a small village. Second, the IMF standard formula requiring countries to reduce fiscal and current account deficits during the crisis had become a subject of controversy. Clearly, the United States had never adopted such draconian measures to pull itself out of its many recessions. Third, the crisis revealed many deficiencies in the way capital was allocated in developing countries as well as undesirable political and economic practices. Lastly, as events would later show, the crisis fostered many historical and positive changes in the region's politics, economics, and corporate governance. Indeed, I now view 1998 as a dividing timeline for Asia in measuring stock market performance.

14

Rising from the Abyss

The year 1999 turned out to be the year of recovery – for the Asian economy, the global stock market, and for myself. In January, however, volatility still ruled the day. One of the Brazilian states defaulted on its debt obligation. The Rial plunged when its central banker quit. The country floated its currency on January 15.

In Hong Kong, the Chinese government decided not to support a state-owned enterprise named GITIC, which had somehow managed to pile up debt of US$2 billion. The Chinese action was unprecedented and it signaled to lenders and investors that the traditional paradigm of unquestioned state support for ailing enterprises had shifted. As a result, investors dumped "H" shares and red chips traded on the Hong Kong Exchange. There were many rumors that China would have to devalue its currency in line with all the other developing countries during the Asian financial crisis.

My discussions and work with Fiduciary Trust continued but the signs were discouraging. Its placement agent had sounded out the company's potential investors and received a lack-of-interest message. The main issue was that the U.S. and European markets were red hot and few investors had any appetite for Asian risks. In the investment world, professionals typically follow a strong herd instinct so few contrarians defied the crowd. Fiduciary tried a couple of other schemes but to no avail. The project was abandoned a few months later.

Markets were down for the first two months of 1999. Because of its currency peg to the U.S. dollar, Hong Kong had an overvalued currency in relation to the rest of Asia. Consequently, asset prices adjusted downward. Following the financial crisis, real estate prices dropped over 50 percent. People who bought properties in early 1997 now had negative equity in their investments if they had taken a typical mortgage loan. Because property investments played such an overwhelming role in the investment portfolios of typical Hong Kong people, asset deflation pushed the economy into a deflationary cycle that would persist for many years. To add to the existing gloom, China began making noises in March about pushing for reunification of Taiwan, which it considers a renegade province.

Surprisingly, Asian markets began to move up in late March, with the regional benchmark index advancing more than 10 percent. The momentum continued into the second quarter. I decided to rebalance the portfolio's allocation in favor of big cap and blue chip stocks. There is a well-known axiom that, at the beginning of a bull market, investors will chase big cap stocks in the most liquid markets. Obviously, the most liquid market in Asia was Hong Kong. For a heartening change, stock prices were moving higher every day. The Bloomberg screen was flashing green numbers instead of red ones. Along with higher prices came higher trading volumes.

Our analyst Eugene Soo Hoo resigned in early April and returned to his home in California. The bear market in Hong Kong in the previous two years had convinced many young men in Hong Kong to look for other career paths or migrate to Canada or Australia. Such was the pattern of young Chinese professionals that they represented the epitome of the classical definition of "labor mobility."

With markets recovering, I returned to the States in June to solicit more business. I found that most potential investors were inclined to wait a bit longer to make sure that the recent advance in markets would not be a "dead cat bounce." Nevertheless, I had a productive time in Jackson Hole, where I met a family from Texas spending the summer there. They showed a potential interest in investing. My state of mind was buoyed. My fund had advanced 37 percent in the second quarter, its best performance ever.

For some time, I had realized I needed to expand my business or face decline. Businesses do not stand still. They either move up or decline. Being a small boutique firm has many disadvantages. Investors worry I might be incapacitated suddenly, leaving the fund unattended. Indeed, many investors have a policy of not investing with a one-man firm. In my case, the age factor came into play as well. These were obvious issues I needed to address. Besides, my goal was to grow my business to become one of the preeminent investment management firms in Asia. I would need one or more partners to help me achieve this goal.

How do you attract a partner without much capital under management? And how do you attract capital without a viable organization? It is a kind of chicken-or-egg problem. Over the years, I had not resolved this central business issue, but I have not given up on the challenge. My idea in 1999 was to enlarge the equity of my firm by attracting additional investors to provide additional working capital. The new resources would enable me to recruit a team of professionals.

With this in mind and with the record of my firm having overcome the difficulties of the Asian financial crisis, I came upon the idea of having my company issue a convertible note with a term of three years. It would carry an option allowing the investor to convert the debt instrument into equity in my company. A typical convertible note carries a low interest coupon while the option would be set low enough to attract conversion of the notes to shares on or before maturity. I thought the project was timely because equity markets were advancing almost every day around the world and risk appetite was growing.

I sounded out the capital-raising project with several investors who had been consistently supportive of what I had been doing. I was also mindful that they might be interested in having a partner in Asia. My initial discussions with prospects turned out to be positive and I thought the project had a good shot at success. I worked out a business plan and drafted an offering memorandum for circulation, sending out a prospectus that summer.

Shortly thereafter, I took a trip to the United States to meet the two potential investors who had expressed the most interest. It was a fruitful trip. We resolved a number of critical issues, including how my enterprise was to be valued and the ultimate shareholding structure. Indeed, the investors were so enthusiastic I was asked to prepare detailed legal documents. I did, convinced that, after being a one-man boutique (or basically a proprietorship) since 1992, PCML would be transformed into a shareholder-owned investment advisory firm.

In late 1998, Kyle Shaw, a fellow director on the board of Flextronics in the early 1990s, decided to leave his employer and strike out on his own. Because of our long relationship, he thought we could form an investment management firm as partners. As I was by now deep into building the public equity business, I knew I couldn't dedicate much effort to his enterprise. Nevertheless, I agreed to collaborate with him and he named the firm Shaw Kwei & Partners. The aim of the enterprise was to raise a fund to invest in private companies that had the potential to go public in a few years. This was much the same strategy I had adopted with ASSET, the fund I organized for Asian Oceanic Group in 1988.

Shaw had recruited an associate and an administrator. As my office was not big enough to accommodate three more people, we had to find more space. Timing turned out to be perfect because my old lease would soon expire. After scouting out several options, we leased a space in Hutchison House.

Property prices were very depressed in 1999, two years after the burst of the real estate bubble in Hong Kong. Hutchison is a Grade "A" office while the office we were in would be rated as Grade "B." Because the rents had dropped about 50 percent, Shaw and I decided to keep our rental expenses at the current level but step up to the upgraded space. We would pay HK$31 per sq. ft. per month for a unit with 1,140 sq. feet, along with a six-month rent-free period.

Before I signed the lease, I had a feng shui master visit the premise to make sure that the office design best aligned the energy flows in the space with the two of us. We had already given our essential personal data such as our birth dates to the master. He was very experienced and, in no time, pointed out the best locations for Shaw, me and the Bloomberg terminal. With the master's pointers, the office designer began his work.

In late September, we moved from the Wilson House office to the newly decorated space in Hutchison House. My office had a window view, overlooking the harbor. Shaw's office, which sat at the other end of the floor, also had a water view. Separating the two offices was the conference room. This was the feng shui master's idea and, now, it appeared to make a lot of sense. I was amazed that, in a single day, all the computers and telephone lines were unplugged in the old office and set up in the new one. Broadband facilities were installed and LCD flat panel screens replaced all CRT monitors.

Our office looked first-rate. I also liked the fact that there was a wonderful Shanghaiese restaurant on street level, along with a post office branch, a convenience store, and a fully staffed HSBC bank branch. These facilities significantly improved office efficiencies. Because Shaw and his staff had joined us, we now had administrative support shared between the two groups.

Now optimistic, I launched our company's first website, using a local design firm headed by a Yale alumnus. The website, www.pcmlhk.com, was launched in November. It contained a brief description of my investment strategies, the company's key personnel profile, monthly letters to investors, an updated performance chart, and key events of our company. Since my company is not registered with the U.S. Securities and Exchange Commission, the website was designed to comply with U.S. regulations related to un-registered investment advisors.

Meanwhile, markets kept moving ahead and technology stocks were particularly strong. Investors' enthusiasm was not only due to euphoria about prospects of the new Internet age (Internet stocks having tripled in the past four years) but also increased orders due to the so-called Y2K problem. The Y2K arose because many old computers had their internal clock set in a way it could not handle the year 2000 and thereafter. All the old machines would need to be upgraded or replaced, thus generating an enormous demand for computer hardware around the world.

Excitement about the Internet as the "new, new thing" grew stronger by the day. Brokers touted any stocks having something to do with information technology. Examining a number of the IT stocks being pushed by U.S. brokers, I found we were entering a period similar to the one I had experienced during the junk bond era in the late 1980s. Financial fundamentals were thrown out of the window. "Progress" was now measured by the number of "eyeballs" per month, that is, the number of visits to the website in question. Earnings and free cash flow, the fundamentals of any valuation, were thrown out the window as techniques only applicable to "old economy" stocks.

We received many offerings of U.S. Internet stocks as well as a few in Asia, particularly several out of China. Almost all these listed companies had no earnings history. Valuing such an enterprise was virtually impossible. The Internet was generally a value destroyer in that users on the Web mostly could get what they want without paying anything. Without doubt, the new technology benefited consumers and raised productivity. But, it wasn't clear how providers of such services could generate any profit with their business models. I decided to stay out of this sector and leave the field to intrepid speculators. Our caution would cost us some short-term gains but avoided major pains in the months ahead as events unfolded later in 2000.

The widespread use of the Internet provided a real source of growth for technology equipment companies as more and more people clamored for PCs and servers to connect them to the World Wide Web. Technology stocks were bid up relentlessly as investors expected the current growth rate to continue for years to come. Sharing the same optimism were telecommunications companies and suppliers such as optical cable makers. Valuation again seemed to take a back seat to optimism that future growth would be boundless. Manufacturers were expanding capacity quickly to meet "anticipated" future demand.

A feeding frenzy developed along the food chains in technology and communications industries. Stock prices of IT companies in Asia, like their counterparts in the States, were rising fast. We raised weighting of technology stocks to over 20 percent of the fund's portfolio. In October and November, our fund gained almost 20 percent.

Asian markets roared back with a fury. Investor interest in the region perked up. On November 5, I made a trip to Bahrain to visit a major Bahraini investment bank with the intent to jointly launch an Asian fund for investors in the Arabian Gulf. I had not visited the region since 1991 when I was in a desperate attempt to stave off bankruptcy for the Asian Oceanic Group, my former employer. I had not been to Bahrain since 1977 when I was working for Citibank. I was eager to return. I was treated like a VIP at the immigration counter. After being escorted around the normal entry procedures, I was driven to the five-star Diplomat Hotel. It was a Saturday morning, a working day in the Gulf.

Over lunch at a Lebanese restaurant, my host bombarded me with questions about the Asian markets. For the next two days I spent in his bank, several senior executives interviewed me about my background and virtually every aspect of my firm's operation. After I returned to Hong Kong, the bank decided to send me US$1 million to start a track record. If the account performed well, they would launch an Asian fund with our firm as the advisor. The prospect of doing business with the Bahrain bank seemed promising.

During my bi-annual road show in the States in December, I hit a milestone. I went to Dallas to meet the family whom I had earlier met in Jackson Hole. In my discussion, I went over the most recent economic development in the Asian region and presented our fund's performance. To my delight, I was told they were interested to open a separate investment account which our firm would manage. The initial capital would be US$3 million, the highest commitment by any one investor in our firm's history. I was so excited about the development I managed to put a little scratch on the rental car when I left the garage to return to the airport.

As the year end approached, the Y2K issue loomed large. In fact, the Securities and Futures Commission (SFC) in Hong Kong required financial firms such as PCML to make hourly reports on the first day of the New Year in order to monitor events as they unfolded. Our firm had long since taken measures to make sure we would not encounter any problems. In any case, as investors' funds were kept in the custodian bank, the latter had been sending updates to the regulator since October. I was sure the situation was under control. I certainly did not lose any sleep over the remote possibility of a catastrophic event.

The fourth quarter of 1999 saw an incredibly strong equity market. ASEIP, our fund, was up 35 percent. Indeed, the fund turned in the best performance in its history. It advanced about 66 percent for the full year before incentive payments were made. The latter payments were a big help. Ever since 1997, I had basically been subsidizing PCML to keep it going. Throughout the year, I had been receiving additional commitments from existing and new investors. As a result of the new capital, but mostly because of the investment gains, ASEIP ended the year with its net asset value at US$22 million. While this was a small sum in the world of investment management, it was big enough to give my morale a major boost. Our fund had outperformed the regional benchmark by a big margin, had survived the crisis, and now had a history of seven years to show the skeptics.

So, the old century, after all the turmoil, ended on a high note. The new millennium was about to begin and a new century to unfold.

Looking back, the Asian financial crisis had made a profound impact on the political landscape in Asia. Except for China, Hong Kong, and Singapore, leaders of all other countries are now freely elected. This was something I had not anticipated back in 1996. For example, I did not expect Indonesia's President Suharto to relinquish power without bloodshed. I did not expect South Korea to turn from a military regime to a democratically elected presidency in such a short period of time. The same transformation occurred in Thailand. While Taiwan was barely touched by the crisis, it would become a full-fledged democracy with the opposition party in power for many years.

Even in China and Hong Kong, people power had gained ascendancy and their governments could no longer rule without taking into account people's aspirations and legitimate rights. Politically, the crisis had accelerated reforms at a pace far greater than anyone could have anticipated. Asia could take considerable pride in that the region's political powers; the fact that it did not go backwards for self-preservation is something that Asia could take much pride in.

In the countries that received IMF funding, governments were committed to pursue financial market reforms to attract foreign capital to expedite recovery. Markets that had restricted foreign participation opened up such as the banking sector in South Korea. Corporate governance improved substantially and regulations and supervision were strengthened. In South Korea, *chaebols* paid a heavy price. Several, including Daewoo, went into liquidation. It is truly remarkable that South Korea paid off its IMF loans of over US$50 billion in just three years. Thailand repaid its IMF loans by 2003.

The speedy recovery reflected the fundamental resilience of Asia's private sectors. Interestingly, the contagion of financial meltdown did not affect the developed economies in the United States and Europe. Amid all the turmoil, China steadfastly held its currency exchange, preventing what would have been a disastrous competitive devaluation cycle. The country suffered several years of deflation but the crisis gave it the opportunity to overtake other countries in the region as the preferred source of foreign direct investment.

While Asia was recovering from its crisis, troubles began to show up in the States. Many had predicted the new, new economy had beaten the old business cycles. That theory was about to be proven wrong in a big hurry. The very exuberance that had characterized the U.S. growth planted the seeds of its downfall.

As I blissfully welcomed the new millennium, another stormy season was gathering for me in only a few months' time.

As the Asian financial crisis turned the corner, I wanted to have a firsthand look at the developments in the countries hit hardest by the turmoil. I mapped out a series of visits to those countries during 2000.

My first stop was to South Korea, where I attended an investors' conference organized by a major global investment bank. I learned all the *chaebol*s and other corporations had put in place programs to improve corporate governance and transparency. I then took a trip to Malaysia to visit companies there. In Kuala Lumpur, I was impressed with the new airport and the twin Petronas Towers, then the tallest buildings in the world. Because of the currency devaluation during the Asian financial crisis, everything seemed to be cheaper than before in U.S. dollar terms. The country had been insulated from the crisis and Mahathir's influence and style of development had not changed much. There were some reforms in the banking sector but I wasn't sure whether the bad loan problems would be resolved expeditiously.

A few days later, I went to Thailand, only to be disappointed by the progress there. The Thais had decided to resolve their nonperforming loan (NPL) problems in a way that protected the families who owned insolvent businesses. When a company became insolvent, its future would not be determined by the creditors or the courts, but by a combination of the debtor, the creditor, and the court together. Clearly, countries with such a convoluted system would recover much more slowly than South Korea, which had taken serious and rigorous reform steps.

During a UBS conference in Hong Kong in late February, I ran into Ching Ju Yeh, an experienced and well-regarded fund manager I first met in Taiwan a few years back. Ching Ju was born in Taiwan and, like many young students in the 1980s, finished her university education in the States and worked there for a couple of years before moving to Hong Kong. When I met her in the conference, she told me she had left the Trust Company of the West because it decided to close its office in Hong Kong. I immediately thought she would be an ideal partner. She was a hard-working person with the utmost integrity and had a good track record in portfolio management. In subsequent weeks, we held several meetings. One idea that appealed to both of us was to launch a new Asian technology fund that would attract U.S. investors. In early April, we agreed to the terms of our collaboration.

On March 18, Taiwan held a presidential election, and the opposition candidate, Chen Shui Bien, won. This was a historical moment. The Nationalist Party, the Kuomintang, or KMT, in power since 1945, was thrown out in a truly democratic election. No one whispered of any irregularities. Chen ran on the platform of distancing Taiwan from the embrace of China, implying the possibility of seeking independence in the future. His platform, of course, infuriated China's leadership. I was relieved that China, while blistering in words, took no hostile action. The market first dropped and then went up on March 21.

As the first quarter ended, I was pleased with a number of developments. My convertible note project was moving ahead to the documentation stage. For the first time in our company's history, we started managing a separate account opened by the Bahrain bank. In addition, the Texas family formally remitted funds to the custodian account, establishing another separate account for our firm. Finally, I was optimistic Ching Ju would come on board to help me build the business. I was making big plans, but little did I realize the U.S. bull run had ended, ushering a market correction that would be the second longest since the Depression years.

Since I turned 55, I had been undergoing annual physical checkups without fail. I knew my cholesterol level was high, probably the result of enjoying too much junk food in my youth.

In March 2000, a routine physical examination indicated my PSA reading had jumped since my checkup a year ago. PSA is a marker indicating potential prostate cancer condition in men. The higher the number, the more likely the chance of having malignant cells. I was asked to look into this but it didn't sound urgent. Given my heavy work schedule, I didn't bother to have further consultation until the summer. Unfortunately, test results by then determined I had a few tumors in my prostate. Dr. Richard Lo, the urologist, recommended I have my prostate removed. Fortunately, a body scan showed no indication the cancer cells had spread outside the prostate.

I decided early on to continue working as if nothing had happened. I told a few close friends, my family members, and only the potential investors in the convertible about my condition. I did not tell anyone in the office except Bela, nor did I tell any investors in my fund. Since my condition was not life threatening, I felt my ailment did not represent a significant material change in my physical condition. Physically I felt no different than before the diagnosis. The procedure would require only 10 days of rest. I scheduled the operation over the Christmas break so it wouldn't be disruptive to work.

While I continued working at my regular pace, I was clearly living in a different state of being. For the first time, I felt vulnerable to forces I couldn't control. The affliction reminded me the aging process was not a walk in the park. My mental and psychological condition were greatly helped by my meditation practice. I knew I had to be strong and let go of any negative thoughts.

One technique I used to control my emotional bearing was to turn to poetic musings. In the period leading to my operation, in quiet moments, I managed to write three poems. I am particularly fond of the one I wrote on my 65th birthday:

On Turning Sixty-Five

The October sky carries signs of the coming winter.
Stepping on fallen leaves that once painted the hills in blazing colors,
My thoughts turn to the mysteries of life that surround us.
I look up and catch the glow of the setting sun.

Many seasons have passed and many roads have been taken.
My life has been marked by swings of up and down.
And yet, I've found no time to reflect on the past and slow down the pace of my work.
I have learned much, but there is much more to learn.

The biting wind tells me it's time to go home.
Walking in the shadow of the setting sun,
I am conscious of the impermanence of body and spirit.
Surely, I will not be spared challenges that come with changing of the season.

Growing old, I am told, is not for the faint of heart.
Even so, let the lotus of wisdom blossom in me, and let the lamp to brighten my awareness be lit.
No anxiety and fear will I harbor,
When there is so much joy and blessing in my journey.

October 22, 2000

My prostate procedure was scheduled for December 21. I went into the hospital the night before as stock markets around the world continued to tumble. I was up early the morning of the 21st, sitting on my bed in the hospital and talked to Ching Ju about several trades. Kathy, my daughter, came early and stayed with me. She accompanied me to the operating room. Her presence calmed my nerves that were working overtime. This operation was the first since my cataract operation in 1964. Over the years, my health had always been very good and I had rarely visited a hospital, let alone found myself lying flat on my back being wheeled around.

The procedure took several hours. I woke up at around 6 pm to find the operation had been successful. I was comforted to be in the company of Kathy, my wife, and Bela. There were many flowers in my room. Kathy placed a small Christmas tree at my bedside. A day later, Clarence came back from New York. We spent a wonderful Christmas Eve in my hospital room. When Dr. Lo came to check up on me early that evening and saw the jovial atmosphere, I could tell from his facial expression he had no doubt my recovery would be a speedy one. Indeed, it was a miracle my recovery proceeded exactly as anticipated. I left the hospital on the morning of the 28th.

My family decided to continue the tradition of holding a big festive dinner party on the 30th. Although I stayed upstairs in my room, I could hear the festivities and knew everybody was having a great time. This made me feel pretty good as well. I had already started walking and we went to the Hong Kong Country Club to welcome the New Year on New Year's Day.

15

Coping with the U.S. Bear Market

The U.S. bull market – no ordinary one – started in 1995 and ended in March 2000. It turned out to be the biggest five-year advance in the Dow Jones Industrial Average history. Many dubbed this "The New Paradigm Era," in which old rules of value did not apply. The Internet revolution opened up many opportunities by changing the way consumers shopped and the way companies did business. E-commerce and technology companies were competing to be the first in their fields. They drew an unprecedented amount of money into fast-growing startups. Businesses, meanwhile, poured millions of dollars into computing systems, storage, and communications networks. Demand for new workers pushed the US unemployment rate down to a 30-year low of 3.9 percent.

The lure of easy money spawned a new generation of day traders who ignored fundamentals. Venture capitalists poured capital into technology companies, increasing investment from US$3 to US$5 billion per year in the mid-1990s to nearly US$100 billion in 2000. To the euphoric investor, the lure of the Internet-based "new economy" suggested low inflation, increasing productivity, and banishment of business cycles. Unfortunately, the newfound investors' confidence was sorely misplaced. It so happened business cycles were still alive and well. And when the prevailing cycle peaked, businesses began to cut spending and orders for manufactured goods fell. Santayana, the great 20th-century philosopher, once said: "Those who do not learn from the past are condemned to repeat it." Investors would soon learn that this period was not a "new era" but rather one of the biggest speculative bubbles in history.

Historically, the price-to-earnings multiple, or P/E ratio, of the S&P 500 Index has averaged around 14 times earnings. But at the beginning of 2000, it was trading at over 30. The NASDAQ, host to many technology firms, saw its P/E reaching astronomical level as half of the large cap technology stocks traded on the market-weighted P/E ratio of 208 times earnings. In short, the market was clearly set up for a free fall.

And the freefall did happen. In April, NASDAQ stocks took a beating, down 25 percent in one month. Stocks continued to drop over the entire year. The relentless descent would leave the market at about 50 percent below its peak by year-end. The intensity of the super bull market in the late 1990s now turned in reverse. In 2000, we witnessed the obliteration of dot-com favorites like Garden.com, Pets.com, and more. Even prices of blue-chip stocks such as Dell Computer, Cisco Systems, Intel, Sun Microsystems, and Lucent Technologies dropped 50 percent or more from the top.

As the U.S. market fell, markets in Asia followed with a depressingly high correlation. On April 14, the Dow Jones was down a whopping 7 percent as technology stocks were being dumped. I was in Singapore and had arranged to visit companies, but the extreme market volatility forced me to cancel most of my meetings. When placing sell orders, I had put a limit of 10 percent drop, much too narrow in the face of indiscriminate selling. As a result, few of my orders were executed. By the end of the day, our fund was down 13 percent. It was such a bloodbath that I dashed off a note to our investors, explaining my actions and what happened in the markets. In addition, I turned down subscriptions by two investors who had remitted their capital to the fund's custodian. I couldn't in good conscience do anything else. By month-end, markets staged a modest recovery and the fund was down around 9 percent for the month.

Through all this, Ching Ju Yeh, who had earlier agreed to join my firm as a partner, began to work on the new technology fund as originally planned. We knew technology stocks were taking a beating, but we thought the market correction represented a good buying opportunity. We didn't anticipate the initial market fall would lead to one of the greatest bear markets in modern times. Meanwhile, my proposal for an investors' conference in May drew four commitments and I decided to go ahead with the annual event.

The first sign that investors were getting cold feet about equity investment came in May when my carefully prepared investors' conference had only one actual attendee. It was awkward for me to have invited several important speakers and not have an audience. To avoid embarrassment, Ching Ju and I scrambled to fill up the space with local contacts. That was the last conference I organized until this very day.

With the market reeling day to day, the chances of our firm raising a new fund focused on Asian technology stocks increasingly dimmed. Nevertheless, since we had done so much spadework on the project, I went to the States to raise as much capital as I could. Ching Ju and I decided that we would launch it if we could find a minimum initial capital of US$8 million.

I made the usual round of stops in the States in June. Besides meeting several prospects, I also met our investors and briefed them about the status of ASEIP. In many ways, raising capital is a probability game. The more people you meet, the more likely you are to find investors. I figured that, having raised ASEIP without any track record, raising the new technology fund with a proven track record would be relatively easy.

EAST TO WEST TO EAST

My marketing trips to the States were always a pleasant change of pace from my focus in equity research in Asia. I'd often be schmoozed with dinners or theater or other entertainment. At times, our meetings would be so casual that I didn't need to make a formal presentation. The highlight of this trip was to spend a wonderful afternoon with a prospect at his home by the bank of the Snake River in Wyoming. The air was clean and crisp. With the majestic Grand Teton rising in the distance, our talk wandered into politics, international relations, and our mutual values.

With my usual optimism and a positive outlook, I returned to Hong Kong with a renewed sense of confidence, even as technology stocks were tanking. I reported to Ching Ju we should proceed with our new project. Additionally, I thought all the issues for the convertible note for my company had been resolved. I was looking to set a closing date some time in September. Meanwhile, markets kept trending down. Our fund was down a whopping 10 percent for the second quarter and another 2.6 percent in July. My old doubts about my ability to steer the fund through volatile periods returned. I felt I had not reacted quickly to market adversity.

Each market downturn is usually different from the other. This one was no exception. The first market crash I experienced was the result of the 1997–1998 Asian financial crises. Now, U.S. stock market sell-offs led to investors dumping their stocks in Asia. While Asian investors still remembered the bear market barely two years ago, what was happening in the U.S. market was quite new to U.S. investors used to seeing stock prices going up on most days. In the months of 2000, U.S. investors, seeing red every day on stock tickers, were losing serious money. The mantra to buy on dips no longer worked. The "buy and hold" strategy that had worked for so many years became a bad idea.

In this scenario, the so-called "long only" funds had become a largely unpopular asset class. Investors flocked to "hedge funds" that promised to make money in bear markets.

I had anticipated the relentless bear market would have a negative impact on my ability to complete the convertible transaction. It came as no surprise in early September when the anchor investor of the convertible note requested the deal be deferred. A week later, another investor essentially made the same request. In the months that followed, market conditions began to improve, but the interest in the convertible could not be rekindled. My serious attempt to reorganize my firm to reach a higher level of corporate structure had come to naught.

After the summer months, stocks were sliding across the board, especially technology stocks. The dot-com fallout coupled with the PC slowdown in the States resulted in slower growth for chipmakers and server producers. Optical networking companies also experienced slowdowns as their primary customers, the telecommunications companies, were having their own problem of inventory glut. Investors began questioning growth rate assumptions, P/E's and valuation. To exacerbate the matter, the U.S. Federal Reserve continued to raise interest rates in its fight against inflation and held its "tightening bias" through November.

It was evident investors' mood had become decidedly negative since my last visit in July. Several were contemplating getting out of my fund. Our portfolio went down by 8 percent in September. South Korea and Taiwan were particularly hard hit. South Korea fell apart because Ford announced, in the middle of the month, that it was abandoning its expected rescue of Daewoo Motors. Taiwan traded down to almost the level reached during the height of the Asian financial crisis in 1998.

Our firm's prospect brightened somewhat when we were approached to be a sub-advisor of a new global emerging market fund. The approach was made by one of my investors, a well-known investment manager specializing in emerging market funds. In October, he sent his partner to our office to make a due diligence trip. I showed him how we made asset allocations, estimated target price for stocks, and conducted financial modeling to determine the intrinsic value of a stock. He seemed impressed. As a result of his visit, we were selected to be the Asian sub-advisor and be part of his management team. My hopes were high that we'd see a major jump in assets under management if the fund could be launched.

The bear market persisted. In mid-October, following the plunging NASDAQ, the Taiwan market dropped at the maximum permitted range of 6 percent per day for two consecutive days. Investors were exiting out of technology shares en masse. Samsung Electronics, the largest stock on the Korea Stock Exchange, plummeted 12 percent in just one single day. Although I had sold some futures in the market, it was of very limited use.

Markets were also unnerved by political events. A terrorist boat in Yemen rammed a U.S. military ship, badly damaging it. Separately, Israeli gunships fired missiles into Palestinian sites, escalating the longstanding conflict that showed no signs of rapprochement. On Friday the 13th, I sold 50 percent of all core holdings at market price. I also sold more futures as I anticipated markets heading in another mindless stampede. My action reflected capitulation, but I thought it wise to be out of the market for the moment.

I was now approaching the ripe age of 65, with no intention of quitting. In fact, I wanted to expand my business. I remained confident the investment management industry in Asia would experience a bright future. I celebrated my birthday by taking the afternoon off and getting my portrait taken by a professional photographer. I visited the Po Lin monastery on Lantau Island, home to a 34-meter-tall bronze Buddha. I climbed the steps to the top and walked around the large statute. I reflected on how much I had gained from studying Buddhism over the years. I had learned to let go of negative thoughts and become detached from daily travails. Celebrating my birthday made me thankful for the teachings that, over the years, had helped me spiritually.

The month of November saw more selling and limit-down days in Taiwan. By the 20th, Taiwan's market dived to a level lower than when I started the fund in 1994! The U.S. election was a messy process as well. The election of George W. Bush as the next president brought few cheers. In the States, the S&P Index, which measures performance of the broad market, lost 10 percent in 2000. Worse still, NASDAQ dropped 40 percent. In Asia, the regional benchmark lost 38 percent. Incredibly, our fund lost more value in 2000 than during the Asian financial crisis. The new millennium was not beginning in the way I had hoped.

At the very beginning of 2001, the Fed surprised investors with a 50 basis point rate cut on the second trading day of the New Year. This action followed indication by the Fed in November 2000 it would now lean toward an easing bias. Interest rates began their downward slide as the U.S. dollar also began to trade lower against other major currencies. The prospect of lower interest rates caused several analysts to forecast rising stock prices. Indeed, this was to be the first of 11 attempts by the U.S. central bank in subsequent months to reverse the economic slide.

The first bad news that hit me was that the Bahrain investor decided to pull out less than a year after they had agreed to work with us to launch an Asian fund in the Gulf region. A few weeks later, my biggest supporter from Boston decided to take out 50 percent of its commitments. The first quarter of 2001 saw the greatest amount of redemption in the fund's history and changed the economics of my business in the most fundamental way.

A year earlier, the firm's assets under management stood at US$25 million. By the end of the first quarter of 2001, the nominal value of the total assets under management had dropped to US$18 million. My business no longer had positive cash flow. I expected more redemptions as U.S. investors took more hits in their home investments and became ever more risk adverse. There was no room for me to cut expenses. I had no choice but to hang tough and ride out this turbulence. Fortunately, I had taken in a good deal of incentive payments earlier in 2000. These came in handy for supporting negative cash flow situation in my firm.

If the year 2000 saw the markets bruised, the year 2001 would witness the markets truly battered. It was also a year of what is known as "head fakes" or "dead cat bounces." For example, markets would go up strongly one day but slump the next day. Profit warnings came flowing in at an alarming rate and fears of a hard landing were rampant. Earnings visibility was bleak and technology spending estimates dropped through the floor. It would be a year when corporations saw their worst profit performance in a decade. In February, Barton Biggs, a prominent global strategist at Morgan Stanley, advised clients the U.S. economy would take a U-shape recovery (i.e., a recession). I knew the economic valley was going to be a very broad one.

U.S. investors suffered their greatest-ever one-week loss during the week of March 12–16. The Dow Jones Industrial Average took three sharp declines in five days, resulting in a loss of 7.7 percent, while the tech-dominated NASDAQ Index fell 8 percent. In the year ending March, the NASDAQ had fallen 63 percent, the biggest percentage drop in a major U.S. stock index since the 1929 crash. In the same period, the S&P was down 25 percent. The combined losses on the NYSE and NASDAQ topped US$4.6 trillion, nearly five times the losses from the Wall Street Crash in October 1987. The sheer magnitude of this bubble burst was staggering. It was said the losses were greater than the combined Social Security and Medicare trust funds and was equivalent to the GDP of the combined economies of Japan and South Korea. So rapid was the collapse in share values U.S. household wealth saw its first net decline since the federal government began keeping such figures in 1945.

The impact of this colossal financial liquidation can be illustrated by the following two examples. One was the huge hit taken by Yahoo, a great name in the stock market. Its market cap fell from US$150 billion in March 2000 to under US$10 billion within a year. Its stock price plunged from US$250 per share to US$17 per share. Even at the lower price, the stock was still vastly overvalued as it was still selling at 140 times earnings. America Online's purchase of Time Warner was another example of a bubble economy deal that ultimately unraveled. Eventually, Time Warner would take charges and write-downs to the tune of US$98.7 billion because of the merger. The stock traded at US$90 at its height, but it dropped all the way to US$10 in mid-2002.

For the first time in a quarter century, all three of the main economic centers of the world – the United States, Japan, and Western Europe – were simultaneously experiencing economic slowdown. Amid relentless selling pressure, I was unable to mount an effective strategy to minimize portfolio losses. Market volatility often upset my hedging strategies and the fund's performance suffered.

In early May, Yale celebrated its 300th anniversary event in Hong Kong. The event was chaired by Patrick Caviness, my erstwhile tennis partner, and assisted by several long-time members of the alumni club in Hong Kong. The occasion provided an opportunity for Yale graduates in the Asian region to meet one another for the first time. Yale's President Rick Levin was in town to lead the celebration, which helped raise the profile of Yale in Hong Kong to a much higher level than before. It was noteworthy that, in celebrating the university's special anniversary, Levin visited only London and Hong Kong outside of the

United States. In the years to follow, Yale University would continue to develop its relationships in the Greater China region as it viewed the region as having a special strategic relevance in the world of higher education.

During this period, investment analysts continued to downgrade earnings of U.S. corporations. A few forecast they would fall as much as 16 percent. On that basis, U.S. corporate earnings performance would be the worst since 1991. Stocks continued to decline from May through August, increasing in magnitude over the summer months. In Hong Kong, shares of Chinese companies suffered particularly high volatility as the authorities cracked down on illegal money flowing out of the country. Our fund's performance did relatively very well, remaining flat for the second quarter against a drop of over 3 percent in the regional benchmark index.

On July 5, Typhoon Urdo, reportedly the biggest one in 20 years, missed Hong Kong but delayed flights and closed schools. Fortunately, the typhoon hit land the day before I was to leave for the States to visit clients. Still, it was raining hard, accompanied by powerful winds. My mood mirrored the state of the weather somewhat in that the objective of my client visits was "damage control." The day before, Marconi, a telecommunications company listed on the London Stock Exchange, dropped 50 percent, which pulled all the markets down further. Later in the month, JDS Uniphase, another New Economy company, wrote down its assets by US$45 billion to reflect the loss of value since the bubble burst.

During my trip, I took time out to attend the wedding of my niece, Stephanie, on July 15 in Ipswich, Massachusetts. The wedding was held at Castle Hill, a beautiful setting overlooking the Atlantic Ocean. On our way there, my son and I stopped by Danvers to take a look at St. John's Preparatory School, where I graduated 47 years ago. For a long time, I reflected on how dramatically my life had evolved since my innocent days as a young boy learning to be part of the American culture.

While I was making client visits, markets were dropping almost every day. I had been unloading shares even though they were valued at below their intrinsic value. It was an ugly time. In any event, the meetings with investors accomplished what I intended – damage control. No new redemptions surfaced and a couple of investors indicated they would add when the market conditions improved. Still, ASEIP's size had declined 40 percent from its peak in 2000 to only US$15 million.

On September 11, 2001 the world's history changed course. Suicide hijackers crashed two airliners into the World Trade Center in New York, causing the 110-story twin towers to collapse. Another hijacked airliner hit the Pentagon and a fourth crashed in a field in Pennsylvania. Some 3,000 people were killed in all.

When the attacks struck, I was in the American Club in Hong Kong for my regular workout. On entering the gym, I noticed several members glued to the television set on the wall. They were watching CNN and the commentator was saying there had been an accident. He said that a commercial airliner had just crashed into one of the World Trade Center towers. As we stared at the incredible sight, we witnessed the second plane slamming into the second tower. Surely, the second crash could not have been an accident. I continued to watch the news as I exercised, feeling dumbfounded. After I finished my workout an hour later, I went to a TV screen in the lounge and caught the horrifying sight of the buildings collapsing. I immediately called my wife and my son, both of whom were in New York City. My wife was home but my son had already gone to work at the Rockefeller Center. I couldn't reach him on the cell phone for 30 minutes. I spent the rest of the evening watching the news on CNN and talking to people I knew in New York. Fortunately, everyone I knew was safe as none of them was near the tragic scene.

On that day of infamy, stock exchanges in New York were closed; airports shut down; borders sealed and offices evacuated, as the United States went into maximum alert. The next day, markets in Asia, as expected, plunged. Hong Kong's market dropped 1,000 points at the opening but recovered some afterwards. South Korea opened late and dropped 15 percent. Taiwan would open a day later and went down by 12 percent in two days. The event was so horrific that everyone I met had to talk about it. Everyone unloaded his grief to another. I wrote a note to my investors, mourning the loss of human lives and inquiring about their safety. I was glad that I received replies from most. The interchange brought us much closer. The good news was all my investors were safe.

There were many thoughtful and thought-provoking commentaries in the days that followed. Two, in particular, mirrored my own views about the implication of the disaster. These are excerpted below. The first is by Amos Oz:

> *It is all too easy and tempting now to fall into all sorts of racist clichés about "Muslim mentality" or "Arab character" and other such rubbish. The horrendous crime committed against the cities of New York and Washington is a sharp reminder that this is not a war between religions, nor a struggle between nations. This is, once more, the battle between fanatics for whom the end – any end, be it religious, nationalistic or ideological – sanctifies the means, and the rest of us who ascribe sanctity to life itself.*
>
> *Let no decent human being forget that the vast majority of Arabs and Muslims are neither accomplices to the crime nor rejoicing in it. They even have some special reason for worrying, as ugly sounds of indiscriminate anti-Islamic feelings can already be heard in some places.*

The second is excerpted from a message attributed to the Dalai Lama:

There are two possible responses to what has occurred today. The first comes from love, the second from fear.

If we come from fear we may panic and do things – as individuals and as nations – that could only cause further damage. If we come from love we will find refuge and strength, even as we provide it to others.

We will set the course for tomorrow, today. At this hour. In this moment. Let us seek not to pinpoint blame, but to pinpoint cause.

Unless we take this time to look at the cause of our experience, we will never remove ourselves from the experiences it creates. Instead, we will forever live in fear of retribution from those within the human family who feel aggrieved, and, likewise, seek retribution from them.

The message we hear from all sources of truth is clear: We are all one.

If we could love even those who have attacked us, and seek to understand why they have done so, what then would be our response? Yet if we meet negativity with negativity, rage with rage, attack with attack, what then will be the outcome?

A central teaching in most spiritual traditions is: What you wish to experience, provide for another.

If you wish to experience peace, provide peace for another. If you wish to know that you are safe, cause [others] to know that they are safe.

If you wish to better understand seemingly incomprehensible things, help another to better understand.

If you wish to heal your own sadness or anger, seek to heal the sadness or anger of another.

Those others are waiting for you now. They are looking to you for guidance, for help, for courage, for strength, for understanding, and for assurance at this hour. Most of all, they are looking to you for love.

Despite the pain and destruction that would last for years, stock markets carried on. In the weeks following the attack, I sold futures to minimize volatility but my action didn't fully buffer the market sell-off. My usual sense of optimism was greatly tested as I feared that the United States would now slide into a recession.

In the spirit of maintaining my work routine, I went to a UBS Korea Conference on September 23. Surprisingly, the Hong Kong airport procedure did not impose any new security safeguards. By month's end, our fund was down 6.3 percent while the regional index was down 16 percent.

I wrote the following note on September 30:

Well, this has been an unbelievable month, a tragic one, a frightening one, and the events in the US could conceivably change the course of history. US is definitely going into a recession and I am not sure how long that would last. The so-called terrorism is now the first global enemy of the US in this new century and there is no precedent to help us combat it. Let's hope that the US doesn't make any foolish mistakes along the way. My expectation is that the culprits won't be found and the conflict will go on for a long time. Another hope is that there won't be some kind of chemical or biological terrorist act in the future. If not contained, the world can go into a major conflagration. The best solution would be for the Arabs to act and get rid of terrorists in their midst and reverse the type of jihad preached by the radicals.

It didn't take long for the United States to take retaliatory action. On October 7, it launched bombing attacks and missile strikes on Afghanistan. A new dimension of the conflict began. Markets were weak but did not tank. I closed my hedge positions even though I wasn't sure the worst was over. Markets seemed to have, by now, digested all the bad news and begun a slow recovery.

In mid-October, the United States faced a new anthrax scare. Bombing continued in Afghanistan. It was evident the Taliban government would eventually fall, but many innocent people were being killed. Meanwhile, markets appeared to be shrugging off the escalating war in Afghanistan and the anthrax attacks and continued to recover. I didn't complain and watched the fund go up 5.8 percent for the month of October, the first positive return since April.

By mid-November, the Taliban government was collapsing. The U.S. military success plus the rate easing by the Fed reversed the bear market sentiment, and equity prices were advancing. However, in early December, Enron, a high-flying utility that had turned into a New Economy favorite, sought Chapter 11 protection after reporting a surprising loss of almost US$700 million the previous month. This was the largest bankruptcy in the history of U.S. business failures at the time, and executive malfeasance was the chief culprit. The U.S. market was clearly unsettled by this corporate disaster.

When I flew to the States in December to brief my investors about the latest regional developments, I found security procedures at the airport significantly tightened. On domestic flights, notebook PCs and other electronic devices had to be checked, and overcoat and shoes had to be separately scanned. The lengthier process meant that one had to arrive at the airport much earlier than before, significantly increasing the time it took to travel from one city to another.

On this trip, I was surprised when several investors indicated they would add to their commitments in the fund. They were apparently happy that the fund's performance had been much better than the market average. The bad news was that my investor's effort to launch the emerging global market fund had to be abandoned for lack of sufficient commitment by prospects. I wasn't surprised as the U.S. market had by now been down for two consecutive years.

For the first time in many years, my family spent Christmas with my brother's family in their home in Wappingers Falls, New York. This was a truly happy occasion. But, unexpectedly, on the 28th, Bela, my assistant in Hong Kong, called me in the middle of the night, telling me that my mother had fallen and fractured her right leg and was in the Canossa Hospital. My mother, 88 years old, was increasingly fragile. My wife and I agreed that I should return to Hong Kong as soon as possible.

I returned to Hong Kong on the 30th and touched down on New Year's Eve. By then, Mother had returned home and I went to visit her the next day. She was being taken care of by the housekeeper who had worked for her for many years. Mother's physical condition had deteriorated much faster than I anticipated. Nevertheless, when I visited her the next day, she appeared alert and reasonably cheerful. I believed the fracture was healing and the episode was likely to be a routine one for someone of her age.

So, the year of 2001 ended with a lot going on in my mind. I was worried about Mother's health; worried about the economic downturn; worried about the unfolding war on terrorism; and worried about my business prospects. Despite the great turmoil in the markets, our fund had gone up almost 1 percent for the year while the regional index lost over 4.5 percent.

―

My mother passed away not long after the New Year. On January 17, she died in her sleep. Like the situation I encountered with my father's unexpected death five years earlier, we never had any last words together. I knew she wanted to have a Buddhist funeral and I arranged it that way.

Mother had led a privileged life in her youth. Unlike many girls in those days, she didn't have to bind her feet. She went to the best girls' school in the city and had a high school degree. She used to tell my brother and me about those days of wealth and privilege. According to her, every one of her siblings had a car attended by a driver. It was also evident that she was a socialite and knew many young men.

Mother said that she was attracted to father because of his educational background and his career achievement. In those days, girls from good families did not work. She had no skills other than those of a wife and a mother. She raised my brother and me and centered her entire adult life on taking care of the family and her kids. In Shanghai, Mother had a happy time.

Her life, like many others of her generation, changed dramatically when the Communists took over Shanghai and the family had to seek exile in Hong Kong. She never accepted Hong Kong as her home and always yearned to return to Shanghai. While in Hong Kong, she made few new friends. It was fortunate that three of her best friends also moved to Hong Kong from Shanghai with their families, and they all stayed in touch.

Mother's life was basically uneventful. Much later, I noticed she had kept copies of Father's daily newspaper editorial writings. After Father died, she threw them all away, and I am guilty of not salvaging any. Slowly, she became reclusive and seemed to lose interest in social activities, except seeing the grandchildren and me. Every month, from 1987 and onward, I would drive her out and have dinner with her on weekends. My wife would occasionally join us and so would my kids when they were in town.

Mother had osteoporosis and her condition slowly deteriorated. In late years, she began having trouble walking. In the last two years or so of her life, she was in a wheelchair most of the time. We continued to go out and eat even as her condition made it very difficult. I admired her spirit and never suggested she might like to just stay home. I realized that she had tried to keep her old habits as a confirmation that she still had a life.

Increasingly, she became less willing to change old habits. I now believe I know why old people behave like this. The real reason is that they sense that every change means giving up what they used to be able to do. For example, because she would fall down at times during her nightly walks to the bathroom, I suggested moving her bed closer and to carpet just the area where she walked. She adamantly refused.

The end came very quickly and unexpectedly. Only two days before her death, Bela and I drove mother to the hospital to check on her leg. After the examination, we were told that the fracture was healing and she should come back in a week. Two days later, she died in her sleep. My wife and Kathy came back to Hong Kong from New York as quickly as they could and so did my brother and his wife. The funeral was a simple affair, attended by our two families and a few close friends.

My father died in 1987 and my mother died in 2002. Their ashes are now in two urns standing in a small chamber in the Cape Collinson Crematorium in Hong Kong. The chamber is covered by a stone slab on which their names, birth and death dates were etched, along with their pictures. The crematorium has four buildings located on a tree-lined hill overlooking Chai Wan at the eastern end of Hong Kong. My parents' place is among many in one of the buildings, on the third floor. It is a restful but windy place.

In Chinese custom, families visit their deceased parents twice a year, once in the spring and once in the fall. At the crematorium, many Chinese families would bring food and blankets and have a picnic right in front of their parental urns. The kids play and the grown-ups chat loudly. I have often wondered if people in other cultures have as much fun on their visits to their dead relatives.

In our case, the ritual is much more subdued. Typically, my wife and I place flowers and fruits in front of the slab covering the urns of my parents. We also bring incense and paper money for burning. At each visit, we light the incense and bow in front of my parents' pictures as a sign of respect. We usually do not stay long.

Although I only go to my parents' burial site twice a year, I remember them in my daily meditation. Over the years, I have always made the visits, rain or shine, since I consider the entire ritual is a way of "taking care" of my parents. The tradition retains connection between the two generations.

There is an old saying that dead ones should be allowed to rest in peace and never be moved. However, in this day and age when the world is a village, I don't think this old admonition is applicable anymore. I would like my body to be cremated and be "buried" close to where my kids can visit me. I wouldn't mind that my urn be moved by subsequent generations so my offspring in later generations can come to visit me occasionally. It would be even better if they would bring their families and have a feast in front of my image.

16

Return of the Bull Market in Asia

Even with low interest rates and liquidity, the U.S. economy was in recession as 2002 began. In the business world, a leading U.S. telecommunications firm, Global Crossing, followed Enron into bankruptcy. Surprisingly, Osama bin Laden and Mullah Mohammed Omar of Afghanistan appeared to have escaped encircling U.S. military forces. Renewed violence erupted in the Middle East and geopolitical risks were clearly rising.

Ching Ju and I went to Shanghai toward the end of January and attended a major conference hosted by UBS. The conference was held at the Grand Hyatt Hotel in Pudong, an area east of the Huangpu River that was transformed from swamp land into a great urban center in only 15 years. The hotel itself was on the upper floors of the Jinmao Building, a muscular, shiny silver skyscraper that is among the world's tallest buildings. My room was on the 58th floor overlooking the vast expanse of the busy city.

The meetings were unremarkable, but the trip to visit Compal's factories in Kun Shan, about 1.5 hours north of Shanghai, turned out to be the highlight. Compal, based in Taiwan, is one of the largest notebook computer makers in the world. As we traveled north from Shanghai, smog and pollution hung over the entire landscape. Looking out of the window of the bus, I could not find any rural scene, just buildings and more buildings.

We first visited the company's CRT monitor plant, then the LCD monitor plant and the notebook PC plant. I was impressed with the scale of the facilities as well as the sense of tight organization and high productivity. The factory workers assembled parts that came from Taiwan and elsewhere. There was nothing high-tech about the work on the production lines. During discussions with factory managers, I learned that in 10 years, the company would expect all the Taiwanese expatriate managers to be replaced by local ones. The continuing drive to cut production costs is a constant challenge in the manufacturing process and the Taiwan management is very good at doing that.

Over 250,000 professionals from Taiwan were working and living in the Greater Shanghai area. Indeed, Taiwanese were among the first foreign investors in China, even though their legal status was murky and unclear. It has been estimated that China has absorbed more than US$10 billion of direct investments from Taiwanese businessmen. In the process, they brought not just money, but also world-class technology, modern management practices, and a global network of contacts. Some say politics typically follows economic interests. If this holds true in the case of Taiwan's relationship with China, then I would not be surprised if the two sides eventually reach a sensible agreement in the political arena.

Ignoring the poor U.S. economic condition and heightened geopolitical risks, markets continued to recover from the lows of the previous September. In the United States, scuttlebutt reported President Bush had already decided to invade Iraq. More ominously, scandals continued to emerge from Wall Street. In March, WorldCom and Qwest disclosed their accounting practices were under investigation. The accounting firm Arthur Andersen was indicted for obstructing justice in the Enron case. Its survival became uncertain. Then, Adelphia Communications revealed it had undisclosed liability of US$2 billion in the form of a corporate guarantee to the Rigas family, which controlled the company. There was no doubt that U.S.

corporate scandals were not going away anytime soon. With these disclosures, there were loud cries for reforms in U.S. corporate governance, particularly in chief executive pay packages.

In May, amid market turbulence, I took off to the States to conduct my semi-annual road show. To my delight, my Asian investment story was well received in meetings in New York, Boston, San Francisco, Atlanta and Dallas. My notable investment track record was beginning to be a major positive factor. In addition, investors appreciated that our company, now into its 10th year of operation, had survived the Asian financial crisis and the U.S. recession. More than usual, I was delighted to meet several prospects who would later become investors.

While sitting in the Atlanta airport waiting for a flight, I saw a CNN feature about a 100-year-old architect, who continued to put in a full day's work, five days a week. He said he had only stopped going to the gym a few months ago. I was inspired that people considerably older than I were working and staying healthy. This story strengthened my resolve to continue to find investors and not slow down.

In June, Arthur Andersen was convicted of malfeasance and the firm was quickly wound up. Then, three CEOs of major U.S. corporations were charged with felonies. Dennis Kozlowski, the Tyco executive, was charged with tax evasion on the sale of six paintings purchased with company funds. Samuel Waksal, the founder of Imclone Systems, was arrested for insider trading. Martin Grass, the former CEO of Rite Aid, was charged with a massive accounting fraud, fabricating board minutes, transferring money to personally controlled entities, and tampering with witnesses. This series of corporate misdoings took a steady toll on the market. By now, the Dow Jones Industrial Average had dropped to an eight-month low. Then, on June 25, WorldCom dropped a bombshell in announcing that it would restate its results for 2001 and 2002, eliminating a staggering US$3.8 billion in its previously reported earnings. The company filed for bankruptcy one month later.

For the first time in recent years, U.S. investors recognized corporate malfeasance risks. With it, risk premium on U.S. equities rose relative to that in Asia. I turned quite positive in expecting funds to return to our region where valuations were low and growth prospects far stronger than elsewhere in the world. Equally important, I could see that Asia, despite the misgivings about North Korea as a member of the so-called "Axis of Evil" – a term coined by President Bush – as well as the tension between Taiwan and China had in fact the most stable political landscape in the world. The only question was: How long would it take international investors to see my point of view?

In Asia, continuing bad news from the States finally started to have an impact. Tech stocks sold down heavily. In the second quarter, Asian markets were down 6.6 percent while our fund was down 4.4 percent. In June, we heard the good news that the prospect who visited our company in May would send US$3 million to our fund. Indeed, we learned that the fund would soon receive a total of US$4.5 million of new subscription. This was the greatest inflow we had ever experienced at any one time.

The capital inflow came not a moment too soon. Our fund's size had now dwindled, due to redemptions and unrealized losses, to a level comparable to that in the depth of the Asian financial crisis in the spring of 1998. The exceptional inflow to our firm was recognition that Asian markets, since the bottom of the market meltdown in the summer of 1998, had outperformed, in the succeeding four years, all other regional markets around the world.

During August, I assigned our summer trainee to study the nascent gas industry in China. A number of relatively new gas companies had been listing in Hong Kong, and brokers were pushing the sector hard. The interesting angle was that these companies had cornered licenses in several cities across China, connecting gas to housing developments and industrial users. As Chinese had traditionally relied on coal as their main source of fuel, this new industry appeared to offer enormous potential.

The analyst and I visited five companies and listened to their strategies. We also pored over their financial accounts. In the end, two main factors caused me to be cautious and stay away from the sector. First, their current income was generated largely from connection fees, which were related more to the construction of pipelines than anything else. Second, gas revenue was still very small and, as regulated by authorities, carried a very narrow margin. Virtually all the listed companies would need additional fundraising rounds because they were all operating with negative cash flow. As things turned out, Wah Sang Gas, a much-touted growth story at that time, was suspended by the exchange in 2004 for having falsified accounts.

The stock markets virtually went into free fall in September. Not only was corporate news from the States bad, investors were unnerved by the warmongering posture taken by the United States to remove Saddam Hussein in Iraq. Bush sent U.S. war planes to bomb Iraqi airfields. Continuing Middle East tension had pushed oil prices up over 50 percent. By the end of the third quarter, U.S. equities were down 29.4 percent. The U.S. market was expected to see three years of consecutive negative return.

Meanwhile, our fund was performing much better than the regional market index. The out-performance of our fund was due to three factors: First, we raised cash to 55 percent of the total portfolio. Second, we reduced IT exposure from over 12 percent in early 2002 to 6 percent by the third quarter. Third, we began to build up a sizable position in South Korea and China, two countries that had bucked the trend of global economic malaise. Finally, we reduced exposure to big cap stocks to only 14 percent of the portfolio.

This U.S. bear market had lasted longer than that of the Asian financial crisis. In early October, Andy Fastow, the CFO of Enron, was charged with conspiracy, money laundering and fraud. The S&P 500 responded by closing at 776, half of the peak it reached back in March 2000. The NASDAQ fell 78 percent, the largest slide by any major index since the Great Depression.

New York Attorney General Eliot Spitzer was on a roll in his efforts to uncover corruption. One of the worst cases of abuse was Morgan Stanley's under-the-table payments to rival firms to issue positive research about Morgan's corporate clients. The investigations concluded with 10 Wall Street firms being fined US$1.4 billion and agreeing to insulate research analysts from investment banking units. U.S. corporate scandals uncovered toward the tail end of the bear market were truly mind boggling in their audacity and scale.

In spite of the war threats and other negative news, worldwide markets began to recover in October, most likely due to the perception that they were much oversold. Additionally, aggressive rate cuts by the U.S. Federal Reserve lowered the risk-free rate to a point where investors began to take equity risk in order to gain a higher return. In Asia, markets were certainly oversold in spite of good economic and earnings growth.

While global economic growth was highly uncertain, Asian economic growth reached 5.6 percent, with China delivering a 7.6 percent growth for the year. Among several economies recovering from the crisis years of 1997–1998, South Korea's turnaround was the most impressive. The country had paid off its debt of US$20 billion to the International Monetary Fund and had now foreign exchange reserves of US$115 billion. Since late 2002, our fund's exposure to South Korean stocks was the largest, amounting to 25% of the fund's assets. Among the long-term holdings were Hyundai Mobis and Hanmi Pharmaceutical, two companies that attracted me during one of my company visits in 2002. Both companies, leaders in their fields, were trading at very low valuation.

The most exciting development in our family was that, Kathy, our daughter, decided to leave Louis Vuitton in Hong Kong and go to London to take up studies in handbag (accessories) design. We were not surprised. Through her work at LV,

Kathy had developed a real interest in the fashion business. What was surprising was her determination to start her own fashion line after graduation. By year-end, she had established her new routine. When I visited her in London, I found her making real progress as she was learning to be an artisan with unique craftsmanship in her work. She had also found a new group of friends to keep her busy.

Going into 2003, all eyes were glued to the ongoing saga of debates in the UN, where the United States tried to convince the rest of the world to support its plan to invade Iraq and to oust Saddam. The news media reported that the U.S. and British governments were already making massive troop deployments. As this international drama unfolded, markets continued to slide. In mid-February, North Korea declared that any economic sanction would be a declaration of war and threatened to tear up the old armistice agreement. Massive demonstrations against Bush's plan to invade Iraq occurred all over the world. In Southern China, a mysterious form of pneumonia, later to be known as SARS, was reported in the media. .

In February, I flew to Seoul to visit companies. Over the span of three days in South Korea, I visited eight companies in the pharmaceutical, industrial and materials sectors. During these company visits, I saw no sign business conditions had deteriorated. People I met were not unduly concerned about the North Korean actions. The new president, Roh Moo-hyun, was expected to push through corporate reform harder than his predecessor – a positive move in the eyes of investors. Overall, the country's economy was in good shape and business prospects appeared positive. Like the Taiwanese, South Korean companies were committing increasing resources to China and were optimistic about prospects there.

Our fund received over US$1 million in early 2003 (a small sum by most standards but a sizable amount for our firm). We anticipated another substantial inflow in April. I flew to the States in early March and made my usual round of calls and meetings. I found the U.S. opinion on the Iraqi war issue sharply divided. Among my investors, a significant number were against U.S. unilateral action in international affairs.

The 2003 invasion of Iraq began on March 20 when forces belonging primarily to the United States and the United Kingdom invaded the country. After approximately three weeks of fighting, the Iraqi government was toppled and the occupation of Iraq began. This war, considered by many as unwise, unjust and unwarranted, was undertaken with substantial opposition from the international community. After many months of searching, the United States eventually announced it was unable to find any evidence Saddam harbored weapons of mass destruction, the purported existence of which had been a major pretext for the invasion.

I returned to Hong Kong on March 26 and while lining up to go through immigration, I noticed for the first time many in the airport were wearing masks. It dawned on me that the respiratory disease known as SARS had become a serious issue in Hong Kong. The next morning, my wife gave me a few masks to use in public. I put one on for the bus ride and noticed every single passenger had one on. Once in the office, there was no need to wear it. The surgical masks were only good for a few hours of use so that I had to keep a packet in my pocket every day.

SARS, or Severe Acute Respiratory Syndrome, caused great damage to the economies of Hong Kong, China, Taiwan and Singapore over the next several months. In Hong Kong, hotels, restaurants and movie theaters were virtually empty. Flights were cancelled as travels to SARS-infected cities were curtailed. In April, the World Health Organization warned against travel to Hong Kong and Southern China. All public functions were cancelled or deferred. Even social plans were cancelled.

Not surprisingly, shopping malls were silent. Even schools were closed for two weeks.

Hong Kong, a bustling city of over 6 million, suddenly became very still. For me, there were no more yoga classes and my weekly Rotary Club lunch meetings were cancelled until further notice. I stopped taking the bus home, flagging down a taxi instead. In our office building, a cleaner was assigned full time to clean elevators. New statistics about the death toll and the number of new infections were featured in daily newspapers. Shaking hands and touching another person were now taboo. The only positive aspect of the SARS episode was Hong Kong launched a major cleanup program in every neighborhood and the city had never, ever been so clean.

SARS was a deadly infectious disease, transmitted easily from person to person through close contact, and from home to home, probably through contaminated hands that happen to touch the person's nose or mouth. SARS appeared to affect older people more easily than younger ones. Even now, we still do not truly understand the nature of the disease.

Starting in late March, SARS spread from Hong Kong and Guangdong to Beijing and other countries in Asia. It also spread to Toronto and some cases were reported in the States. Fortunately, the epidemic was short-lived as unprecedented worldwide medical cooperation led to early steps to screen passengers and quarantine infected areas in Hong Kong and elsewhere. In Hong Kong, the number of infections began to show a significant downtrend in early May. By late May, Hong Kong was declared free of SARS and by July 5, WHO declared that the outbreak had been contained. Still, Hong Kong estimated the epidemic cut economic growth by 2 percent in 2003.

SARS, however, brought out innovative solutions. In Hong Kong, classrooms went "virtual" as classes in universities were conducted over the Internet. In May, CLSA, a prominent regional broker, hosted a "virtual" Asia forum in the Grand Hyatt Hotel in the midst of the crisis. A few fund managers in

Hong Kong attended, but the proceedings were watched on the web by other investors around the world. Instead of facing live presentations, we sat in a room with a holographic flat screen set on a stage. The speaker sat in front of a camera in a studio in his home city, which could be anywhere in the world. We watched his live image in color and in three-dimensions and listened to his talk. Questions could be raised by anyone in the room or elsewhere in the world and the speaker could hear them. The technology was so advanced it was instant news on the media. I was truly impressed.

In April, despite the threat of SARS, I toured factories in Southern China, where I found the workers donning masks and cleaning the machines every few hours. Interestingly, throughout China, there was no reporting of SARS in the factories. I attributed this to the fact that factory workers were mostly very young, between 18 and 22, and the factories were located outside of urban centers. As a result, China's economy barely slowed down.

In mid 2003, our investor from Texas added US$1 million to her account, signifying her confidence in our work. Her timing was good as the global economy was on the mend. Despite SARS, the war in Iraq and the threat from North Korea, our fund did well in the second quarter. It was up 11.5 percent. Our strategy to stay with an overweight position in stocks of companies having substantial business interest in China proved to be right on the money. In June, China shares trading in Hong Kong advanced sharply, and the momentum spilled over to China-related shares in Hong Kong and Taiwan. In addition, our focus on smaller cap stocks and value was the key to out-performing the regional benchmark.

China's economic growth was surprisingly unaffected by SARS. In April (which was the worst month of the spread of the disease), China's GDP grew 8.9 percent year-on-year, with industrial production up 15 percent and retail sales up 7.7 percent. Throughout the first six months of the year, China continued to attract foreign direct investments, which jumped 26 percent year-on-year.

Given the positive economic backdrop, markets that sank in March began to recover in late April and continued their advance over the next two months. Helping the markets was U.S. Federal Reserve's interest rate cut by another 25 basis points in June. Chairman Alan Greenspan of the US Federal Reserve Bank was adopting an aggressive easing bias to reflate the U.S. economy. The continuing buildup of excess liquidity in the system was finding its way into equities. Our fund recorded a gain of almost 12 percent in the second quarter.

A historical event took place in Hong Kong on July 1 when over 500,000 people marched peacefully to protest against the imminent passing of the so-called Article 23 Anti-sedition Act. The protest took place on the sixth anniversary of Hong Kong's handover to China. The marchers endured insufferable heat, waiting for hours to join the march in streets, and, in the process, displayed people power to the halls of the Hong Kong government and those in Beijing. My assistant's husband walked the entire length of the march and so did an analyst in our company. I joined the march only in the Central district, near where the march ended. Most marchers, by then, were tired and sweating profusely. Still, plenty of people were shouting slogans while others held up flags and large canvases proclaiming their desire for democracy and freedom of speech. It was a stirring moment to stand alongside people who chose to stand up for their beliefs in this massive demonstration.

This act of peaceful defiance put to rest any lingering doubts the Hong Kong people were entirely apolitical. Then, on the 9th, another demonstration of 35,000 took place in Central to demand the bill be submitted only when real democracy had been established. This act of peaceful protest notably did not arouse China's instinct for repression. Instead, the proposed Article 23 legislation was deferred indefinitely. This incident was the first time the Hong Kong government listened and responded to the people's views.

A significant event materialized unexpectedly in early May. Ching Ju, my partner and director of my company, said that she was considering two job offers. One offer was to head the asset management group at Citic Capital, a prominent investment bank owned by a conglomerate under the control of the Chinese government. When she approached me with the news, I was taken by surprise. Although times had been tough since she joined the firm in 1999, I thought recent increases in subscriptions signaled a positive future to her. I thought we formed a good team because we had similar instincts and we were both avid stock pickers. On the other hand, the new job offered her a far greater scope of responsibilities and challenges than her work with me. She left our firm at the beginning of August.

Following the SARS outbreak in the second quarter, the region's economies recovered quickly. In July, Hong Kong's exports were up 7.6 percent year-on-year and Taiwan's exports grew 4.5 percent, while South Korea's exports rose a substantial 16 percent. China reported export growth of 32.6 percent in June with imports up 40 percent year-on-year. Industrial production was up 17 percent in June and auto production was up a whopping 83 percent!

Given all the good news, markets roared ahead in the summer of 2003. Analysts were now starting to upgrade earning numbers. Liquidity improved and trading volume increased, thus building upside momentum. After rising 11.5 percent in the second quarter, our fund gained 16.3 percent in the third quarter.

Following Ching Ju's departure, I began a search for another partner. This process, by its nature, took time. Meanwhile, I needed an analyst to help in the research work. Since I knew a number of analysts working in various brokerages, I called them for help. Soon, I received several names of interested candidates.

I eventually hired Dennis Lam, a young man who had three years of research experience in a local brokerage house. Dennis had an honors degree in molecular biology from the University of Toronto. He was bright, enthusiastic, and productive in his work.

Ever since I started my fund, all my new clients came from word-of-mouth referrals. I rarely cold called anyone. The limitation of my marketing program made the process of growing my firm's asset base extremely slow. Since I visited the States no more than four times a year, and as each visit lasted no more than three weeks, my marketing initiatives lacked intensity. In this extremely competitive business, not having a continuous marketing program was the major reason for the firm's slow progress.

Of course, I wanted to grow my business faster. However, I could not find any third-party marketing agent to help me because my firm's asset base was too small. This is a chicken-and-egg situation. Third-party marketing agents typically only work with firms that have an asset base of at least US$100 million. Until my firm could reach that size, I had to find investors on my own. Having referrals from my clients was the only channel to reach prospects.

The most important client of our firm was also my biggest supporter. For over a year, their officer had made several attempts for me to meet the CEO of the advisory firm, Institute of Private Investors (IPI). IPI specializes in serving the private family offices established by wealthy investors. In the summer of 2003, I finally had the opportunity to meet that CEO. The meeting was highly productive and I was subsequently invited to speak at a forum in New York City in October on a topic related to China.

IPI is an organization for managers of private family offices to meet fund managers, to network with people in the same business, and to have a platform where relevant issues can be discussed. On the morning of October 9, I spoke in front of about 45 participants for an hour. I had worked on the presentation for over a month and thought this occasion would help me locate future prospects. After the talk, which I gathered went well, a number of listeners met me and I received a total of 15 cards. My prospect list had just expanded by the number of cards I had in my hand.

There is no question investors' interest in investment opportunities in China had greatly improved over the past two years. For one thing, markets in Asia had out-performed the United States and other major markets since 2000. For another, China's impact on the U.S. economy, whether hurting it due to manufacturing outsourcing or helping it due to price deflation as a result of cheap Chinese imports, had become a topic of conversation and news reports on an almost daily basis. China was rapidly emerging as a global economic power.

To illustrate the outsourcing phenomenon, there is no better example than Yue Yuen's shoe-making plants in Shenzhen, located on the other side of Hong Kong's northern border with China. Yue Yuen is a Taiwanese company listed on the Hong Kong Stock Exchange. In one location, an entire plant was built to make athletic shoes for only one major US client. The complex housed some 80,000 young, single female workers. Production lines were neatly planned and work was efficiently organized. Making shoes is highly labor intensive, involving more than 500 steps. What distinguished Yue Yuen was its vertically integrated production process which included dyeing the leather as the first step in its production process. The dyeing plant, almost as large as an enclosed football field, housed equipment to cut the leather and dye and dry the pieces. Yue Yuen is now the largest athletic shoemaker in the world, serving all major brands including Nike, Adidas and New Balance.

South China's attractiveness for outsourcing was not just its low labor costs. Other factors such as worker productivity, dexterity, and a strong work ethic also counted. China is one of a few countries (including the United States) where worker mobility is built into its social fabric. In countries rife with unemployment, such as Indonesia, it would be difficult to recruit young women from the countryside to move to a distant factory near a city. But in China, young women from farms didn't hesitate to make a big move to the factories. As a result, foreign direct investment kept pouring into China to make things of all kinds for the world's markets.

In the final two months of 2003, equity markets remained buoyant. Interest rates were expected to remain low and liquidity strong. Geopolitical events, while difficult and unpredictable, were not expected to throw a monkey wrench in this economic upturn. In November, South Korea reported a rise of exports by 22.5 percent year-on-year, while China's export growth reached 34 percent and Taiwan's went up 16 percent. These were encouraging numbers, particularly as the region had been beset by the SARS episode early in the year.

I took time off in December to ski in Killington, Vermont with my family and several old friends in the States. It was time for me to have a break, at least one long weekend away from the markets. Asian influence had reached even the remote corner of the State of Vermont. I saw many Asian faces on the slopes and some clearly from mainland China. One of the two main restaurants near the lifts offered Chinese fried noodles along with hot dogs.

Our fund finished 2003 with a gain of 44 percent, beating the regional index by about two percentage points. Looking back on 2003, an outstanding year for Asian markets, we were vindicated in our earlier judgment that the Greater China markets would outperform all others in the region. By year-end, the "H" share market was up 152 percent! Hong Kong and Taiwan were up more than 32 percent each. From a bottom-up stock-picking perspective, our stock picks in mid-cap and smaller-cap companies were well rewarded. Among the fund's large holdings, Hyundai Mobis was up 169 percent; Huaneng Power was up 96 percent; Samsung Electronics was up 50 percent; and Li & Fung was up 76 percent.

By the end of January 2004, our flagship product, Asian Select Equity Investment Partnership, completed its 10th year of operation. With a decade of experience under our belt, we felt gratified that the fund beat the regional benchmark by a wide margin. During this period, ASEIP returned 37.4 percent while the benchmark returned a negative 35 percent. To put it in another perspective, our fund outperformed the benchmark by 72 percent in the span of a decade, a decade that saw two horrendous periods – the Asian financial crisis in 1997–1998 and the U.S. market collapse in 2000–2002. When I set out to launch this fund in the winter of 1993, the world felt distinctly less complicated than now. The great thing about where we are today is that so much progress has been made in Asia, and China has astonished the world by becoming the industrial base for the world's many consumer and IT products.

Going into 2004, China's GDP per capita exceeded US$1,000 for the first time. Crossing this threshold meant the Chinese had entered the consumer society. Since China set about reforming its economy two decades earlier, its GDP has expanded at an annual rate of 9.5 percent. Its economy has doubled nearly three times in the past 30 years. In a recent report by the Central Intelligence Agency, China has already become the second largest economy in the world, with a GDP – expressed in purchasing power parity – of US$6.5 trillion. It makes more sense to think of China's economy as closer to two-thirds the size of the U.S. economy than to one-seventh.

China's comparative advantage in labor costs and productivity is primarily responsible for the country's sustained growth. It is driven by the booming private sector as the country transits from a planned economy to a market economy. Across China, banks are increasingly lending on a commercial basis and prices of many products and services are set by market players. Another reason China's growth is so fast is that the world keeps feeding it capital. In 2003, China, taking in US$53.5 billion in foreign direct investment, surpassed the United States for the first time. With foreign investments came knowledge about markets, products, technology, and modern management practices.

The growth of China is rattling businesses around the world. Nothing like this has ever happened before. It has become the world's dominant supplier of whole categories of products. It is the largest producer of shoes and clothing and other low-cost, labor intensive goods. Foreign investments have helped push China up the technological ladder. It is now the world's largest maker of consumer electronics, making more TVs, DVD players, and cell phones than any other country. It is making computers, building cars, making parts for Boeing, and exploring space with its own rockets. It is also fast becoming a center for research and development. For example, Motorola alone has 19 research labs in China that develop technology for both the local and global markets. In more ways than one, the Chinese economy is rapidly catching up to the West.

China's demand for industrial materials to feed its factories and cities had raised global prices for oil and raw materials of every kind. The government, realizing its super-fast economic growth could lead to excess capital spending and inflation, decided to put on the brakes. In early May, China announced policy measures to rein in investments in certain overheated sectors such as real estate, steel, aluminum, and cement. Lending restrictions were imposed on banks. These actions led to widespread debates about their effectiveness. Skeptics of the move expected hard landing while optimists claimed there would be "no landing."

When uncertainty rises, investors' sentiment can turn on a dime. In this case, China's new credit tightening measures took place alongside increasing oil prices to over $40 a barrel. At the same time, the U.S. Federal Reserve notched up short-term interest rates. In March and April, markets in Taiwan and Hong Kong took a beating. Commodity and base metal stocks slumped as fears of a hard landing in China became a mainstream mantra. On May 10, the "H" shares dropped 8 percent and South Korea was down 6 percent. Then on May 17, "H" shares of commodity companies plunged 15 percent.

In this chaotic market condition, I took cut-loss measures with the limit set at 15 percent from the closing prices in the previous month. My orders were filled. Unfortunately, shortly afterwards, the markets rebounded. I chose not to put money back into the market because of the prevailing high volatility. At the end of May, our fund had 40 percent cash. On hindsight, this was not a good decision in terms of keeping up with the benchmark performance. On the other hand, I took the view that preserving capital was in the best interest of our investors.

Having made a good impression at the IPI Forum in October 2003, I was invited to host IPI's visit to Hong Kong as part of their "Destination China" program in June 2004. I was delighted by the invitation and prepared an interesting program for the group's 45 visitors. I booked a large conference room in the Hong Kong Club and gave a talk on the markets in Hong Kong and China. This was followed by two speakers I invited to participate. The first was the CEO of a mid-size consumer products company. He talked about how he was transforming his company from an OEM manufacturer to a global brand manager. The second was the managing director of *Asian Wall Street Journal,* who spoke on the rise of consumerism in China.

After lunch, I took the group to visit the Hong Kong Stock Exchange, where the deputy CEO gave a very interesting talk about the history of the exchange and told some anecdotes that showed how the market in Hong Kong had matured dramatically over the past few years.

According to feedback from IPI, the entire program was a great success. The group left Hong Kong the next morning and visited Shanghai and Beijing in the following five days. They heard presentations by government officials and U.S. businessmen. When I met several in a later trip to the States, I was told they thought the trip was useful but it raised more questions than it answered. Several said they remained extremely cautious about investing in China.

In the fall, John Lee joined our firm to assist me with portfolio management and marketing. John is a U.S.-born Chinese who had previously worked in the hedge fund industry. My intention was to groom him to take over the work of making cold calls and expanding our network of contacts. His main task was to help me market our services to U.S. clients. In addition, he would help me make company visits and provide specific stock ideas. In the early months of our collaboration, I was hopeful John would replace Ching Ju, who left the firm in 2003.

In the United States, George W. Bush was elected to a second term as the country's president. This represented both good news and bad news from my perspective. The good news was that Bush was pro business and the stock market would welcome the continuity in Washington. The bad news was, with his unwavering attitude toward the war in Iraq, the geopolitical situation in the Middle East would remain hghly unstable. As a result, the price of oil would probably remain high, if not rise higher. The world had become less safe than before the invasion.

There is no doubt that sentiment in the United States toward China is a mixture of euphoria, fear, and admiration. By 2010, China's economy will be double that of Germany's, now the world's third largest. By 2020, China is expected to surpass Japan as the world's second largest economy. The boom in China's world trade has left few sectors untouched. Multinational companies of all sizes are now sourcing products from China, either to reduce costs or to procure more of what they make with cheaper prices. China is now a price setter with the lowest price possible. According to one estimate, between 1998 and 2004, prices in the States fell in nearly every product category where China was the top exporter.

China's increasing economic power has already made an impact on its relationship with its neighbors from South Korea to Indonesia. In many areas of trade, China's growing power has made trade deals that have strained its relationship with the United States. Its trade deals with Russia and Iran have been a source of concern for U.S. authorities.

In late 2004, IBM announced it would sell its PC business to a Chinese company, Lenovo. This raised great concern among many in the States who feared loss of national security. Such clashes between business and political interests will only increase in the years ahead as China's commercial and business interests spread throughout the world.

China runs a large trade surplus with the United States. In 2004, China sold US$160 billion more in goods than they bought. By early 2005, China's export surplus resulted in its foreign reserves topping US$600 billion. And the dollar had declined in two years, by 55 percent against the euro and 22 percent against the yen.

The fall of the dollar is the outgrowth of an unbalanced world economy. China's surplus has been recycled by the purchase of billions of dollars in US Treasury securities. This process protects China's exports while keeping U.S. interest rates low. The destinities of China and the United States are now tightly interwoven and interdependent. This interdependency was characterized by former U.S. Treasury Secretary Lawrence Summers as a "balance of financial terror." How all these ties get sorted out surely define the future of the world in economic and geopolitical terms.

17

Merger for the Future

While the Iraq war continued without relief, interest rates were ratcheted up by the Fed and oil prices stayed high. Nevertheless, stock markets were on an up trend, particularly in emerging markets globally. Signs of inflation were reflected in strong metal and commodity prices. These helped emerging economies achieve attractive economic growth. High oil prices and huge spending by the U.S. government in the Arabian Gulf produced a financial bonanza to countries such as the United Arab Emirates, Qatar, Kuwait, and Saudi Arabia. In short, there was ample liquidity in the world to support stock prices.

Another newly observed phenomenon is that in spite of the increasing short-term interest rates, the U.S. long-term bond yield had stayed remarkably unchanged. No one knows exactly why, but the consensus attributes lower bond yield to demand by Asian central banks, flush with U.S. dollars earned through increasing exports to the United States. In other words, there was a virtual cycle going on. Asian countries were subsidizing U.S. trade and current account deficits by buying up credit papers without limits. This is a dangerous partnership but the world was enjoying the benefit while ignoring the potential downside.

Going into 2005, the Asian markets had already delivered two years of double-digit advances. The key question was: How should we position our portfolio strategically to ensure that it would produce superior return consistent with our investment philosophy – that of finding value in growth companies?

We worked on this question among ourselves and with a couple of strategists from investment banks. Our conclusion we reached was we would continue to overweigh China stocks to capture the country's extraordinary opportunities. We also decided to overweigh in two broad sectors: domestic spending, particularly in China, and IT sub-sectors focused on components in handsets. As events turned out, these decisions served us well during the year.

In my trips to the States, I realized investors were becoming increasingly more comfortable with investing in Asia. Just about every month in 2005, there was considerable inflow of funds to the region. Our firm benefited from this trend and signed up several new clients. However, with me at the helm and spending little time in marketing and calling on prospects, growth in new capital remained inconsequential.

Among my most memorable experiences in 2005 was attending Elliott Goldstein's 90th birthday celebration in late October. Elliott was one of my first investors from my first trip to Atlanta in 1993. Since then, he had become a close friend and we have developed an immense respect for one another. Earlier in the year, I flew to Atlanta to go to his wife's grave as I had been unable to attend her funeral service.

I decided I couldn't miss the celebration. Elliott was in great shape and was overwhelmed by all the accolades that went on for more than an hour after dinner. I was reminded that I have been most fortunate in having some of the finest individuals as clients. Meeting them and sharing ideas with them has been so rewarding that I have not found it wanting that my fund size has not advanced as much as I would have expected.

There was much to celebrate in my family life. Kathy graduated from the London Institute of Fashion with a master's degree in accessories design and moved to New York, hoping to launch her own line of high-end bags and accessories. This was an audacious plan on her part and I supported it. I was happy that she had found a career she could commit to and therefore would not hesitate to help her to make it a success. Clarence, my son, had abandoned his own venture and opted to work in a major corporation. He joined Time Warner in New York and had been working his way up the ladder and assuming greater responsibilities in their website production projects.

I completed my 70th year on earth in November 2005. I thought I should celebrate this occasion, something I had not done on all my previous birthdays. My brother told me that he didn't think hitting 70 was a big deal. The average American lifespan was 76, he said, and until he could beat the average, there was nothing to crow about.

I didn't buy his argument. So, on October 26, I hosted a dinner party in the Hong Kong Club. I invited only friends who were not connected with my business, with two exceptions: Bela Chu, my long-serving assistant and her husband, and Ching Ju Yeh, my ex-partner, who has remained a good friend. The eight other couples were friends with whom I went hiking, practiced yoga, or played tennis. Kathy, my daughter, flew into Hong Kong from New York a few days ahead to join the celebration.

To make the dinner lively, I asked Patrick Caviness, my tennis partner and close friend, to be the master of ceremony. Because of my fondness for American folk and popular songs from the 1960s to the early 1990s, I decided to have a songfest after dinner. Patrick, a wonderful guitarist and singer of country and folk songs, agreed to lead the way. To assist him, I asked Cary Abrams, a gifted professional musician, to accompany him with the playing and singing. The Club put together two dining tables at one side of the Victoria Suite. Bela ordered lovely flower arrangements for the tables and Patrick brought shaker eggs to keep the beat going while singing. The shakers came in different colors and were great decorative items on the tables. My wife surprised me by displaying many copies of photos taken of me since I was an infant. She had these pictures enclosed in paper mounts and placed them on the tables for all to see.

Patrick was wonderful in his MC role, making the evening lively and enjoyable. The better part of the evening was spent in singing folk and popular songs by such favorites as Gordon Lightfoot, Eric Andersen, Pete Seeger, and Paul Simon. We ended the session with John Lennon's "Imagine," waving our white table napkins during the final verse, a symbol of our unity and friendship.

Before we started singing, several guests gave flattering toasts. Kathy, however, gave the most touching toast of all. One guest later told me that she was greatly touched by the sentiment. Let me quote an extract of her words:

> *Although I always joke about how old I think you are, I know you are still young at heart, which is what matters the most. I must proudly admit I don't know any other 70 year-old man who can do a head stand, let alone want to do one, plus play tennis, do yoga, ski black diamonds, hike and exercise as much as you do.*
>
> *We want you to know that you have a lot to celebrate. You have loving family and friends, an extremely successful career that has taken us all over the world, strong health and an active and enlightened mind. These traits are hard to live up to and I know Clarence and I are thankful every day to have you as a role model.*
>
> *Dad has taught us about being honest with our feelings, goals and dreams. He has taught us to bear the weight of our choices, our decisions and then to pursue them with passion, determination and sincerity. We have learned to respect and cherish hard work, as well as our relations with our family and*

friends. And, finally, to value fulfillment of the mind and spirit above everything else.

Dad has learned the perfect balance between not over-parenting and not under-parenting. I believe that my father has recognized that what my brother and I really need in our lives is a person who will love us all along the way, as we continue to learn and make our mistakes. In the end it is his love and complete devotion that will always make him the most important man, husband, friend, mentor and father to us.

Feeling elated by so many good friends making the evening a big celebration, I was reminded of my great-great-grandfather's much-uttered words, as recorded by his son. He said that one's life should be judged not by his material possessions but by the love and respect of his family and friends. These were my exact sentiments as I sat among those who meant so much to me in my life.

Meanwhile, the Iraq War continued to rage and political stability in Afghanistan was nowhere in sight. Interest rates were rising and the U.S. Federal Reserve Fund's rate stood at 4.25 percent going into 2006. Oil prices had risen 50 percent in 2005 from US$40 a barrel to US$60. Yet, economies managed to weather rising rates and oil prices. Global GDP was up an estimated 3.2 percent while the Asian regional GDP advanced 6.9 percent. China's economy continued to barrel ahead, with exports jumping 28 percent and trade surplus reaching US$102 billion by the end of 2005. Global emerging markets were up 32 percent in 2005, outpacing Asia ex-Japan region's gain of 18 percent. Our fund performed well, gaining 16.4 percent after all expenses and fees.

Our firm had a complete overhaul of professional personnel at the end of 2005. Dennis Lam, our analyst, decided to return to the sell side. John Lee resigned to seek employment elsewhere. We also moved to a new location because our landlord had decided to raise rent by 70 percent. Violet Chong, who left the firm after John Lee came on board, returned to work with me. Soon after 2006 commenced, I recruited an analyst to fill our staffing needs.

There is no doubt that one of the principal challenges of owning and running a boutique firm is having a viable succession plan for its principal. From the very outset, I realized that being a one-man band has many limitations. They all boiled down to the issue of what happens to the business if the principal becomes incapacitated. In fact, many investors have a policy of not putting money with such boutique investment management firms, no matter how outstanding their investment track record is.

In Hong Kong, many Chinese businesses have remained in the family's hands because one or more of the offspring steps up and succeeds his father. I, for one, never tried to persuade any of my children to consider joining my practice. And, none of them ever volunteered. They knew what I was doing but they had their own career interests. Judging from how they are enjoying what they have embarked upon, I have no regrets.

I have, along the way, made several attempts to bring in a working partner or a strategic partner. As the years progressed, the need for a viable succession plan became all the more apparent. The logical alternative is that investors would simply withdraw their accounts in my fund should I become incapacitated or decide to retire. This outcome is not uncommon in other professional services. The fact that a practice ceases when its principal retires is common among medical doctors, small law firms, accounting firms, headhunters, advertising agencies, real estate brokers, and others. In theory, I should view this outcome with complete acceptance.

While I share this attitude, I am not one who will give up pursuing my goal of transferring my business more or less intact to a partner when and if I wish to step aside. In late 2005, in a lecture on Buddhism in Hong Kong, I ran into a French investment manager, whose path had crossed mine some years earlier. Fabrice Jacob had set up his own boutique investment firm in 1998 and saw it grow to a size comparable to my own. His organization is identical to mine in that he has one portfolio manager and one analyst. We met and exchanged ideas on stocks. I found he is just as much of a value investor as I am.

In spring 2006, Fabrice and I started planning to merge our two licensed fund management firms into one jointly owned company. This merger would create a new firm with close to US$80 million in managed assets and a team of six professionals. Together, we would have three funds under management. The biggest one was the Asian regional fund, which I managed. Fabrice had two funds, one focusing on China and the other, interestingly, was a global distressed bond fund. While my client base was U.S. private families and endowment funds, his client base was mainly Swiss banks with private accounts.

We had three major objectives. First, we wished to create a new "brand" to cross-sell our products around the world. This would require some technical changes to our funds but these would not constitute serious impediments. Second, we believed, together, we would improve our investment management process. With more analysts, we could conduct more in-depth research. Third, we believed that we could realize some cost savings by combining our forces. If all went well, I hoped our combined business would reach a much higher level in terms of market recognition and fundraising potential. This change would allow my business to grow at a much faster pace than when it was a one-man show.

Throughout 2006, merger discussions continued and along with them, the two groups started working closer together. We held weekly meetings going over stock ideas and discussing our views on the market. Because Fabrice's equity focus was on China, discussions would be principally about stocks that traded in Hong Kong. Still, having an exchange of views was helpful. Besides, we found that we had a similar due diligence approach.

In the fall of 2006, Fabrice and I instituted a quarterly conference call with clients and prospects to supplement my periodic visits. These calls gave us a chance to communicate with both clients and prospects at least once every quarter. This initiative turned out to be a major success. Since then, I have noticed a greater number of participants in each succeeding conference call.

Another noteworthy initiative we took was to appoint Alex Leung, one of our senior staff members, to be the compliance officer. We engaged a third party service provider to prepare a compliance manual for the firm and help us in all related matters. Slowly but surely, our firm progressed to becoming an investment management firm of institutional quality.

The global economy remained resilient in 2006. By midyear, however, oil prices reached over US$70 a barrel and the U.S. Federal Reserve Fund's rate increased to 5.25 percent. In Asia, China, South Korea, Hong Kong, and Taiwan had also raised rates to control growth and inflationary pressure. With the lack of progress in Iraq and increased tension with Iran (sparked by the latter's aspiration to become a nuclear power), geopolitical risks remained high. As a result of these negative factors, market performance became volatile during the second quarter. Nevertheless, liquidity remained strong and capital inflow into Asia, particularly China, accelerated.

The big story of 2006 was the arrival of the long awaited re-rating of China shares. When that happened, momentum was far greater than expected. The "A" shares traded in Shanghai jumped over 125 percent while "H" shares traded in Hong Kong rose more than 90 percent. Stocks in Hong Kong had a great run as well, up 34 percent. Just to cite a couple of examples, in December alone, Ping An Insurance, the second largest life insurance company in China, saw its stock surge 44 percent.

China Construction Bank's stock price moved up over 20 percent in the same month.

As a result of the strong market trend, our fund delivered a return of almost 30 percent, net of all expenses and fees. Our assets under management grew from US$35 million to over US$45 million. Economists were generally bullish about global economic conditions. In addition to ample liquidity in the region, I believed our markets would benefit from China's success in restructuring its industries, allowing a slower but steadier appreciation of its currency.

At the end of 2006, I had much to celebrate. The fund had a great year. Fabrice and I were steadily working towards merging our two firms. My health was good even though I underwent an angioplasty procedure in September. My routine of tennis, yoga, and regular exercises was keeping me fit and healthy.

In October, I had the great fortune of locating my long-lost relatives in Father's birthplace in Sichuan, China (an encounter described in a later chapter.) In addition, my daughter Kathy started her own handbag business in late 2005, using the brand name Katherine Kwei. She produced her first collection of upscale leather handbags in April 2006 and found a prominent showroom run by Cynthia O'Connor to handle sales. This first effort turned out to be an unexpected success. She had no trouble finding buyers, including Lane Crawford, a very prestigious department store in Hong Kong. *Women's Wear Daily*, a fashion trade newspaper, which has the largest circulation in the industry in the States, featured Kathy on the cover page of one of their fall issues.

Still, there were signs that challenged the bull market's sustainability. In October 2006, I had dinner with a real-estate broker from Northern California and was astonished to hear that, in her town, inventory of unsold property had reached 15 months. From newspaper reports, I learned that U.S. housing prices topped out in 2005 and had been sliding throughout 2006. Home sales had been falling as well. With interest rates rising, it would not take much time for real estate market problems to affect the broader economy in the States.

In Asia too, there were signs that made me uneasy about the future momentum of stock markets. We have had four years of a bull run and my experience had taught me that bull runs do not go on forever. It would be just a matter of time before some adverse economic change would trigger a major sell-off. Looking at the shape of the prevailing financial landscape, I saw at least two major issues that called for caution and concern.

First, for over a decade, trade between the United States and China had produced a massive imbalance between the two countries. China's trade surplus had been rising annually while U.S. trade and current account deficits continued to escalate. This was clearly not a sustainable situation. Second, U.S. banks and other institutions as well as consumers had been borrowing massive amounts of money to support consumption growth. This was also not sustainable. I knew when the day of reckoning came, de-leveraging would bring down the house of cards just as it did in previous financial crises.

Second, as we waded into 2007, the U.S. banking system had started unraveling at the seams. On April 2, New Century Financial, the largest U.S. subprime lender, filed for Chapter 11 bankruptcy. In financial jargon, I learned the full meaning of the term "subprime" mortgages, which had been extended to borrowers with dubious ability to pay back the loan. Banks became increasingly cautious in extending credit, even amongst themselves. Credit conditions tightened. Over the summer, the subprime crisis in the United States spread to Europe. I first became aware of the magnitude of the credit crunch when the European Central Bank put nearly $210 billion into European financial institutions in early August. Then, the U.S. Federal Reserve injected US$100 billion into the U.S. banking system.

To add fire to the emerging credit crisis, the prices of oil, gold, coal, and other commodities continued their upward spiral, supported not only by fundamental demand growth in countries such as India and China, but also fueled by speculative purchases by hedge funds and other investors hedging against dollar weakness. By late 2007, oil prices had ascended from around US$60 per barrel to close to US$100 per barrel. The twin threats of inflation and credit crunch would soon bring the rising stock market to a screeching halt.

During the first half of 2007, I focused my efforts on completing the merger of my company with Fabrice Jacob's company. Although I had worked on several mergers and acquisitions projects in my professional career, this was the first time I was a principal in the transaction. The financial part of the merger was simple, since we ran very simple businesses. More contentious were issues related to the new organizational structure, name of the newly merged firm, and a business plan for the new entity. We needed to find a new location to accommodate our joint resources. Thankfully in this process, we had the capable assistance of Ming Lee's advice and counsel.

Ming Lee is a person of exceptional skills and talents. She is smart, multi-talented, resourceful, and experienced. Professionally, she would soon become the head of one of the largest German private banks' Asian investment operation. Outside her professional career, Ming is a renowned yoga teacher. I had attended her yoga retreats in Thailand, China, and Bhutan.

I found Ming's work on a number of sensitive issues was extremely useful in conflict resolution. With her help, we settled big issues such as the organizational structure and small ones such as the color and font we would use for our website. The merger agreement was signed on August 10. We named the new entity JK Capital Management Ltd. J stands for the initial of Fabrice's last name and K stands for the initial of my last name. We also agreed to use JK as the brand for all our investment products.

It would take another three months before our merger officially took place as we waited for approval by the Securities and Futures Commission of Hong Kong. Meanwhile, Fabrice, Ming and I found a new space in a small building in the middle of the Central district. With the booming stock market and business conditions, rentals had taken a big jump. The building we found was probably two notches down from grade "A." While we tried to minimize rental expense, all three of us agreed to make our new office a grade "A" space and not economize on design or furnishing.

Back in 2006, I was introduced to a fund of funds operation based in Connecticut. Its head of investments sought a manager experienced in Asian equities. My first round of discussions was encouraging and I was told they would monitor my performance to determine whether they would pursue the discussion. This prospect was particularly important because, if approved, we would receive an allocation of at least US$10 million in capital. By mid-2007, I felt they were virtually ready to make a commitment, except they were not allowed to allocate funds to off-shore investment entities. Their mandate required us to organize a U.S.-based firm registered with the Securities and Exchange Commission of the United States.

In the fall of 2007, a fund manager whom I had met some years earlier in Seoul contacted me. Jiyoung Kim was then working for Credit Suisse in New York, running its technology and healthcare investments. She was a graduate of Harvard College, majoring in biochemistry. Her earlier career had been with Fred Algiers and PIMCO. Jiyoung is a bright, thoughtful and experienced portfolio manager. In 2007, she left Credit Suisse to take a sabbatical in her home country, South Korea. When she returned to New York, she decided to explore an entrepreneurial opportunity more challenging and rewarding than working for another big hedge fund. As it turned out, she and I found that we had compatible views on investment strategy and methodology.

In December, Jiyoung spent a week in Hong Kong to become familiar with our operation and people. I decided to allocate the technology and healthcare sectors in our portfolios to her management. More importantly, Jiyoung and I decided to launch a new fund to invest in innovative companies in leading-edge industries in the Pacific region, spanning from Japan to India.

The fund would initially focus on the information technology, healthcare, alternative energy, and educational services industries. It would employ a long/short strategy that would qualify it to be marketed as a hedge fund. We believed this fund was unique in concept and execution. Our rationale and enthusiasm for the project were based on our conviction that Asia needed to transform itself from a largely manufacturing-led economy into one with more broader knowledge-based and higher value-added enterprises. Our aim was to invest in winners of tomorrow as the region undergoes the transformation.

Jiyoung and I were passionate about this investment theme. Whether or not we would be able to find funding initially, however, was a different matter.

My plan was to set up a separate firm in New York, headed by Jiyoung. It would be a small operation since the basic research and trade execution would continue under JK Capital Management. The U.S. firm would be registered with the SEC. Assuming we received the mandate from the Connecticut firm, the fee income would cover much of the operational expenses and we would have time to raise the new hedge fund without a lot of cash flow pressure.

For most of 2007, investors in Asia seemed to ignore the financial crisis brewing in the Western world. Aside from two small corrections, Asian stock markets roared ahead, reaching historical heights. Economic conditions in China remained buoyant. Its exports had now moved from largely labor-intensive industries such as footwear, garment, and toy to encompass high-valued merchandise such as cell-phone, laptop computer, and many cutting-edge consumer electronic products. With market reforms, shares traded in China doubled in 2006 and doubled again in 2007. The Chinese central bank raised reserve requirements several times and raised lending rates to sterilize foreign exchange inflows. It also allowed the Chinese currency to appreciate more rapidly against the U.S. dollar.

As early as June, I advised investors that I had become cautious about the roaring stock market in Asia. I started taking profit and raising cash. I thought investors were too complacent, given record oil prices, record write-downs in U.S. financial institutions, and other bad news such as a steadily climbing unemployment rate. To hedge against expected volatility ahead, I searched for a derivative instrument that would work best for our fund. I was fortunate Commerzbank structured an Asian basket reverse certificate (RC), which has the effect of buying a "put." The basket consisted of Asian indices that mirror our country allocation. This instrument gave us the advantage of hedging market risk efficiently and at low cost, because it did not trade with either a premium or a discount to its intrinsic value.

During these buoyant days, my fund grew rapidly due to the rising market and increased number of investors. This was indeed a kind of virtual circle when our superior performance (relative to the U.S. markets) attracted more investors. By now, my investors' pool came from four areas: Boston, New York, Atlanta and Louisville, Kentucky. As a result, my travels generally included these four cities plus Jackson Hole in Wyoming and either Dallas or Scottsdale, Arizona where I had several important clients.

Asian economies continued to do well throughout 2007. For example, South Korea reported an increase in exports of 24 percent year-on-year in October. Exports from China grew 22 percent year-on-year as its trade surplus reached a new high of US$257 billion. At the peak of the bull market, which ended in October 2007, assets under my management had grown to US$63 million. My partner had US$24 million under management. As such, JK Capital Management had close to US$90 million of assets under management. While this was not a big number, it was still much larger than what I could have imagined just a few years earlier.

The expected reversal of market direction came in November. By then, a series of bad news had been coming out of the United States and Europe. In June, Bear Stearns pledged a collateralized loan of up to US$3.2 trillion to "bail out" one of its funds; in August, American Home Mortgage, the tenth largest mortgage lender in the States, announced it would file bankruptcy; and in September, Northern Rock, a large consumer bank in the United Kingdom, became insolvent and was nationalized. And this was just the beginning.

Starting in September, it seemed all the skeletons began to come out of the closet. UBS AG, a multinational investment bank based in Switzerland, warned that it would write down US$3.4 billion in assets. Its chairman resigned soon thereafter. In October, Merrill Lynch announced a US$5.5 billion of write-down of subprime-linked mortgages, and its CEO, Stanley O'Neal, was soon dismissed. Citicorp then shocked the public by writing down US$5.6 billion in its third quarter results, leading to the ouster of its CEO, Chuck Prince. Meanwhile, the Fed started reducing rates to ease the credit crunch.

Asian markets began a selling frenzy in November, down almost 10 percent in a month. China shares traded in Hong Kong dropped more than 14 percent. Foreign selling reached US$13 billion, the second largest outflow as a percentage of market capitalization in history. My hunch was that the five-year bull market in Asian equities had ended and this would be followed by a bear phase of many months.

Looking ahead during the closing days of 2007, I expected our newly constituted investment management firm to face both challenges and opportunities. Our greatest challenge was using the new platform to build assets under management. Next., we both recognized that we would need, over time, to resolve a number of open organizational issues to maximize value creation and make our merger a truly successful venture. Right after the merger, we faced the onset of a new bear market. This turn of events made it difficult to accomplish our merger goals. Investors turned bearish and raising capital would be virtually impossible until market sentiment turned favorable.

Still, my business prospects had improved already. My investors and prospects no longer viewed JK as a one-man show. With Ming Lee's help, we prepared a set of due diligence questionnaires for institutional prospects. Our presentation material was now visibly more attractive than before. In short, I was convinced the JK platform would lead to opportunities not possible when I was running my own business.

Recognizing my story certainly hasn't ended, I have decided to end my manuscript here. Although dark clouds have gathered over the financial landscape, I see them as a temporary setback that will form a strong foundation for our business to prosper in the years ahead. While always vigilant about risks that may arise from anywhere on any day, I remain optimistic about the future and about our newly formed firm. I am happy and proud that both of my children have matured and are growing in their work and enjoying life. I am thankful my health and energy have not waned much over the years. On both the professional and personal level, I am much blessed.

PART III

Roots, Recreations, Reflections

18

In Search of Family Roots

Early sowing of seeds with much talent and quality,
Yielding bumper crops with exceptional loyalty.
The root grows big and bright; aspiration, far and wide.
Famous and reputable do branches become as they multiply.

This poem's title, date and author are unknown. Yet, it contains part of the code that eventually helped me crack the puzzle of my family history. The poem was once lost behind a curtain of fear during the Cultural Revolution of China.

The story goes back to my father. The fact he had said very little about his family in Sichuan Province has always been a mystery to me. The only thing I knew about him was he was born during the last days of the Qing Dynasty, in the city of Kaixian to a well-to-do family. He passed the court's examination to pursue studies in Beijing. He never talked about his parents, his siblings, or anyone else in his family.

Looking back, it dawned on me how little interest or curiosity I had in finding out about my father's family and ancestors when he was still alive. Like most young people, I had my priorities in what was lying ahead instead of what was behind. After I turned 55, this all changed and I suddenly had an urge to discover my roots. I began to pepper my mother with questions. It had already been a few years since my father passed away. As it turned out, Mother also knew little about Father's family because she never visited Kaixian or anywhere outside of Shanghai during the days she and Father were living in China. I was left to use my initiative and intuition to solve the puzzle.

In 2004, I was 69 years old by the Western calendar, but 70 years old according to the Chinese calendar. I decided to visit Kaixian that year because it is auspicious to visit one's ancestral place at the age of 70. Another reason was the Three Gorges Dam project would, in three to five years, flood much of the town where my father had lived as a boy, obliterating the site. This homecoming project eventually became a reality when my two enthusiastic children agreed to come along with us.

Prior to the visit, I had communicated with a Mr. Lu, a relative on my paternal grandmother's side. Lu lives in Chengdu, the capital of Sichuan Province, and is familiar with Kaixian and its surrounding areas. Now retired, he had been a high school teacher in Wanzhou, a town about two-and-a-half hours' drive south of Kaixian along the Yangtze River. When I asked him to visit Father's hometown with me, he was delighted. He volunteered to take me to Kaixian and show me where my father's old house was located. His son, Lu Jr., agreed to drive us there in his SUV, one of the latest model on the market.

On December 26, 2004, my family of four, plus a friend of my son, took off from Hong Kong to embark on this unique homecoming journey. Sadly, it was also the day when the devastating Asian tsunami engulfed towns and villages around the Indian Ocean, eventually consuming more than 200,000 lives. We did not learn about this catastrophe until we checked into our hotel in Chongqing.

The weather was cold and wet and the city was fogged in after sunset. We used Chongqing as the staging point because there is no airport in Kaixian. On the morning of December 27, we set out for Kaixian, a five-hour drive east. We drove on paved highways for two hours, then unpaved dirt and finally gravel roads over mountainous terrain.

Kaixian, situated on a mountainous slope, is one of the three most prosperous towns in the area. We reached the city from a high point as we drove down from the top of the mountain. A great deal of construction work was going on, with wide areas being leveled for roads and housing to accommodate up to 100,000 people. These citizens were to be relocated from the lower part of the town when flooded by the Three Gorges Dam in three to five years.

This city of 250,000 has a new and an old section. The new section was dotted with modest six-story apartment blocks. As our car descended down into the old section, the streets, clean, tree-lined, and flanked with two-story old brick houses, were full of people, either walking or biking. The landscape appeared not to have changed over many decades.

Soon, Lu Jr. turned his car left into a narrow street just wide enough to accommodate one vehicle. Dong Jie (meaning East Street) was crowded with shoppers who were unconcerned that a car was trying to make its way through. The sidewalk was full of peddlers selling fruits and vegetables. It was a bustling scene. We soon stopped in front of a three-story stone building – probably the tallest and biggest on the street. Lu asked us to disembark. "Here," he pointed at the house and said, "was where your father lived in his youth."

The home that my father told me about had long been demolished. The present building housed an office and several homes in the back. "At last!" I thought, "I am standing where Father had once played!"

We walked around and observed the street scene, full of people crowding into tea houses and shops selling clothes, medicine, and home appliances. I thought, if this street scene were approximately the same as when Father lived there, he would have been happy growing up in this neighborhood.

Lu does not know too much about our family. He said that during the Cultural Revolution, families were discouraged from talking about members who were abroad. To be associated with someone abroad meant you were one of the "five stinky categories" and which constituted a crime. Had any of our family members known about my father, they would certainly have feared to talk about him. So, sadly, a generation later, the history of the older generation was lost.

To my astonishment, Lu said that my father wasn't born in Kaixian. Instead, he was born in a village called Chenjia (Chen's House). My grandfather apparently came to Kaixian after father was born when he was appointed a treasury official in the city government. This new piece of information prompted us to leave Kaixian and head toward Chenjia, which was another hour's drive south on a dirt road, but this time straight up into the mountains.

The drive became more difficult. By then, it was already late in the day and daylight was receding fast. After an hour's drive, Lu turned left into a dirt lane, which wound itself left and then right slightly on a decline. We then stopped in an open area overlooking a valley on the left. "This was where your father was born," Lu said.

The site of my father's birth was now a small grove of orange trees to the left of the road. According to Lu, Chenjia is famous for its red oranges sold throughout the country. We befriended an old woman who was curious about the visitors and came to offer her help. To everyone's great surprise, she said that about 200 Kweis lived down the road some distance away. This came to us as incredible news. Even Lu wasn't aware of this fact. However, because the road was unlit and fog had started descending around us, we decided not to venture further.

It was pitch dark when we left the little village and headed south toward Wanzhou, where we would stay overnight. Visibility was bad. It was foggy and very dark. There were no lights on the road up the mountain. We kept going uphill for a long time, on a two-lane road that was partly dirt and partly gravel. At a high point, our car was stopped by a guard who told Lu Jr. we had to wait for vehicles traveling from the other side to pass before we could drive on. The very enterprising and cheerful Lu Jr. thought that the wait could last an hour or so. To speed things up, he offered the guard a single cigarette and we were allowed to proceed.

About 20 minutes later, on the high mountain, we suddenly saw a caravan of lights heading toward us. This was the traffic from the other direction that the guard had indicated earlier. Lu Jr. skillfully steered the SUV to the side, allowing mostly trucks to pass. I thought, "It must have been on this very mountain where my father, sitting on a sedan, confronted the robbers."

We reached Wanzhou in two hours. Wanzhou is a city of 500,000 people located on the Yangtze River. As much as one-third of the city would be eventually flooded by the Three Gorges Dam. After having spent eleven hours on the road that day, most of it a bumpy ride, we finally reached our hotel. We stayed overnight and returned to Hong Kong the next day.

Somehow, while immensely gratifying, my homecoming trip felt incomplete. My curiosity about the mountain and the Kwei community in Chenjia was heightened and I knew then I had to return again to probe more deeply into my family's ancestral past.

An opportunity to revisit Chenjia came in October 2006 – two years after my first visit – when I attended an investors' conference in Chongqing. Since the discovery of a Kwei tribe in Chenjia, I had asked Lu and a few others to find out if anyone there might remember my father and my grandfather. In the two years since, Lu's efforts had yielded no results. As I was planning to go to the conference, my travel agent located a certain Mr. Zhang, who was an area administrator in Chenjia. The agent provided him with the names of my father and grandfather. According to Zhang, he had made enquiries but he too came up empty-handed.

I wasn't going to give up easily, because I couldn't be sure whether any serious effort had been made in response to my request. I decided I should spend at least one day to do some digging in Chenjia for more information about my family. I knew the odds of finding my relatives were remote, but I just couldn't rest until I did my own research. My plan was simply to go from door to door to try my luck.

At 7:20 in the morning, on October 20, my driver, an interpreter, and I left Chongqing and headed east to Wanzhou. The drive took three hours. From Wanzhou, we drove further north to Chenjia. We drove uphill on a two-lane highway, crossed a long bridge, and headed north to our destination. Along the way, I took many pictures of the awesome mountain ranges where I believed my father, at the age of eleven, had taken the very same route when he left home to go to Beijing. When we reached the top of the rise, there was a long tunnel. After we navigated through the tunnel, the road started on a descent.

Unlike two years earlier, the roads we drove on were now mostly paved. Interestingly, I did not arrive at the place that we reached in the previous trip. Instead, we descended down the slope into a small town with one paved road. There, the interpreter picked up Zhang, the area administrator. After we exchanged greetings, Zhang assured me there were lots of Kweis in the village. Zhang was in his mid 40s and a pleasant fellow. He said he did not have any real information about my family but was happy to take us around on our search.

We headed to the village by turning off the main road onto a nondescript small lane that turned into a dirt road in the middle of the countryside. I had the strange feeling the street we just left behind was merely a stage set. The real world lay beyond the main street and in the farms along the dirt path.

Seeing rows of mostly two-story houses, Zhang said that we had reached the village. We stopped at the first of the houses where a few people stood outside. The old man who stepped forward to greet me had my middle name, Zheng. He said his father had the same middle name as my father and his daughter had the same middle name as my daughter,. It was obvious this fellow was somehow related to me.

The old man went into the house and soon came out with a red book entitled the *Book of Kwei*. This book, according to him, was compiled some years ago by several village elders. He tried to identify our family branch in the book. Unfortunately, nothing in the names came close. The old man then asked Zhang to take me to another Kwei who had worked on the book. Along the way, Zhang told me that Kweis live in houses after houses along winding paths in the middle of rice paddies.

We stopped in front of a house where four men were playing mahjong at the front door. Zhang knew this old Kwei, who was short and very nearsighted. He took us into his one-room farmhouse, which was dark and sparsely furnished. He looked at my sheet of names and started talking loudly, speculating about a lot of names and connections. According to him, three branches of Kweis were living in Chenjia and the surrounding area. I asked him how the Kweis first arrived in this area. He speculated that, during the Ming Dynasty, a lot of people were forcibly moved to new areas and that was likely the reason the Kweis' came to Chenjia. He mentioned another Kwei who might know something about our branch of the family.

We piled into the mini-van and drove to another field and stopped in front of a brick house. This was a distinguished two-story structure amid one-story farm houses. Zhang went in and shortly came out accompanied by an old man with white hair. He wore a suit, a tie, and a shirt. I couldn't believe I could find a "scholar" in this patch of farmland. He invited us to his living room, where there were two small sofas. This Kwei was retired but had been a school principal. It turned out that we found someone who really had known about my family.

"Scholar Kwei" was 80 and looked healthy. His middle name was also Zheng. Up and down the generation, the middle name of his family members was exactly like ours. I realized that the

Chinese naming system is extremely useful in tracking down relatives. This Kwei knew a lot about our family. He knew that Father went to study in Beijing, lived in Shanghai, and was a lawyer. He knew that Father had two sons but didn't know that we were twins. Most importantly, he knew where a daughter of my father's younger brother lived and mentioned this to Zhang. This old Mr. Kwei took out his copy of the red *Book of Kwei* I had seen earlier and showed it to me. To my pleasant surprise, he gave me his own copy when I was about to leave!

We had a good conversation. His wife was very short and really friendly. She kept shoving oranges at us as a sign of hospitality. This Kwei said that, in the old days, before the Cultural Revolution, the Kwei clan used to meet in the neighborhood once a year to exchange news. It was also an occasion when the rich members would help the poor. He said that Father's father was sent to Kaixian to be the treasurer of the city. It was a big deal in the eyes of the Kwei families living in the farm.

Zhang then drove us to a different village, about 20 minutes away. When we finally came across several houses on the left, Zhang asked the driver to stop. I stayed in the car while he walked ahead into a small housing compound. Soon, a woman smiling broadly came out of the compound and waved at me wildly.

Little did I know at that moment my own cousin was waving at me. Her name is Kwei Zheng Yu. We greeted each other on the dirt road. The first thing I noticed about her was that she was barefooted. She took us into the compound but not the house. We sat down on a small chair outside the house and chatted. After checking the middle names, it was evident we were indeed cousins. I was thrilled to finally locate a close relative. Yu appeared to be a simple and kind person. She had a pleasant demeanor. She was immensely surprised to find a stranger showing up unexpectedly at her door on this sunny afternoon and discover he was her cousin!

Yu is a farmer who grew rice and corn. She looked quite healthy and spoke in a direct way. Her husband, Chang, is a school teacher. When she found out who I was, she immediately sent word to fetch him. Her father – my father's brother – was a teacher who died in 1984. Yu was only 54, being the youngest of my uncle's children. Her son is now working in a factory in Shenzhen, close to Hong Kong.

Soon, Yu's husband showed up. To my surprise, he knew a lot about us. He knew that Lu had met us in Hong Kong some years ago. He knew that Father's first wife was an American. He said that soon after Father left for Beijing, the family's fortune declined. He said that my father was famous in Kaixian. His name had been recorded as one of the "city's notable sons."

Although my visit was short, I knew this would not be my only visit to see Yu. I was sure I was going to get to know her family. Even though we had just met, I had a sense that we were part of the same family, and there was an unspoken bond between us.

About My Genealogy

Our family has followed the traditional practice of writing a special poem and then assigning characters sequentially in the poem to each generation. In Chinese names, the surname is generally only one character and comes first, followed by the first and second names. Under this naming practice, a family would select a particular character in a chosen poem for the first name of all its members.

Our family's chosen poem is the one I have included in the beginning of this chapter. Beautifully written, it consists of four stanzas, each of which contains five characters. The Chinese characters are written vertically and read from top to bottom. In the "genealogy poem," each character is used for one generation in the order it is positioned in the poem. Each generation is to select the first name for his offspring by choosing the character that is the next lower to the one designated for him.

When my brother and I were born, Father located the appropriate character, next to his own, in the poem to give me my first name, "Zheng," (note I used "Chen" in the first chapter for my first name as it was part of my legal name) which is also the name of my brother. My father's brother would have the same first name as my father and he would have used the same first name as mine for his offspring. On these points I was proven right during my genealogy hunt in Sichuan Province.

To check the authenticity of this poem, I traced the first name of several generations from my generation to earlier ones and found the method to be absolutely accurate. According to the poem, I was born in the 10th generation. Therefore, including my offspring, this poem is to be used for another 10 generations as it contains 20 characters. I have already told my kids what they should use as the first name of their offspring.

Beyond the traceable genealogy of the direct branch of my family, the history of the Kwei tribe can be traced to as far back as the Zhou Dynasty (221 B.C.–11 B.C.). It was thanks to a book prepared by my great-grandfather that I came to know the long history behind our family name.

The book was mailed to me by my brother, who found it in Mother's apartment during his trip to attend her funeral in 2002. He did not mention it to me until two years later. The book had two parts. The main body of the book was a manuscript written by my great-great-grandfather about the geology of the Hubei Province and which was presented to the Qing Dynasty's emperor for his private collection. Such an honor was only possible because the book was highly regarded by officials in the court.

The book now in my possession is a copy prepared by his son, my great-grandfather, possibly for private distribution. What interested me most was not the main manuscript discussing the geology, but a long appendix in the back that outlined the Kwei family's history. Indeed, this outline represented a major breakthrough in my quest.

Along with this book, I now possess another book about the Kwei clan from Chenjia. Together, these two books constitute the sum of everything I know about my family's genealogy.

Here is a summary of my findings:

According to records on some stone carvings – generally viewed as legends that may not be historically accurate – one of our family members was a court scholar and teacher during the late Zhou Dynasty. It was then he was given the name of Kwei. Previously, the family's name was Ji, which, according to historical records, was the family name of the Zhou Emperor. During the Zhou Dynasty, our ancestors lived in today's Xian, in Shansi Province. According to another source, there was a square stone plaque of the Kwei family in Xian.

The first "story" I managed to find about one of my ancestors was of Kwei Zheng. He lived in Shangdong on the northeast coast of China in a village named Yue Zhou. He lived during the Qin Dynasty (221 B.C.–206 B.C.) and he was the first Kwei whose life history was preserved on record.

Kwei Zheng was an unusual person with great scholarship and wisdom. By the time he was 21, he had completed his education in all the classic literature. A famous scholar, he was made Minister of Education and promoted to the highest official rank in the emperor's court. Kwei Zheng was also a teacher for the emperor's children.

In his ruthless way of consolidating power and eliminating rivals, the emperor decided to burn all the books and eliminate all the scholars. Many scholars were caught and buried alive. Fortunately, Kwei Zheng escaped to a place known as Lingzhou in Henan Province. There, to avoid arrest, he changed his name to Shan Zheng. In this process, his works were lost but his reputation survived down the generations. He was said to have died after eating a turtle brain.

During the 700-some years between the Han Dynasty and the Tang Dynasty, the Kwei tribe expanded across 41 generations and branches of the tribe multiplied. It was in the Tang Dynasty

(618–907) when the Kwei family's history started to appear in official records. Between 907 and 960, there was much turmoil in the land and many families moved south across the Yangtze River for safety. From there, they spread out to the Jiangsu and Jiangxi regions. Kwei Zhi Lan, fearful of a barbarian named An Lu Shan who tried to overthrow the government, moved his family south and settled in Jiangnan in the Zhejiang area.

Kwei Zhi Lan's grandson, Kwei Zhong Wu, moved his family to Fujian, then a remote territory in the south of China. He was an official in charge of civil administration of the territory. His responsibilities included defense and military inspection.

Four generations later, in the Sung Dynasty (960–1279), a certain Kwei Chung Hue moved to Gansi, south of Hubei Province. Nothing was written about him. His grandson, Kwei Tang, moved further east to Zhejiang. There, one branch (the middle of six sons) of the family clan and his later generations formed our family's direct lineage. One of the offspring was so highly regarded that a temple was dedicated to him. It was in the Sung period that the Kwei clan spread itself across many areas of the country, some to the south, others to the west while still others remained.

The first group of Kwei from Hunan arrived in Sichuan during the middle of the Ming Dynasty (1368–1644) and settled in the area of Wanghou and Kaixian, where I found my cousin in 2006. It was a period of social and political turmoil, leading to economic hardship and perhaps even famine. Initially, the families encountered many hardships and difficulties because of the primitive conditions in the region.

In the early Qing Dynasty (1644–1911), a Kwei You Yue moved to Hunan Province and served as a high-ranking officer in charge of penal facilities. His son moved to Guangdong and lived in Nanhai, which is about two hours' drive north of the present-day city of Guangzhou. His son, Kwei Hong, became a prominent and respected person. He passed the court examination in 1786 and later served as a governor of Jing County in Anhui Province. His social status was elevated to that of a noble family.

Kwei Hong's son, Kwei Ze Ji, served as a military defense official in Weihai, which is in the Gannan region in Hunan Province. He had six sons. One of the sons, Kwei Wen Hui – my great-great-grandfather – was the author of the book about Hubei's geology my brother passed on to me. In the appendix of that book, my great-grandfather wrote about his father, Kwei Wen Hui, a gentleman who was a prominent scholar and officer, serving the emperor in many important assignments.

One of the assignments that Kwei Wen Hui handled was a project related to the defense of Guangdong's coastline against the British Naval forces during the Opium War. Another project was to set up a bureau in Fujian to help families whose men had gone off to work in Peru and became unaccounted for through untimely death. He was also a great scholar who wrote many books that were preserved in the emperor's private library. He died at the age of 62 in Hubei, where he was serving as a county governor.

From Kwei Zheng down through generations, the family tree noted 41 generations before moving to Sichuan. Since then, there has been another 67 generations.

With the mystery of the past resolved, my remaining challenge was to find the history of my father's father, son of the one who wrote the appendix that contained much of the information I related above.

The Last Piece of the Puzzle

Since the earlier trip to Sichuan when I met my cousin Yu, I knew I had to return to talk to her and her siblings about what they know about my father's family. In early 2008, I learned that my cousin Yu, whom I met outside her home in Chenjia, was diagnosed with cancer of the digestive tract. I decided to visit her to check on her health and learn more about her life. This intent somehow morphed into a plan to meet all her siblings. A lunch was planned in Wanzhou, a nearby city on the Yangtze River, for the family's get together.

At this point, I was communicating with Yu and her niece Chen Lin, a third-year college student majoring in English at Chongqing University. Lin and my travel agent helped me organize the entire event. Zhang, who saw me in 2006, brought Yu's brothers and sisters and a few of their offspring to the occasion.

On Saturday, April 26, 2008, in a restaurant in Wanzhou, I met the surviving offspring of my uncle, Kwei Zhong Zheng. They included the wife of his first son and their daughter as well as his second son and his wife. I also met his first daughter and her daughter and, of course, cousin Yu, who is my uncle's youngest daughter, and her husband. They brought along their daughter, Chen Ke Fang, and her husband.

Over a long lunch, we chatted about our family's history. I learned my grandfather, Kwei Xiao San (also known as Kwei Ling Kui), was a successful businessman in Kaixian. He was a large landlord and ran a grain business. He also served as an official for the city, collecting taxes from farmers tilling the land around the city. According to some of my guests, he had at least three wives.

Grandfather had five daughters by one wife and four sons by another wife. The four sons included my father, the eldest; a second son who died in childhood; Kwei Zhong Zheng, the third son; and a fourth son who served in the army and was killed during the Second World War. Of the girls, the youngest one married Lu Zheng Ying. She is the mother of the Lu who had escorted our family on our first trip to Kaixian.

Contrary to what Lu told me during my first homecoming trip, my relatives at the table said father was indeed born in Kaixian, not in Chenjia. They also told me shortly after my birth in 1935, my grandfather passed away.

After the family patriarch died, the family fortune quickly faded. No one seemed to know how or why. However, it emerged that one or more of his wives had the habit of smoking opium, an expensive habit. Financial losses could also have occurred in the Great Depression, which probably had a major impact on grain prices. Perhaps the sons couldn't manage the business well. Perhaps Grandfather had debts that were unknown to the family until he died. I figured the Second World War must have had an adverse impact as well. Whatever the reasons, the family eventually went bankrupt.

It was too bad I could not visit grandfather's grave. It had been obliterated when a new highway went through the family plot in the upper part of Kaixian.

Kwei Zhong Zheng, the third son of my grandfather, was remembered by my family members as having a long white beard. He was a primary school teacher. I learned, in the 1930s, he went to Shanghai twice to ask for Father's help to find work. He intended to move his family to Shanghai but the war interrupted the plan. He stayed behind in Kaixian instead.

In 1951, shortly after the Communists had taken over China, my uncle's family was branded members of the landlord class and mistreated. That was why he couldn't find work. Uncle sent one of his sons and his two daughters to Chenjia, where a big clan of Kweis was known to be living. His eldest son remained in Kaixian.

When he arrived in the village in 1951, my uncle started a primary school. It didn't last long because the government decided there would be no private education. His own kids received little education and became farmers. My uncle's school building was supposed to be close to Yu's home. I discovered it had been razed and a residential house built on the plot. Uncle died in 1984 at the age of 73.

Out of his four children, the only living son, Kwei Chen Hua, was now 66 years old. He had been a farmer all his life. He told me he had only two years of schooling. This is surprising considering that his father was a teacher. He told me that schooling was "unfashionable" when he was young and he thought he would be better off being a farmer. What he didn't say was that he grew up in the worst of times in China, when sons of good families were forced to work in hard labor.

Kwei Chen Hua told me that he plants rice, corn, and barley, sufficient only for his family. Their three sons worked in Shanghai, but he did not know what they were doing. When I asked him what would happen when he retired, he said he didn't know, but one thing was for sure: The land would go back to the government. He expected his sons to support him in his retirement. Neither pension nor any benefits were expected from the government.

Another relative, Kwei Chen Yu is also a farmer. She was my cousin who appeared barefooted on that sunny afternoon back in 2006, waving her arms wildly to greet me. Only in her early 50s, she is the youngest of the four children. She was more refined in her demeanor than the others. In the two letters she wrote me after we met in 2006, she ended them with short poems. She had cancer in her digestive tract and had an operation in a Wanzhou hospital in February. The operation was fortunately successful.

Yu's husband, Mr. Chen, is a teacher who knows about my father's history. He and Yu have a son and a daughter. The son works in Shenzhen where he has lived for the past 10 years. He is married to a local Chenjia woman who also works in Shenzhen. While they work in a distant city, their children stay with their grandmother in Chenjia. I understand this is a typical family situation in Chenjia. All the young people have left the village for work in far away cities, leaving behind only the older farmers to care for the farm and grandchildren.

Life on a Chinese farm is hard. Typically, the day starts at 4 a.m. Over many decades, little has changed. The chief difference is they now use fertilizer instead of manure. The farmers grow rice, corn, and oranges, but only enough to feed their own families. There is no vacation at all.

Cousin Yu's daughter, Chen Ke Fang, met me at the airport and accompanied me in every activity during the weekend. Born in 1975 in Chenjia, Fang grew up as a farmer's daughter.

She now lives in Chongqing, is married to a Mr. Yang and they have two daughters, one around 4 and the other around 11.

The person who spent the most time with me was Chen Lin. She was born in Chenjia to the brother of my cousin Yu's husband. Her parents left her 10 years ago to work in Xinjiang Province, where they now own a pig farm with 200 pigs. Lin was raised by her relatives and attended different schools every few years. Lin is the only child from the Kwei families in Chenjia who has made it to college. With some pride, she told me about 70 percent of her high school classmates are in college. Like everybody else of her generation, she sees no future in going back to Chenjia. She wants to travel overseas and work in an office environment in Chongqing.

The next person I spent a lot of time with was Kwei Beng Ying. Her father was the oldest son of my uncle Kwei Zhong Zheng. Ying is married and has a daughter, a doctor working in Chengdu. Ying and her husband, surnamed Deng, work in a state-owned military machinery plant in the city. It is clear that she and her husband have moved up the social ladder to the emerging middle class in China.

There was not much I could learn from my relatives about the older generations. It seems that, during their youth, little had been passed on from their parents. Perhaps for the same reason that his brother didn't inform his offspring, my father was silent with us for fear any disclosures might jeopardize his relatives in his hometown. Being from a former landlord class – even a bankrupt family – remaining silent was preferable to making a remark that might lead to unfortunate consequences in faraway China.

My quest for my father's family roots has come to a satisfying end. It I had learned many of my ancestral fathers had been scholars and mid-level officials of high repute. Father was born in a small village in Western China, but he was the odd son who left his hometown and became a lawyer and a journalist in the Western style. He never tried to return to his hometown. Who would have thought that one of his children would go back to reconnect with the family that he had left behind so many decades ago?

Even though my father's brother moved to a farming village due to political and economic circumstances in 1951, his grandchildren have all left the farms and sought work and life in the big cities. While none of them is well educated, my young niece, Chen Lin, is in college and she will no doubt scale the social and economic heights denied to the elder generation.

My journey to seek my family's roots found a kind of closure. I believe the relationships I developed represent a beginning that will be nourished by those in our family who care to remain connected with one another. This connection represents a link among the disparate Kwei members who, today, encompass not just the Chinese ethnicity but also span more than one continent. Michael Crichton once wrote: "If you don't know your family's history, then you don't know anything. You are a leaf that does not know it is part of a tree."

In the future, as the Kwei family members move out of their rural surroundings, some may well adopt the values my family and I hold. It may sound incredible, but I find that in my relatives' simple existence in rural China, there is a sense of dignity in their outlook absent in some of the people I deal with every day.

The roots of our family's history give us a sense of who we are. They serve as an anchor against many vicissitudes we often face in living in the fast lanes.

"There are only two lasting bequests we can give our children; one is roots, the other, wings."

– Anonymous

19

My Life-long Hobbies

Over the years, no matter how busy my studies, work, or family responsibilities have been, I have consistently maintained a number of hobbies. These pastimes inspire me spiritually and keep me physically fit. Music has always played a major role in my life. So has reading. In sports, I have played tennis, hiked, and skied for most of my life. In my later years, I took up the practice of yoga. Not only have I enjoyed many good times pursuing these interests, I have also developed wonderful friendships along the way.

Tennis

I have been an avid tennis fan and player for many years. The first serious tennis game I remember was the one I played with my brother in the summer of 1953. We had wooden rackets that we bought with money we made while working as ditch diggers at Maryknoll Seminary in New York. Although I don't recall who won, I remember we had a tough game and I was scoring some serious points with my backhand swings. My brother was able to make the school team but I did not.

I didn't have any opportunities to play tennis until much later, after I moved to Hong Kong in 1980. We lived in a house in Strawberry Hills, a luxurious housing compound on the Peak, which came with a tennis court. I also belonged to the Hong Kong Country Club, which had many courts.

My first tennis buddy was my neighbor, Robert Fallon, who worked for Citibank at the time. Later, he moved to Tokyo and worked for Drexel Burnham until it folded in 1989. In 2004, he became the CEO of Korea Exchange Bank. Over the years, we have managed to stay in touch.

It is too bad that I neglected the game during my prime years. I didn't belong to any clubs and finding courts in New York City and Boston was difficult. Still, I saw many tournament games in Forest Hills, Queens. My favorite players in the old days were Australian – Rod Laver and Ken Roswell. Later on, my admiration switched to the great Swedish player, Stefan Edberg, and of course, John McEnroe. My all around favorites were Pete Sampras, Jimmy Connors and Ivan Lendl. My current favorite male player is Roger Federer.

Tennis rackets went through several evolutions – from wood to graphite and then to metal. The rackets got bigger when Prince introduced its revolutionary design in the 1980s, enlarging the racket surface while keeping its stiffness. Players got taller and bigger. Balls went back and forth faster and faster. Soon, most players would win with a heavy serve and sharp volley.

After we left Hong Kong and moved back to New York in 1983, I was determined to keep up my game. I enrolled in classes held in the Armory on the Upper East Side. I played with my son, Clarence, who was then 8 years old. We played in a public court by the East River Drive just below East 96th Street. The court was small and the surface hard and uneven. But, it was the best I could find. Even today, when he visits Hong Kong on holidays, Clarence and I continue to play tennis every chance we get.

After we returned to Hong Kong in 1983, we moved back to Strawberry Hill and I rejoined the Hong Kong Country Club. Robert had gone to Tokyo by then. I usually played with three partners until the end of the decade. The first was Andrew Choa, who was head of the Hong Kong office of Russell Reynolds, an executive search firm based in New York. He was older but a much better player. Andrew and I played together every Sunday until he moved back to New York in 1996. The second was my neighbor, Roger King, who is married to the sister of Tung Chee Hwa, the first Chief Executive of Hong Kong after the handover in 1997. Along with Roger was Tung Chee Hwa's brother, C. C. Tung, who headed a large publicly listed shipping company while his older brother served the post of Chief Executive. Unfortunately, our games were terminated in the mid 1990s when Roger decided not to play and C.C. found other partners.

In the late 1990s, my most frequent partner was Michael Hui, a lawyer who was running the real estate business in China for the family of Robert Kuok Hock-Nien, the Malaysian property and media tycoon. We played mostly at the Aberdeen Marina Club, a Kuok property. The Club is a vertical complex with courts on the rooftop. We were about even in skills so that our games were always tight. After playing, we would enjoy a drink and a delightful meal in the Shangri-La tradition. Later, Michael retired from his work, moved his family to Seattle, bought a large property, subdivided it for sale, and lived as a neighbor of Bill Gates.

From the year 2000 until 2006, my steadiest tennis partner was Patrick Caviness, Yale class of 1964. He was from Arkansas and a great sportsman. Pat's game level was better than mine. Playing him, my game had actually improved. Patrick, a natural athlete, had been a linebacker and a champion boxer at Yale and very competitive. Even in middle age, his lateral and forward movements remained formidable. Needless to say, my chances of winning entirely depended on whether he had an off day. Our favorite court was the American Club in Tai Tam. After our game, we would drink and eat and talk about the books we were reading and hold summit meetings on all the world's major problems. Sharing those times together was exhilarating and memorable for both of us.

I am now playing with Jesse Friedlander, the grandson of Elliott Goldstein, one of my early investors from Atlanta, Georgia. Elliott was a war hero during the Battle of the Bulge in the Second World War. He went on to receive his law degree from the Yale Law School in 1951 and proceeded to become one of the most prominent lawyers in Georgia. Jesse is working for a large U.S.-based hedge fund. A 2001 Yale graduate, Jesse has a great interest in China's economic development. We used to be an even match but he has had an upper hand for at least two years now.

Over the years, I have taken several coaching lessons. Still, my game has never been great. My serve is erratic and my eye-hand coordination slow. I am not good at playing doubles because I am particularly useless at the net. However, I have a reasonably good passing shot and I run around a lot, even now. My best moment was when I competed in a senior tournament in the American Club in 1998 and won second place.

As I write this piece, I am winning few matches but I remain a competitive player, using control and placement to win points. My stamina is still reasonably good and my knees, even though they are not strong enough for serious hiking and skiing, are holding up fine. Having had a cataract condition since the mid-1990s, I do not see the ball as well as before, but this is definitely not a good excuse for missing shots.

SKIING

Tom, my brother, introduced me to skiing back in 1961. I don't know how he found out about this great sport unless it was from his then fiancée, Amy. We were both working at IBM in Poughkeepsie, New York. From then until I moved to Philadelphia in 1968, I would go skiing in New York, Vermont, and New Hampshire almost every weekend during the winter months.

In the early days of skiing, skis were made of wood that had to be waxed every day. The standard practice was to use a ski whose length reached the bottom of your palm as you stretched your arm upward. The ski pole should go up to the armpit.

When I was at IBM, I skied with my housemate, Jack Moreschi, a classmate at the Columbia Graduate School of Business. We were both bachelors then. Jack later left IBM and joined Arthur D. Little in Boston and was my roommate again when I moved to Boston in 1966. Jack is of Italian descent and his father owned an Italian lasagna and spaghetti factory in Hartford. Eventually, he went back to his family business and took control of it.

My favorite skiing mountains were Stowe, Sugarbush, and Killington in Vermont. But the most notable ski trip I had was to Jay Peak in upper Vermont. This was in December, 1962. There, I learned parallel skiing. In one of the lessons, a student sprained an ankle and couldn't go on. The instructor took a look at me and asked me to escort the rest of the group to the base. I was delighted he showed such confidence in me. After I joined Citibank, I lived outside of the United States most of the time. However, when we were back during 1978–1980, I would take my wife and two kids to ski. We went mostly to the Poconos in Pennsylvania because it was close to New York and the slopes were easy. There, my kids had their first lessons and developed a real joy for the sport. My wife, though not really into sports, came along and skied with us. We always had a great time.

After we moved to Hong Kong in 1980, my skiing activity dropped off significantly. However in 1986, we did take one interesting trip to Mount Zao, two hours north of Tokyo in Japan. We joined a group of parents of Hong Kong International School's students and stayed in a Japanese inn. We slept on tatamis. The inn was made of wood and there was no heating at night. Every morning, in absolute chill, I would get out from under my warm blankets to turn on the heat. There was only one sink and one Western-style toilet for all 20 of us. Somehow, we all managed. Food was mostly Japanese but mixed with some

Western dishes. The best part of the experience was relaxing in the natural hot spring pool every day after skiing.

I didn't have a chance to ski again until 1997, during one of my innumerable trips to the States to meet investors and prospects. Among my most valuable and supportive investors is Tom Chrystie, a retired vice chairman of Merrill Lynch. Tom is a fine athlete, about two years older than me. He lives on a beautiful ranch in Jackson Hole, Wyoming. In December that year, I spoke to a group of guests, invited by Tom, about Asia and my investment style and strategies.

After the talk, we went to the Grand Teton ski area. The weather was perfect, sunny and not a cloud in the sky. The mountain was magnificent and the air extremely cold and dry. As Tom and I are of the same build, Eliza, his wife, gave me a ski outfit of his, which fit me perfectly. The slopes were in fine condition, and they were not crowded. Although the temperature was below zero, I didn't feel cold. I grew tired quickly because I was not used to skiing at such a high altitude (about 9,000 feet). My legs and, in particular, my knees, felt sore, and I was short of breath after only a few runs. After lunch, I could only handle two more runs and asked Tom to quit. The mountain air was thin and dry and the sun was strong. I felt somewhat dizzy and nauseated. Apparently, I was dehydrated. After we returned to Tom's home and luxuriated in the steam bath, Jacuzzi, and sauna, all was well again.

The most recent skiing trip was in February, 2008 when Clarence and I took a few days off to ski at Lake Tahoe. The skiing conditions on the West Coast are quite different from those on the East Coast. The slopes are longer and broader and the snow is deep and solid. It was sunny and not too cold while we were there. The two of us had a great time, taking our runs leisurely. I no longer try to do difficult trails. Instead, I am happy to ski down intermediate slopes that give me time to enjoy the magnificent scenery and take in fresh, unpolluted air. My knees do not bother me, which is a great comfort. And I pace myself so that I don't feel exhausted at the end of the day's workout.

I intend to continue skiing every chance I have. I still thrill at the feeling of speeding down the slope, balanced first on one leg and then the other. I like the often spectacular landscape and experiencing magnificence of nature from the top of the mountains. I enjoy the incredible beauty of snow-capped trees along the trails. I like the feeling of cold air brushing over my face. I like the feeling of sweating while everything is cold around me. Finally, the taste of a cup of hot chocolate is never better than when taken after a long ski run.

Hiking

I have always liked to be outdoors. If there were previous lives, I must have been a farmer or a paleontologist. Below is a fleeting brush of my hiking experiences. As I write this note, I realize I haven't hiked for a couple of years. My old hiking group has disbanded due to "retirement" and transfers out of Hong Kong.

I did most of my early hikes between 1964 and 1968 when I was living in Boston. I used to hike in the mountains of Massachusetts, New York, Vermont, and New Hampshire with members of a Chinese fraternity named Rho Psi, which I had joined. In those days, because racial prejudice against Chinese was fairly common, Chinese students formed their own social organizations to network and meet each other.

We used to go to a state park in Massachusetts or New Hampshire, set up tents and then spend the afternoon hiking on trails. If we were close to the Berkshires, we would go to listen to the Boston Pops under starlight. Many times, we would lie on blankets and listen to the beautiful music coming from the music shell. We never had money to buy a seat inside the shell.

During my bachelor days in the early 1960s, the most challenging hike I did was one up Mount Marcy, the highest mountain in New York State. Powen Huang, who was two years behind me at Yale, led the hike. Po eventually became a banker and also lived in Hong Kong for many years.

The hike up the mountain was quite difficult. It was hot at ground level but we brought ski clothing with us because we knew it would be freezing at the top. Halfway up the mountain, we found a place to set up tents. After feasting on barbecue, we made a big fire and sang campfire songs. During the night, we heard scratching sounds outside and wondered if bears were rummaging through our campsite.

The next morning, we packed up and set out for the top. I still remember crossing some streams and the climb becoming difficult and strenuous. We made it by noon and all of us were blown away by the grand vista around us. The weather was perfect, sunny, cold, and calm. We didn't stay long because the hike down the slope promised to be even more difficult than the ascent. By the time we got to the bottom, it was after 5 p.m. and we were all exhausted. My bones ached for the next few days, but the wonderful time we had together, meeting the challenges, made it all worthwhile. My hiking career came to an abrupt stop when I moved to Pennsylvania to start my business. Marriage, family, and a series of career moves outside of the United States followed quickly. When the dust eventually settled in 1984, I found myself in Hong Kong, heading a regional bank and starting the Yale Club of Hong Kong with a couple of other Yale graduates. The first president of the club was none other than Powen Huang.

Po and I decided to make hiking a regular feature of the club's activities. One very early group member was Bob Bonds. He was instrumental in holding the club together until 2004 when he moved to Germany. For his contribution to the club's well-being, Bob was awarded the Yale Medal, the highest honor Yale bestows on its alumni.

EAST TO WEST TO EAST

Since 2000, I have completed two very challenging hikes.

On January 15, 2000, I joined Pat Caviness and other members of the Yale Club to climb the Sharp Peak in Sai Kung. I had a hiking stick with me and used it extensively. The hike was the toughest I had ever done. The ascent and descent took five hours. It was dangerous, too, as the trail was less than 12 inches wide at times and, at other times, there was no trail at all. We had to hug the mountain to avoid slipping down into the abyss. The final climb up the hill had no path and we scrambled on our hands and knees around boulders and rocks. The peak was only large enough to accommodate the 25 of us. Coming down, our leader lost his way and we walked in a dense jungle of trees without a visible path for hours. We wound up on a beautiful and peaceful beach. But then, we realized we were still one-and-a-half hours from the bus stop and had to climb two hills to get there. That news didn't sit well with me, as I was already pretty tired. The place was so remote that cell phones didn't work. As we made our way to the end, I was far behind everyone. Trying to bring up the rear, I was not helped by the fact that there was no light on the trail. Somehow, I found enough strength to finish the hike and joined the others for a well-deserved dinner.

The most recent hike I made was when I joined Ming Lee's yoga retreat in the Kingdom of Bhutan in February 2007. One bright day, after an early yoga session, the group took a bus and reached the base station to climb to the Taktsang (Tiger's Nest) Monastery, over 1,000 meters up, situated on top of a sheer cliff. At the top, the monastery is about 3,000 meters above the Paro Valley. According to legend, Guru Rinpoche was said to have flown on a tiger to the cave one thousand years ago to bring the Buddhist Dharma from Tibet to Bhutan. He meditated there for many years, giving his blessings for peace to the world below.

The hike up took me three hours. The trail was well-marked but the ascent was relentless. After about two hours, I felt increasingly tired. To keep going, I focused on breathing and taking one step at a time. The guide kept my spirits up. When I reached the monastery, there were snow patches on the ground. It was quite cold and windy.

We were told that the wooden monastery was burned down in 1982. The structure standing in front of us was the restored version. I was truly bone tired but still walked upstairs to see the sacred room. My feet were freezing by then, but I had to take off my shoes. Soon, everyone appeared from downstairs. Ming Lee decided to have a meditation session. A monk took out rugs and spread them on the floor by the back of the room. We sat there for at least 15 minutes. It was a good time for me to rest, but my head was pounding, either because I was tired or because of altitude sickness.

We then left the monastery and walked down to the bridge connecting one side of the cliff to the other side of the mountain. After crossing, we had to walk up the slope before descending again. Along the way, I saw a family picnicking in a corner of a ledge. I think the kids were laughing at how tired I looked. Eventually, I reached the top of the other side of the mountain. I thought going down would hurt my knees, but it didn't. I walked fairly fast. After a simple lunch midway down, I was refreshed and continued downhill without much difficulty. At the end of the day, we felt like we had achieved something good and fulfilling.

I hope to continue hiking in the future, as long as my knees hold up. I'd like to close this section by quoting an excerpt from *A Walk in the Woods* by Bill Bryson:

> *There comes a moment when I look up and notice the amazing complex delicacy of the woods, the casual ease with which elemental things come together to form a composition that is – whatever the season, wherever I put my besotted gaze – perfect. Not just very fine or splendid, but perfect, unimprovable.*

I would change Bryson's next statement to a context more appropriate to my situation:

You don't have to walk miles up mountains to achieve this, climb steps upon steps on steep slopes burdened by bottles of water and other paraphernalia, slip sputtering in mud, be drenched in sweat or bitten by mosquitoes on trails covered by foliage, push yourself hour after hour to the edge of your limits – but, believe me, it helps.

Yoga

To keep in shape, I used to work out in the fitness center in the American Club. I had a routine that included lifting some weights, working on the NordicTrack for 20 minutes, running on the treadmill for about 10 minutes, and toning my knee and leg muscles. Since I turned 70, the routine somehow was reduced to twice a week instead of three times a week.

To supplement my workout, I took up Iyenga yoga. In 1998, during the tail end of the Asian financial crisis, I wanted to find an exercise that would calm down my anxiety as markets kept losing altitude. I was diagnosed with high blood pressure – the result of the high level of stress I had to deal with every day. Exercising, tennis, and hiking were not exactly the remedy for reducing stress.

By chance, Pat Caviness, my tennis partner and long-time friend, was working for a firm whose senior partner's wife was a yoga teacher. Kathy Cook became my yoga instructor. She is a patient and caring teacher and she teaches in a location convenient for me. Once a week, as long as I am in Hong Kong, I go to practice in her class. I have been her student for over eight years now.

Although yoga gurus around the world are usually male, I have noticed most yoga practitioners are of the opposite gender. I rarely meet people of my age in yoga class. Most practitioners are in their mid-30s to late-40s. It is unfortunate older people are not attracted to yoga. I believe yoga is particularly helpful when your bones become brittle and the muscles less supple. By stretching and twisting body parts in ways not common in a person's regular routine, yoga helps to prevent your physical body from going into atrophy. Its practice of breathing through discomfort and cultivating the ability to stay in the pose has one important benefit. You learn to endure discomfort at the edge of pain and discover, after a few moments, that such pain passes. Recognizing this, you are less likely to panic or go into distress in moments of difficulties.

Over the years, my yoga skill level has not improved much. Because my bone structure is pretty stiff, partly due to age, I cannot keep up with several basic exercises. Although I do not consider myself a beginner, I have not progressed much beyond that level. This does not discourage me at all as I am not in the class to compete with anyone. More importantly, I feel refreshed after each class. I should add that yoga offers, beyond the physical benefits, a way for the practitioner to achieve harmony between his mind, body and spirit.

Beyond the regular weekly routine, I have participated in Ming Lee's annual yoga retreats in several exotic locations. In 2005, her yoga students met in Hua Hin in Thailand. In 2006, Ming took us to Zhongdian, Yunnan, considered to be China's Shangri-La. Zhongdian is located on a plateau near Tibet at an altitude of around 12,000 feet.

In 2007, Ming led her students to Bhutan where we scaled the heights to reach the world famous Taktsang Monastery perched on a mountain cliff about 3,000 meters above sea level. During each of these retreats, we practiced yoga for one-and-a-half hours in the morning and again in the evening. In between, Ming would organize trips to see famous sights. At the end of such trips, I feel invigorated – as if I were almost 30 years younger! But, alas, this feeling only lasts a few days.

Reading

I have been an avid reader since an early age. When I was six or seven, my father required that we read the Chinese classics. These included the Confucius Analects and Tang Dynasty poetry. In addition, I read romantic novels Mother bought. I also read Chinese translations of many of the Tarzan books. Other favorites were the famous detective stories of Sherlock Holmes and Watson. I read old Chinese classic novels such as *The Three Kingdoms* and *The Monkey's Journey to the West* while I was in grade school in Shanghai. Later, during junior high and high school years, I had little time for leisure reading as school work was very demanding.

From the time I was a bachelor up to my early 40s, my reading habit was an on-again, off-again, affair. There were simply too many distractions and my evening hours were mostly tied up in entertainment. If there was any spare time at all, chances were I would watch a late-night movie. For better or for worse, my reading picked up when my energy level started sliding. I was in my 50s then. Nowadays, I read every evening for at least 30 minutes before I go to sleep.

In the years before I reached 50, I used to read only novels, mostly based on recommendations by the Book-of-the-Month Club, of which I had been a member for a long time. I have now virtually abandoned reading novels. To me, real life is more exciting, unpredictable, and complicated than a writer's imagination. I know this is not a fair way of looking at novels but, by and large, this statement should be partially correct. I rarely read anything about business and current events.

My main interest lies in books about history, biography, religion, and science. Over the years, I have read many, many fine books. Here, I would like to mention those that have influenced the way I view the world and my place in it:

First, the history books. The book that started my interest in history was Barbara Tuchman's *Stilwell and the China Experience*. It was an account of the U.S. involvement with the Nationalist Party under President Chiang Kai Shek during the Second World War. What astonished me was that Tuchman's account was vastly different from what I had learned from school and my friends. The book was not just outstanding in its scholarship and storytelling but, more importantly, it changed my views about the role of Chiang in the war against the Japanese and the Communists. Since then, I have read almost every book Tuchman has written. They include *The Guns of August*, a first rate account of the events leading to the First World War and *Bible and Sword*, an account of the Crusade that arguably started a history of bloodshed in the land of Palestine.

Another great historian and writer whom I thoroughly enjoy is Jonathan Spence, a professor of history at Yale University. His *The Search for Modern China* is a seminal work on the history of China from the 16th century to 1989. I also enjoyed *God's Chinese Son*, an account of the Tai Ping Revolution between 1850 and 1864.

There are just too many great books for me to comment on, but I wanted to mention some names that have had a strong impact on my development of historical knowledge:

- *The Great Game* by Peter Hopkirk, a compelling story about great powers struggling to control Afghanistan in the early 20th century
- *Balkan Ghosts* by Robert D. Kaplan, an anecdotal account of the Balkan's tragic and bloody history
- *King Leopold's Ghost* by Adam Hochschild, a history of Belgium's colonial occupation of Africa.

- *Parting the Waters* by Taylor Branch, a detailed history of the civil rights struggles in the early 1960s in the United States
- *A World Lit Only by Fire* by William Manchester, a great account of major figures of the 14th century, including Martin Luther and Ferdinand Magellan
- *A Peace to End All Peace* by David Fromkin, a very well-written history of the events leading to the end of the First World War
- *Paris 1919,* by Margaret Macmillan and Richard Holbrooke, another very-well written history of how the big powers carved up the Ottoman Empire after the First World War
- *Let the Sea Make a Noise* by Walter A. McDougall, a delightful history of the development of the territories around the Pacific Ocean
- *The General and his Labyrinth* by Gabriel Garcia Marquez, a fictionalized story of General Bolivar, the liberator of South American, in his dying days
- *A Bright Shining Lie* by Neil Sheehan, a moving and at times gripping and painful story of the Vietnam War tragedy
- *The Empire* by Henry Kamen, a sweeping history of the troubled Spanish empire in the 16th and 17th centuries and its conquest of South America

My second list includes biographies of people who have made a difference in history. Here are some of my favorites:

- *Truman* by David McCullough
- *Churchill* by Martin Gilbert
- *Lincoln* by David Herbert Donald
- *Personal History* by Katharine Graham

- *Benjamin Franklin* by Edmund Morgan
- *Joan of Arc* by Régine Pernoud, Marie-Véronique Clin, and Jeremy duQuesnay Adams
- *Peter the Great*, by Robert Massie

My third list concerns spiritual and scientific reading. Long ago, Plato was the first thinker who proposed that the philosopher could reach a profound understanding of God through the study of Nature, His Creation. I have found this comment to be entirely true in my search to understand what I observe and my inner thoughts.

- *Chaos* by James Gleick, a good explanation of the chaos theory
- *Genome* by Matt Ridley, a fascinating book about the fundamental building blocks of our body
- *Fabric of the Cosmos* by Brian Greene, a well-written account of the latest scientific views about cosmology and the search for a unified theory of physics
- The Bible
- *Elegant Universe* by Brian Greene, a scholarly and at times erudite explanation of the string theory
- *A Short History of Nearly Everything* by Bill Bryson, a sweeping summary of man's knowledge of the physical universe
- *Beyond Belief* by Elaine Pagels, for readers who want to know what is not included in the Christian Bible
- *In Search of Zarathustra* by Paul Kriwaczek

The pleasure and joy of reading is a free gift. Anyone can exercise it. If you watch TV or a film, you have to continuously pay attention to the screen to not miss anything. Your gaze is controlled by the flickering images in front of you. If you turn your head in a different direction, you miss something on the screen. When reading, you are in control. You control the pace of events to unfold, dialogues to proceed and ideas to inform. You can stop at any word and chew on it. You can go back and re-read words that you may have missed. You can read at a fast pace or a slow pace, and there is never any commercial to interrupt the flow of words. More importantly, you are in direct communication with the author. No intermediaries. No actors to interpret what the author had in mind. You form, in your imagination, scenes, images, and ideas the author has put on paper. You are the interpreter. That's all there is to it.

So, every weekend, I wait in excitement to read the next *New York Times Book Review* for another book that I might want to read. Reading the noted book review is a delightful and informative experience. Every so often, I visit Amazon's website to browse. It is incredible that new writers emerge every day with something to say, with another perspective on events long past and on new discoveries and events yet to happen. There are only 26 letters in the English alphabet. And yet, there are infinite ways of combining them so that every book in its way is unique, first born, and not entirely replicable. I will continue to immerse myself in the pleasure of reading, in the hopes my life will thus be made more whole, in knowledge, wisdom, and compassion.

Music

Music is the passion of my life. I have music in my head all the time. In younger days, I could create music by sitting around and concentrating my thoughts. If there were previous lives, I must have had been a musician or a composer in one of my incarnations. I love to listen to music of all kinds, tried to play a few instruments, and have been an aficionado of the latest music reproduction equipment for many years.

When I was a child, our home in Shanghai had a floor-standing RCA radio and record player. This machine gave me the first exposure to music I can remember. Our family only had a few records of popular songs of the time – both American and Chinese. But my brother and I enjoyed listening to them immensely.

My first instrument was a harmonica. The harmonica was very popular with kids then because they could be used as a toy or something more serious. I was twelve when I started to play the accordion. My parents never bothered to introduce me to the piano or violin because they were not very keen on music. Perhaps, our family didn't have sufficient financial resources to invest in an expensive instrument. We did have a teacher for the accordion and we practiced simple classical pieces until we left Shanghai. I wasn't very interested in the sound of the accordion but liked the sound of the harmonica. I became a better player with practice.

While in Shanghai, my brother and I were introduced to a harmonica teacher by the name of Chamber Huang. He was a short young man with an extraordinary gift of playing the harmonica like a violin. He smiled all the time and never seemed to be flustered about anything. He played a number of different harmonicas, including a bass and a chord harmonica. Later, he moved to Hong Kong and then to New York. Playing with him inspired me greatly as I tried in vain to match his versatility.

Huang later developed a harmonica and had it made in China. Until then, Hohner, a German company, made almost all harmonicas. In addition to teaching, he became a classical harmonica player. I believe a concerto was written for him. Huang is one of the rare breed of musicians who was ever energetic in promoting his craft and experimenting with new sound. Harmonica has a distinct sound, which is often not appreciated by music listeners. It has a limited range as well. Like the oboe, it has a clear and haunting sound, but it is not easy to extract a great tone from the metal reeds. When we studied in Hong Kong, my brother and I were invited to perform harmonica duets in sports events attended by large crowds as well as to the programs featuring young musical talents hosted by one of Hong Kong's radio stations, Rediffusion. By then, we could play simple classical pieces that were about 5 minutes long. Our repertoire included waltzes by Strauss, marches by Souza, and others.

Meanwhile, the technology of recorded music made a number of advances beyond the shellac record. First, music could be played on a metal string roll. The sound was not much better than the one from shellac material but it was more portable. The far greater improvements came from the 5-inch diameter 45-rpm record and the twelve-inch diameter long playing (LP) record, both made out of vinyl. The 45-rpm would be used as a medium for popular music and the LP for classical pieces. I believe these new media came to the market in around 1950. The LP was mainly responsible for making classical music popular around the world.

In Hong Kong during the 1950s, an LP record was very expensive and so was the player. I could not afford them. So, I often went to a friend's home to listen. I was introduced to Beethoven, Tchaikovsky, Mozart, and other great classical composers. I was hooked. Nearly every Saturday afternoon, I would go to this friend's house, play basketball and listen to music. My parents, at the same time, bought records by Doris Day, Perry Como, and other popular American singers from the 1950s. I also listened to the music of Benny Goodman and Glenn Miller and became interested in jazz from the 1930s and the New Orleans sound.

After I entered St. John's Preparatory School in Danvers, Massachusetts, I found a piano in the music room and became intensely interested in learning how to play it. I would spend afternoons reading simple scores, trying to play the instrument without a teacher or even a guide. Hanging out in the music room gave me an opportunity to meet the kids playing in a dance band. There was one piano player, one drummer, one trumpet player, and one bass player. When I heard them play, I thought I could make them sound better. So, I decided to do some orchestration work. I learned simple techniques by reading a few books on orchestration. I am fortunate to have perfect pitch and an intuitive feel for harmonic progressions. Having listened to so much music, I found this was something I didn't have to be taught.

In addition to helping out on orchestration at St. John, I became a substitute drummer. I was also a featured harmonica soloist. I continued to see Huang, who became my mentor. At one time, I could play a Vivaldi violin concerto on the harmonica. Huang made a living as a teacher and a professional player in nightclubs and summer resorts. In his home, he had the latest professional tape recorder by Ampex and the best available sound reproduction system and speakers. It was sheer joy for me to be in his home in Riverdale, New York, and listen to music. He persuaded Tom and me to form a trio, with Tom on the bass harmonica and me on the chord harmonica. I practiced seriously in the summer of 1950 and was ready to be booked for an act by his agent. Unfortunately, we were never invited.

During my years at Yale, my taste for classical music blossomed. Being an usher at Woolsey Hall was definitely a catalyst. Also, my financial situation improved somewhat and I could afford to buy one LP every month. I found that I enjoyed music of all eras, from Bach to Stravinsky. I also became interested in American jazz. In my graduate school years, I became fascinated by folk music, not just American, but also from other parts of the world.

Working at the Yale Audio Center made it possible for me to work with professional audio equipment and appreciate sound quality at the highest level attainable. Stereophonic music came into existence in the mid 1950s. Reproduction of sound from two speakers brought realism to a new level of enjoyment. It was a heady time for the audio equipment industry as new startups abounded. There were two companies that sold equipment parts with instructions for assembly. One was named Heathkit. The equipment was of high quality but sold at a fraction of the cost of assembled brand names. My brother and I would order preamps and amplifiers from Heathkit, and spend hours assembling them. We got to be very good at it. Studying electrical engineering at the time also helped to make the assembly job easier.

In the 1960s, I began playing the folk guitar and the banjo. There was a time when I also had a 12-string guitar, the instrument of choice for Leadbelly, (Huddie Ledbetter) the famous black singer who wrote and sang some of the best songs in his time. I played and sang at parties, emulating Pete Seeger. I sang with my brother Tom and his wife Amy, at parties and, particularly, on ski trips with friends. By that time, I no longer played the harmonica. I stopped playing the guitar after I got married in 1972. I didn't start again until much later in 2001, when I bought a new guitar and tried to play classical pieces. I soon gave it up, as I could not get the sound I wanted.

As the 1970s rolled along, my nomadic lifestyle took shape. Still, I lugged the latest preamp and amp and record player, as well as my collection of tapes and records, from country to country. As my kids grew up, they were immersed in classical music of every sort. The interesting thing is that neither of them developed any interest in classical music after they grew up. Their musical taste hugged the contour of the latest hard rock and its many manifestations until today.

While living in Scarsdale in 1978–1979, Kathy and I took piano lessons. My approach to piano playing was somewhat unorthodox. Because I already read music scores with ease and had a basic understanding of the piano, I started playing slow, short pieces by some of my favorite composers such as Chopin, Schubert, and Mozart. I was extremely fond of playing the piano and seemed to have a flair for it, at least up to a certain level of competence. For example, I was able to play a few of Schubert's Impromptus and Chopin's Nocturnes. I continued playing piano until 1987, after which circumstances would not allow me to continue.

The final element in my love for music is an obsession for the perfect sound. Even when I was financially strapped as a college student, I would save every dollar I could to buy the best available equipment. I would spend hours comparing performance data on competing brands and visiting showrooms and trade fairs to make a hearing test. My knowledge was acquired happily when I worked part-time in the Yale Audio Center and in summer jobs at Electro Voice and Fairchild Audio Equipment Co. One benefit from my intensive research is I kept equipment I bought in use for a long time – well over 10 years. My most prized unit was a preamp by Apt Holman Inc. that I bought at least 25 years ago and used for some 20 years.

Sound systems have evolved and improved greatly over the years. The challenge has always been to reproduce sound as in a concert stage or in a jazz club with realism in all its multidimensional facets. Dolby was one technique that proved commercially successful. I used to play Dolby-encoded LPs. I have used a number of innovative speakers including the Ohm speakers. I have also used surround sound systems to emulate more realistic acoustic quality from five speakers with two on the side.

When CDs came along in the 1980s, the digital era unfolded. Digital sound was superior to analog in many ways. However, some purists would argue that it was not as realistic as that produced in the old analog way. Since MP3 and iPod arrived a few years ago, data compression moved to a higher level technologically. Still, most music is produced over two channels. With the left and the right speakers only, the sound has a hole in the middle, unless recording balance happens to be perfect. This is achieved only rarely. In the past few years, recording technology had taken another step forward, with the availability of DVD Audio and SACD formats. More importantly, leveraging on the new home theater systems with 5.1 channels, sound more akin to live performance has become possible. There is now a third speaker in the middle. Nevertheless, anyone who goes to a live concert knows that replication of live music in the home is always a second choice.

My love for music has sustained me for most of my life. Its sounds have a way of resonating in the deepest reaches of my psyche. I still hear music in my head but I have never put the notes down on paper. I do not go to concerts as much as I used to, five to 10 years ago. I no longer acquire the latest audio equipment. Worse, it is now hard for me to discover new music and learn to appreciate it. Music that I have enjoyed since my college days gives me comfort, like old friends. I return to it constantly but realize I need to show more interest in new sounds and new selections.

Of all the pieces of music that I have known, there is one particular piece that I would enjoy at my funeral. It is the second movement of Brahms' *A German Requiem*:

> *All flesh is like grass,*
> *And men's glories are like flowers of the grass.*
> *Grass will wither and flowers will fade away.*

20

Reflections

My journey on this planet Earth has surely been a long one – surpassing "three score and ten," the age that people in the olden days believed to be the span of a lifetime. In many ways, my mind has retained the same sense of curiosity as that of a teenager, eager to explore. I am ready to better understand everything happening around me, meet new people, and explore new ways of doing things. I get up every morning with a positive attitude. I look forward to what I need to accomplish and to the meetings scheduled for the day and/or making plans for my next trips. However, in managing our investment portfolios, I am always on guard for adversities, which could come from any direction – whether they are from company announcements, big sell-offs in the United States, or unexpected notice from regulators. While the only thing that is certain in life is uncertainties, I don't let these potential troubles bother me.

When I get together with old friends from the States, all of whom having retired, I am often asked when I will join the retirement ranks. My answer, as always, is that I won't, unless my health prevents me from working. I do not think I am a driven person. I simply enjoy my work. I have been blessed with good health and a positive outlook and these gifts should not be wasted in leisure and self-serving activities. Although my current work may not make the world better, I am spending what available time I have to do what I can to help the less fortunate or to give my time to help young people to better their opportunities in life. So, I continue soldiering on, in good spirits.

I read with great interest an article in *The New York Times* dated January 24, 2005, by William Safire, who was quitting his job after writing polemics for some 30 years. At the age of 75, he thought it was high time for him to change his line of work. Safire wrote: "When you're through changing, you are through." His words reminded me that my life has been blessed by another factor – that I have had three careers in the past 44 years: information technology, banking, and then investments. Each brought new challenges and different rewards. According to Safire, not quitting but continuing to try something new is a winning longevity strategy.

Looking back on my own life and that of my parents, it is clear that our chronicles have been swept up in the great social transformation in China and the United States. On that fateful day when my father took the sedan ride from Kaixian to Beijing in the late Qing Dynasty, he had broken from his family's roots and sought a new way of life. He was one of the first batches of Chinese students to study in the States and, in his own way, responded to new opportunities that were not available to most in China. Since then, our family has met challenges and taken opportunities that came with the times.

Father was part of a growing wave of the Chinese diaspora, which had developed in a historically unique way. With his U.S. education, he saw the good side of capitalism and rejected Communism, the two paths being sought by many common people in his youth, struggling to rid their country of colonial suppression. After China fell to Communists, father migrated to the States, not simply for economic reasons, but because of his lifelong belief in freedom and liberty for individuals.

In my generation, many Asian students who studied in the States returned to their own countries. Some became leaders in politics, business, and science. To many, their experience in the

States had been positive and they would form a group of core supporters of U.S. policies in the years that followed.

Since the mid 1980s, China began to move toward the capitalist model in its economic management. Gradually, foreign investments poured into the country. Most of the capital initially came from the Chinese communities in Taiwan, Hong Kong, and the rest of Asia. This was a natural process as Chinese living abroad had good connections in China and felt more at home than Westerners in doing business in uncharted situations. This influx of capital as well as technical and management skills from overseas Chinese greatly facilitated the rapid economic progress that we have witnessed in China over the past decade.

The overseas Chinese investors took great risks at an early stage, lost great amounts of money, but persisted. Someday, when historians look back at the development of emerging economies, they will find the Chinese diaspora as the principal contributing factor in enabling China to develop more quickly than other developing countries that did not have the same overseas support. We are justifiably proud to see that China has been accepted as a major nation in the world of nations.

Today, we enjoy unprecedented material well-being, supported by rapid advances in physics, medicine, biotechnology, and so on. GDP per capita has been steadily rising. Productivity gains and advances in science have given more people in the world better living standards than at any time in the history of mankind. However, on the liability side of the ledger, the world is facing the threat of nuclear destruction, unsustainable levels of pollution and environmental degradation, and an ever-growing divide between the rich and the poor. Will the positive trends outpace the negative ones in the years ahead?

The heightened political risks we face today may be attributable partly to the rise of U.S hegemony and partly to the consequences of the policies of colonial powers in the past two centuries. Like other superpowers in history, the United States today is expanding its economic interests by proselytizing a rhetorical set of beliefs that transcend its real hard line interests. The rhetorical beliefs are represented by the twin ideologues of democracy and private enterprise (free markets) that promise to bring peace and prosperity to the world. As the superpower in the world, the United States cannot help but embark on this path of imperialism. The opportunity cost of not doing it, that is, the cost of not having its economic interests expand around the world, is not going to be acceptable to its own people. Nothing can stand still – it will eithr grow or retreat. This historical force, of course, is sowing its own seed of implosion, like every superpower in the history of mankind.

Force begets force. This is Newtonian logic. Today, U.S. imperialism is meeting resistance from Muslims in the Middle East. If you ask any Arab, he will tell you that the so-called terrorism of today reflects an increasingly radical view of people who want to rid their world of Western influence. These people had been dominated by the colonial powers of Britain, France, and Russia and now by the United States, which seized Iraq and Afghanistan in 2003. To them, the U.S. prime interest is about oil and short-term economic gain. It should come as no surprise that the preaching of democracy by the United States rings hollow and definitely sounds hypocritical.

I don't see any solution to this conflict because the United States will not give up and go away from the Middle East, and the Arabic people are too divided to respond effectively to the U.S. power play. I don't believe the United States will trust Muslims and genuinely listen to their hopes and grievances. As the United States is mired down in its interest to preserve vital oil supplies from that region, a third force, China, is increasingly exerting its economic and political influence. China, in the next 10 years, will become important in the global political scene but will be even more of a factor in the Asian region. With its economic power, China will lift Asia to such a level it will become the dominant force to strategically challenge the U.S. position in the world.

What will likely hasten the United States' decline in global dominance is its over-reliance on foreign treasuries to fund its fiscal and trade deficits. The country is spending beyond its means, whether it is the federal or the local governments or the consumers and financial institutions. While Asia saves, the United States spends. Thus far, Asian countries, particularly Japan and China, have largely financed the U.S. deficits. How all this imbalance will be unwound is difficult to foretell. Like the Spanish Empire, the Roman Empire, and the British Empire in history, the United States will find itself financially exhausted and its people disillusioned and weakened by their intense focus on short-term rewards and attempts to hang onto their current lofty status.

Are we leaving a better world to the next generation? While the potential negatives are all known by experts, the potential positives are left mostly to one's confidence and optimism. Fortunately, mankind has managed to survive through much devastations in history without going backwards in terms of measurable parameters such as forms of government, material gains, and size of population and the like. It doesn't take much imagination to suggest that more of the same will follow today's human condition.

By now, I have seen over half a century's worth of political events and wars among nation states. I have seen terrible things happen to people under both authoritarian and democratic governments. So what is an ideal political system?

I believe the question of an ideal political system is no more obvious today than 2,500 years ago when the Greek philosophers were debating this issue. How does a group of people determine an ideal leader to lead them? I am not sure, but there is room to explore a system that has characteristics somewhere between one-man rule and rule by the people.

China, as it evolves from a totalitarian state into a system that gives increasing voice to its people, is developing its own model. It may not turn into a parliamentary democracy like that in the United Kingdom, or a presidential democracy in American style. Nevertheless, the ongoing experimentation is a very interesting and significant one for the future of societies. Thus far, China has managed to put enlightened and responsible people at the highest level of government even though the selection process is undemocratic. The success of its political system has been underappreciated by most, because outside opinions have been colored by China's continuing use of the label "communist," which is completely meaningless as an ideology in practice.

Having observed the capitalist system at work for many years, I have developed some reservations about the way it is practiced and promoted today. In too many instances, the relentless drive for short-term private gain has caused great harm to most people in the society. In the United States, I have witnessed the savings bank scandal of the 1980s, the junk bond craze of the early 1990s, the Internet bubble at the turn of the new century, and, most recently, the subprime mortgage crisis, which has wrought untold damages to the nation's financial institutions. These so-called market adjustments, or creative destruction, have wreaked havoc on people's lives.

In the case of the Enron scandal, thousands of the company's employees saw their entire savings wiped out. Today's highly leveraged world is a direct result of unfettered use of liquidity to make money for the benefit of a few. When the house of cards falls, the perpetrators will have already made their fortune, but the pieces will surely be put together on the back of taxpayer money.

I do not have any solution to the ills we face. However, I do think it is high time we listen to people and scholars who are critical of the kind of capitalist system that is being touted by the United States. We need to be cautious in forming our own opinions and not be led by unchallenged mainstream views. It will be useful to debate how to balance private versus public interest to create a new economic system. We need to rein in unfettered greed and unregulated financial markets, which have demonstrated time and again that they serve society poorly in the long term.

When I reached 60 years of age, something inside me started to stir up an interest in metaphysics. I suppose I was like many people of that age, perceiving mortality as a distinct threat and thinking about its implications. I started asking questions. What will happen to me after death? What does religion tell us about how to deal with death? Why are we, human beings, on earth? Who created the universe in which we live? When was the beginning of time and space or was there a beginning? What is the overall scheme of things in this great universe and how do human beings fit into it?

These questions led me to explore, for the first time, spiritual learning, which was almost completely absent in my studies in my younger days. Since then, I have read many books and found many people searching for answers to the same kinds of questions. I found, for one thing, that there is something common between science and metaphysics. Both deal with the unknown and both are seeking answers to questions that have engaged thinkers throughout the ages.

In my search for answers, I have found empathy with Buddhism. It has given me the most comfort and grounding in my spiritual beliefs. I agree with Buddha that each of us has to find his own answer to his own set of questions. I am, like many others, traveling on a path, seeking Truth and Enlightenment. I have read books on Buddhism, the entire Bible, some sections a couple of times. I have also read works on Islam and Judaism. I have gone to church services, attended Buddhist rituals, and participated in meditation retreats, all to experience what believers find essential in furthering their goals of spiritual awakening.

Here is where I stand on my spiritual path:

There is a good chance that just as there is a beginning and an end to life, there is no beginning and no end to a non-life. Similarly, there is likely a non-physical world as well as a physical world. There is a good chance though my body is finite in time, my spirit is not. I come to this understanding by looking at the world and seeing the contrast in everything. Good versus bad; thin versus fat; light versus. darkness; black versus white, etc. It appears that a balance in nature is struck in having opposites in everything. It would be quite out of character if there were no contrast to the very thing called "life." Similarly, if there is a physical world or universe, then there must be a non-physical world or a non-universe.

To understand death, one has to understand birth. The most important observation is that birth is a miracle. To make a human is an incredible feat. This is true with every living organism. Is there a reasonable chance that birth is actually a process that involves a higher level of abilities that is, as an act, a "superhuman" undertaking? If so, is this not an example of how human beings have "superhuman" traits not even we know about?

One question is whether we come from the womb of our mothers or whether the mother's womb is an instrument with which we achieve birth. If we are only made in the womb, then there is nothing before birth. If that is the case, there is surely nothing after death. Life is just a chance phenomenon. If one thinks about this deeply, it becomes difficult to accept that such is the order of the cosmos that living beings just come and go and nothing is left afterwards.

I learned that each person has a pair of genomes, one from his father, and one from his mother. This is the stuff of immortality. My genome is with Kathy and Clarence. When I die, the roadmap of me is with them and they will give it to their children, if any. Perhaps, this means that, physically, one can achieve immortality. When my body dies and my cells die, I have already left the essential elements to my offspring.

Cosmology has opened my eyes to things like multi-dimensionalism, quantum jitters, non-locality and the three-bane world. Another interesting idea is parallel universes may exist around us. Thus far, no one has been able to go back to the origin of time and theorize what happened at the very beginning, the fuzzy part of the early expansion. It may be that time and space are made of components we don't know anything about. The fact that 90 percent of the entire universe is made of elements physically not measurable is a sobering one.

If the cosmos has been around for 17 billion years and this planet Earth has been in existence for only a few billion years, it raises the question of what God had in mind when He first created this physical phenomenon. If all the beautiful things of this world weren't included in the early days of Creation, what was Creation designed for?

One should look at death as an adventure. If pain is part of the process, then one has to pay that price for the adventure. If one is traveling down the path in the right way, then one should be pretty relaxed about death. I don't know whether there is life after death or no life after death; whether I will be reborn as another me or as someone totally different. Simply, one will never know what goes on in the non-physical world. The only way I will find out is to exit this world when I die.

If, at death, as books have suggested, one feels peace and sees a bright light, then I have already experienced it. When I was anesthetized for my retina detachment operation in 1964 in New York, I remembered the sensation of floating in space toward a very bright light. I was very happy and I saw mountains and streams as I drifted upward. I didn't want to "come back" even though I knew I had to. This sensation is common among people who have had near-death experiences.

I believe that we will never know the ultimate truth. We are just not given the gift of discovering it. Nevertheless, we need to keep searching, if for no other reason than the thought that abandoning this quest is unthinkable. Looking at the universe around us, whether we are contemplating the vastness and the mystery of the cosmos or observing the growth of a cell, whether we are holding a newborn baby or a flower petal in our hands, it is almost impossible not to admit that there is a Creator, a force or being so great and unfathomable that is involved in what is happening, in this tiny corner of the vast cosmos.

I disagree with T. H. Huxley who said in the 19th century that one should follow reason as far as it will take you and not to accept conclusions that are not demonstrable. In my mind, one has to go beyond the limitations of fact-based knowledge. Otherwise, one's spiritual path would surely come to a dead end.

At this moment, I believe I have gained a degree of insight – that I have reached a point where I know the limits of such inquiry. I am now calm and accept the fact that some answers are beyond my abilities to grasp. While I will continue to search, I am no longer doing so in an agitated state.

Nowadays, people who meet me for the first time often remark that I look a lot younger than my age. I know this is a compliment and I have come to enjoy it. Some ask me how I do it, especially since I keep a pretty heavy workload on a daily basis and my business is known to be in a high-pressure industry.

I don't have a good answer to this question. Perhaps, my biological clock is simply retarded. More likely, I am just simply lucky as I have inherited good genes from my parents. Both lived to a ripe old age.

Beyond my inherited piece of good luck, I have followed certain principles. I believe they have helped me remain balanced in my life's journey. The following comments could be construed as my golden rules.

First, I believe it is absolutely necessary one is happy and content with one's state of affairs. I am blessed that I seem to have an innate ability to stay positive in moments of pressure and anxiety, and an ability to find "joy" and "gratification" from an inner depth in everyday life's observations and engagements. I am also particularly sensitive to the "present moment." That said, without a long-term vision, a person will surely stumble in the short term. Another aspect about being content is seeking balance in everything that touches you. If there is any bad thing, then think about the good thing that comes with the bad. Everything on earth is balanced with positive and negative energies.

Second, one needs to have a positive attitude about oneself. This sense of positivism includes a heavy dosage of self-confidence. If you have it, then anything is possible in this world. Pursue your aspirations. At the same time, keep in mind life's journey is a tough road. Unless you are very lucky and extremely bright, pursuing one's aspiration does not necessarily lead to material success. It may not lead to success on your own terms. Still, I think a life dedicated to doing something you like is better than one spent on compromising.

There is another insight I wish to share. Each one of us is made of unique stuff. Some have a knack for making money. Others do not. In the end, there is no difference. The wealthiest person will tell you that money does not buy true happiness. As long as what you want to do does not lead to abject poverty, I think your goals should not be focused largely on making money or getting the next promotion. If you are good at something, somebody will pay you for your services.

Third, it is imperative to "know thyself." Be honest about your character and ability and take responsibility for your thoughts and actions. Life requires a fine balance between striving and accepting. It is okay for you to excel in what you like to do, but it is not okay to do so to the point of destroying balance. All too often we do not see things objectively, being consumed with self-righteousness or a mistaken sense of self-interest. Each of us needs to have a sense of fulfillment, but it cannot come from seeking external rewards; it can only come from within. There are two Confucian dialects I am reminded of:

> *A gentleman avoids four faults: being careless in considering issues; being inflexible; being dogmatic and being self-centered.*
>
> *A gentleman looks to himself for wants; a person of poor character looks to others for wants.*

Fourth, one should never be lazy or aimless in life. It is best if one can find some activity one feels deeply passionate about. Even at my age, he should be actively engaged. It is not necessary for you to be working in business, but it is important to be engaged in a craft or a profession that demands your mental energies and challenges your ability to think. It must have certain deadlines so you do not wake up in the morning and wonder what to do the whole day. Idleness breeds a lot of distractions that are usually not in the best interest of the victim. Indeed, I hold a strong belief that one should never truly retire. As life expectancy has been rising in recent years, the body and the brain need to march together with a common purpose. Extending the life of the body means little if the life of the mind is neglected.

Fifth, it is vital to stay healthy. This means one should be careful in diet and engage in regular exercise or sports. My mother, like every other mother, often nagged me about my poor eating habits in my youth - too much meat, ice cream, chocolate, cakes, candies, and potato chips, not enough vegetables and fruits. Now that my cholesterol level is high, I realize that there is a natural quota for consuming unhealthy food in one's lifetime. Mine was met some years ago. For the past ten years or so, I have been a vegetarian, consuming mostly vegetables and fruit with a smattering of fish and chicken. I play tennis, work out in a gym, hike, ski, and practice yoga. All of these activities, I believe, make my body flexible, supple, and strong. They may be contributing to delaying my aging process.

Sixth, it is highly desirable to be grounded in a spiritual belief. This is because we are spiritual animals. Each of us carries his or her own spiritual seeds. Each person has to find his/hers. If going to church or belonging to a religious organization helps, then by all means, this is the right thing to do. However, if you are like me, more of an individualist, you will find yourself trying to find your own answers. If you take time, such as in meditation, and let your inner thoughts come through, you will be on your way. To have a spiritual grounding gives you greater awareness of all the wonders of the world and a sense of emotional peace you won't find in other pursuits.

Seventh, we human beings generally have a deep-seated need for an "anchor," or "roots." We have a basic need for order, which means regularity in some important aspects of our lives. In this respect, it is important to have a partner in life and a close circle of true friends. Along that same idea, I think it helpful to be organized at work. I have found it helpful I manage my daily routines pretty much in the same way, no matter what assignments I am working on or what continents I am in. Being anchored and organized are important elements that help maximize one's potential in life.

Eighth, don't take yourself too seriously. I certainly don't. Even as I greatly enjoy my work today, I know I can chuck it all and do something totally different. I am also profoundly aware that fortune can turn the other cheek at any time and one should be emotionally and psychologically prepared for just such an occurrence.

By now, I have been picking stocks, managing market volatility, living on the right side of securities regulations and seeking investors for over a dozen years. Along the way, I have learned something about the business of fund management and, in particular, have found my own style or approach to investing.

My investment approach has been greatly influenced by Benjamin Graham, who wrote a book called Security Analysis with David Dodd in 1934. Luckily for me, I studied under Professor Dodd during my years in the MBA program at the Columbia Graduate School of Business. The book was the first attempt to treat buying stock as an investment rather than short-term speculation. According to Graham, the stock market, in the long run, would value stocks in relation to their earnings prospects, balance sheet structure, management, and other fundamental factors.

A stock, whether it is a high-tech company or a retailer or a petrochemical plant, has its own intrinsic value – the present value of its future expected stream of cash flow. In the long run, the price of the stock reflects this economic value, although in the short run, its price could deviate substantially from it due to market psychology. I have used the Graham investment principle as my core approach to stock picking and investing. Having now been in the business for over a decade, I am confident that this is the only sensible way of investing in stocks.

Putting this very simple approach into practice has not been easy. Markets in Asia have been notoriously volatile. There are several factors, I believe, that contribute to the market volatility. Daily trading in Asian markets is often dominated by foreign investors who enter or exit because of exchange rate movements, short-term market strategies, and other reasons that have nothing to do with a company's fundamentals. The rise of hedge funds has added a large dose of volatility because they try to make money on short trades for a very small amount of gains over very large volumes. Today, investors have made more financial commitments to the stock market but trust it less.

Fund managers and analysts are paid to seek out companies that create shareholder value in the long term. Instead, many fund managers are concerned mostly with whether a company will make its next quarterly earnings estimates. They tend to be trading oriented, buying and selling stocks of companies based on market rumors and short-term swings of business conditions. There is no doubt that this short-term bias has played a large part in rewarding corporate executives for short-term performance. The irony, of course, is that true shareholder values are not created overnight; they can only be created over years. Since Asian markets are relatively small compared with developed markets in the West, such trading strategies have made a huge impact on trading volume and volatility.

Because Asian economies are highly dependent on external trades with the United States, its stock markets have a high correlation with U.S. stock markets. I have noticed that in times of high U.S. market volatility, the correlation ratio becomes very high. The reverse is also true, however. The good news is that Asian markets are beginning to decouple from the U.S. market. The decoupling with reduced volatility will accelerate as Asia continues to develop its financial markets in size and depth, resulting from new securities offerings, more market participants of all types, and greater sophistication.

The way to get alpha or out-performance in Asian markets is to seek out high-growth companies that have attained high return-on-equity, earnings growth, and attractive profitability, and those that have strong balance sheets. Asia, fortunately, is full of companies that meet these criteria, thanks to the abundance of entrepreneurship in the region.

We are primarily "bottom-up" stock pickers. We strongly believe in doing primary research, but we also use brokers' research extensively. Our ideas come from many sources. We go to regional conferences several times a year and our team typically visits more than 300 companies in a year. We have an extensive network of contacts, in and out of the fund management industry, that often give us ideas to pursue. Finally, we use our own scanning tool to flush out companies that meet our quantitative criteria.

Making an investment decision with informed judgment is far different from making one without a systematic process or on the basis of so-called "market feel." In our firm, decisions are typically driven by a combination of quantitative analysis and judgment about the company's management capabilities gained from company and factory visits. We try to take emotional elements out of the decision-making process and consider each holding with total objectivity. This is harder than one would think. It is all too human for an advocate of a company to hold onto his enthusiasm and refuse to waver in the face of bad news.

Investing in the emerging markets of Asia requires an active management style. This is not just because many stocks listed in the exchanges are relatively unseasoned. They are often relatively small and illiquid. One of the most difficult management challenges in our work is to determine when to cut losses. Even as we have a bias for holding a stock through inevitable cycles, we need to make a decision on whether to hold onto a stock during a panic selling spree. Such stomach-churning volatility may arise from any number of factors, such as a general market sell-off, an unfounded market rumor, manipulation by hedge funds, or a change in the fundamentals due to sudden alteration in external factors or an internal management mishap. In most instances, markets move with incredible speed and no one has the time to do an analysis and make a dispassionate decision. Often, a stock can go down 15 percent within minutes. By then, the question becomes a binary one: hold or sell.

By its nature, cut-loss action tends to be controversial. Sometimes, in hindsight, it may be seen as a wise move. Sometimes, such action may be made exactly when the stock had reached bottom and the trade became a victim of market volatility. We are not good market timers but we continue to practice cut-loss actions because we view preservation of capital as the most important strategy in managing an equity portfolio.

All investors will inevitably develop their own style when it comes to finding the right investments for themselves and knowing when to buy and sell. My way of doing things is not for everyone. The fact that it has generated satisfactory performance over the long run is not a guarantee that it will produce the same kind of results in the future. Still, I hope some readers will find what I do useful in forming their own approach to making investments.

Postscript

It has been some eight months since I completed the book that I started writing almost two years ago. From my experience, I learned writing takes discipline, persistence, and concentration. I have enjoyed the work even though there were moments when I thought I would never complete what I set out to do. Now that I have finished my manuscript, I should just find an editor and a publisher to publish it. However, as a number of significant events have been unfolding since the end of 2007, I have decided to add a postscript.

The housing crisis that became major headline news in the middle of July 2007 turned into a gale-force wind sweeping across the globe. Throughout the first half of 2008, major banks kept reporting huge write-downs. The following are a few examples: US$18 billion reported by Citigroup in January and a further US$19 billion in April; US$19 billion by UBS in April; US$5.1 billion by JP Morgan; US$2 billion by Lehman Brothers in June, and US$13 billion by Wachovia in July. Meanwhile, more fundraising was needed for banks to stay afloat: US$9 billion by Merrill Lynch in two attempts, US$5 billion by Citigroup, US$6 billion by JP Morgan, US$7.5 billion by Wachovia, and US$16 billion by UBS.

By mid-2008, publicly listed banks globally had write-downs totaling over US$500 billion and they had raised over US$300 billion in equity capital. In the process, much of the new capital was provided not by Wall Street firms, but by institutions far from the shores of the United States. Let me cite a few examples: In November 2007, Citigroup sold US$7.5 billion of equity-linked notes to the Abu Dhabi Investment Authority, giving them 5 percent of the bank. UBS sold US$11 billion of convertible bonds to GIC of Singapore in December. In the same month, Merrill Lynch sold US$4.4 billion of common stock to Temasek Holdings, a government-owned investment house in Singapore. Then in January 2008, Citicorp raised another US$21 billion from investors including the Kuwait Investment Authority.

In March 2008, Bear Stearns became the first significant market casualty when the Federal Reserve led its sale to JP Morgan for US$2 a share. This was backed by the Federal Reserve Bank, which provided US$30 billion of liquidity in exchange for questionable notes and paper. This instance represented only the tip of the iceberg of the U.S. financial woes yet to come.

Almost US$17 trillion has been lost by equity investors since the peak in October 2007. With such staggering losses, stock prices of banks have fallen to the ground. For example, by August 2008, Citigroup's stock price has plummeted from US$60 per share at its height to just US$9. Wachovia's stock slid from US$60 per share to US$14. Washington Mutual's stock dropped from US$40 to US$3. Even General Motors' stock has been trashed, falling from US$60 to US$4 per share.

Already in September 2007 I had turned cautious and begun to raise cash. By the end of the year, our fund had 16 percent of its assets in cash and hedges. I should note that 2007 marked the 10th anniversary of the onset of the Asian financial crisis, the great economic calamity that brought the Asian markets down 70 percent from mid-1997 to mid-1998. Since then, Asian markets have been in recovery, except for the sharp correction experienced in 2001–2002 (down 57 percent) due to the bursting of the U.S. technology stock market bubble. Our fund, over the past 10 turbulent years, managed to deliver a compounded return of 12 percent per year. This is 37 percent better than its regional benchmark, a record we are justly proud of.

When investors hit the exit doors, they dumped everything in sight. Beginning in January 2008, Asian markets kept going down. I continued raising cash and hedges. By the end of August, the fund had 42 percent of its assets in them. Still, our fund performed poorly even though it beat the benchmark by a pretty wide margin. More importantly, our company's revenue, which is a percentage of assets under management, has been seriously eroded.

In the first quarter of 2008, I continued my discussion with Jiyoung Kim regarding the launch of a new long-short strategy mentioned in an earlier chapter. Fortunately, with the help of Mark Barth, my legal counsel at Akin Gump Strauss Hauer & Feld LLP, Jiyoung signed on in April and was named managing director of my new firm in New York, JKC Advisors LLC. Because I also own 50 percent of JK Capital Management Ltd. in Hong Kong, the two entities are considered affiliates. My idea is to use the Hong Kong–based firm to support the businesses that we hope to generate in the States. With the staffing in place, we proceeded to apply for registration with the Securities and Exchange Commission which was granted in August. More importantly, with the SEC registration, I have high hopes that when market conditions improve, we will grow our assets under management far more effectively than in the past. Whether or not my expectation will be realized is a subject that will be left for another book in the future.

While the global economy has been sliding since the U.S. subprime crisis hit the front page, Kathy, my daughter, has continued to build her handbag business in New York. A most pleasant surprise was her winning the Best Independent Handbag Design Award in New York in June 2007. With the help of her showroom and her appealing design, as well as her participation in several international trade shows in New York and Paris, Kathy began to receive orders from a number of high-end fashion powerhouses such as Nieman Marcus and Nordstrom in the States, and Saks Fifth Avenue in the Middle East. Her merchandise is now carried in many parts of the world.

Even more important than her business success, Kathy decided to marry Teddy Wong, who runs his own fund of funds business in New York. Teddy and I share a number of common traits in life. First, we were both born in the Year of the Pig. Second, we did not pursue careers for which we had studied in college. He has a medical doctor degree while I majored in engineering. Third, we are both in the investment management business. So, Kathy may have picked as her partner someone who might be a younger version of her dad.

The wedding took place in Bali on August 8, 2008 (the day when the Olympic Games opened in Beijing), a very auspicious day for such a happy occasion. Using an old cliché, I was the proudest and the happiest father on earth when I walked her down the aisle on the beach of the Amanusa resort. Almost 200 guests came from around the world to celebrate the wedding with us. Since then, I have received abundant feedback from friends who thought the wedding was an event no one will ever forget.

Not to be outdone by his sister, our son Clarence has moved steadily up the ladder at Time Warner. He is now the executive producer for both People.com and EW.com online magazines. The two magazines are the most popular weekly publications in the United States. In February 2008, Clarence and I went skiing at Lake Tahoe, enjoying the exercise and comradeship, though the trip was a short one.

I am writing this chapter in September 2008 as the U.S. economy appears to be heading into a recession.

Through August 2008, ten U.S. banks were closed by the Federal Deposit Insurance Corporation (FDIC), costing taxpayers hundreds of millions of dollars. Then, in September, the government bailed out Fannie Mae and Freddie Mac, as well as American International Group (AIG), once the world's biggest insurer. The takeover in the form of a conservatorship was aimed to provide a slight degree of stability to the U.S. financial market.

In the same month, Lehman Brothers, the fourth largest investment bank in the United States, was allowed to go under. Another mainstay of Wall Street, Merrill Lynch, was sold to Bank of America in a desperate attempt to keep that institution afloat. Before the month was over, the government made the largest bank seizure in American history by taking over the troubled savings and loan, Washington Mutual, and selling pieces of it to JPMorgan. This series of shocking events led the government to consider an emergency bailout plan of US$700 billion. When it passed in Congress, this rescue package was the largest ever in U.S. history.

This book is not a place for me to expound on the causes and effects of the ongoing credit crisis in any detail. I echo Paul Volcker, former Federal Reserve chairman, who said recently that the "U.S. financial system has broken down." He said: "Growth in the U.S. economy this decade will be the slowest of any decade since the Great Depression." In his view, "a lot" more losses from the collapse in the mortgage-backed debt market can be expected. His insistence on changes echoed calls from politicians and academicians. I agree it is high time for the government to reexamine the framework of a financial system that has the regulators, accountants, rating agencies, politicians, and the exchanges all in the same boat with the investment bankers and where virtually no checks and balances exist.

As I see it, the longer-term effect of this U.S.–made financial debacle will be to transfer financial muscle from U.S. banks to banks in Asia and countries that are able to decouple from the U.S.–centric slowdown. In the years ahead, we will look back on this episode as the second leg in the transfer of economic power from the West to the East, the first leg being in manufacturing.

Today, the top global banks belong to the Chinese. No longer do Citicorp, Goldman Sachs, and Merrill Lynch sit on top of the league table. Asian firms now make billion-dollar deals globally and are on the acquisition trail. For example, the value of Asian-Pacific outbound merger-and-acquisition deals in 2007 hit a staggering US$433 billion, more than double the sum in 2006. To mention just one deal, Doosan Infracore of Korea made a US$4.9 billion takeover of Ingersoll Rand Co.'s Bobcat excavator business. The biggest purchase, so far, has been the purchase of a 20 percent interest in Africa's Standard Bank by ICBC of China for US$5.5 billion.

We are in the midst of a "de-leveraging" process, to unwind the past excessive leverage. Credit contraction is the result and it is a painful exercise. In particular, no bull market has ever been built under such a scenario. I fear there is no silver bullet that either financial engineering or government intervention can produce to bring this process to an early end.

Remarkably, even as the economic situation appears to be getting worse, my life carries on, pretty much as it always has over so many years. Ming Lee has said a number of times that "consistency" is the hallmark of my character. I think she is right. I am still doing my yoga and playing tennis every week, as well as working out at least twice a week. I still put in a 10-hour day, although, at times, I take a 10-minute nap in the Hong Kong Club after lunch. I work at least six days a week and often go to the office for a couple of hours on Sundays. I travel quite a bit, typically one trip a month in the region, visiting companies or attending corporate conferences.

I have made a few adjustments that I ought to mention. On transcontinental flights, I no longer go to the back and sit in the Economy section. I need my sleep, lying flat in Business Class. I have spaced my appointments so that I no longer try to catch a meeting in two cities on a single day. Unprecedented foul-ups that go with US air travel due to delayed and often cancelled flights have made the more leisurely pace necessary.

A recent physical checkup indicated my physical condition has remained the same as a year ago. I continue to travel to visit companies and my ever-expanding group of clients. I continue to be excited about opportunities I see in the years ahead. I intend, perhaps unlike earlier years, to spend more time away from Hong Kong, to take a journey annually to a new destination. These holiday breaks will no doubt allow me to find a better balance in my life.

At my age, I still feel that there is much to do and much to learn. As the saying goes, if you are in the traffic, you are bound to run into new ideas to be explored, new deals to be done, and new friendships to be formed. If my good karma stays with me, I may write a sequel to this book in the next decade.

List of Photographs

Mother in her socialite days (1930s) 185
Father in his Shanghai office (1930s) 185
Me and my twin brother (on the left) with mother (1936) 186
Family in 1948, brother on the right 186
Me and brother (on the left) just after high school, 1954 ... 187
College graduation day, June 1958 187
Wedding day, April 1970 188
Opening a Citibank branch in Ras al Khaimah (1976) 189
Clarence (son) and Kathy (daughter) in their late teens
   (1991) 189
Making a presentation to prospects, 2003 190
Father's old home site, Kaixian, Sichuan, China (2004) 190
Brother and I at 50th reunion (brother on the left), 2008 .. 191
My wife, Teresa, and kids (2006) 191
Trekking to Taktsang Monastery, Bhutan (2007) 192
In my office (March 2009) 192

Index

A

Abrams, Cary 265
Abu Dhabi 78, 79, 90
Abu Dhabi Investment Authority 340
Adelphia 244
AE 108, 110, 111, 116, 117
AEB 97, 98, 103, 104, 105, 107, 114, 117, 118
Afghanistan 133, 237, 243, 267, 312, 325
Ahnert, Ed 132, 143, 144
AIG Group 7
Algiers, Fred 274
American Club 102, 152, 172, 180, 234, 301, 302, 309
American Express Bank xvii, 95, 96, 97, 114, 116, 128, 162
American Home Mortgage 277
American International Assurance 7
American International Group 25, 342
Anhui 8, 292
An Lu Shan 292
AOG 131, 133, 134, 135, 136, 137, 138, 139, 140, 141, 142, 173
Apt Holman 320
Arshad, Guli xvii, 158
Arthur Andersen 244, 245
Arthur D. Little 303
ASEIP 155, 156, 159, 161, 162, 166, 169, 170, 172, 173, 175, 176, 177, 180, 181, 182, 198, 201, 204, 205, 217, 226, 234, 258
Asian Cultural Council 162, 177
Asian economies 114, 197, 199, 208, 276, 336
Asian markets 156, 166, 168, 176, 177, 178, 179, 181, 195–197, 206, 210, 216, 246, 257, 263, 277, 335, 336, 340, 341
Asian Oceanic Group 128, 131, 144, 160, 162, 200, 212, 215. *See also* AOG
Asian Select Equity Investment Partnership. *See also* ASEIP
Asian Special Situation Equity Trust 132
AsiaSat 181
Astra 117, 119, 120
Atlanta Historical Center 162, 175, 198
Austin Asset Management 157
Aweida, Jesse 36, 42
Aziz, Shaukat 96

B

Bahrain 76, 78, 215, 220, 230
Baleno 178, 180
Bancom 98
Bankers Trust 98
Bank Indosuez 132
Bank of America 343
Barth, Mark 155, 341
Beadleston, Al 111
Beam, Bill 98, 101, 111, 112
Bear Stearns 277, 340
Becker, Boris 149

Beijing 4, 5, 120, 136, 176, 181, 251, 253, 260, 281, 286, 288, 289, 323, 342
Beijing Enterprises 181
Bersten, Joe 57
Bhutan 273, 307, 310
Biggs, Barton 231
bin Laden 87, 243
Black, Mark 106
Black Monday 124, 125, 126
Blake, Peter 25
Bliss, Dick xvii, 98, 99, 101, 111, 112, 128, 131, 134, 135, 139, 140, 160, 161, 162, 177
Bonds, Bob 306
Book of Kwei, The 287, 288
Boston Pops 305
Bowen, Lou 132
Boxer Rebellion 5
Branch, Taylor 312
Bryson, Bill 308, 314
Buddhism 229, 268, 328
Buffet, Warren x, 152
Bullock, Bill 158
Burroughs 60
Butterfield Bank & Trust. *See* N.T. Butterfield Bank & Trust

C

Caviness, Patrick 232, 265, 301, 307, 309
CDC 60
CDPC 54, 55
CEF 132, 143
Central Bank of Japan 124
Century City group 131
chaebols 105, 107, 108, 201, 218, 219
Chang, Laurence 175, 197, 288
Chenjia 284, 285, 286, 287, 291, 293, 294, 295, 296, 297
Chen Ke Fang 294, 296
Chen Lin 294, 297, 298
Chen Shui Bien 220
Chep Lap Kok 203
Cheung Kong 114, 132
Chiang Kai Shek 312

China Construction Bank 270
China Data Processing Center (CDPC) 54
Chinavest 132
Choa, Andrew 117, 300
Chongqing 12, 282, 285, 286, 294, 297
Chou, Howell 55
Chrystie, Tom xvii, 158, 161, 198, 203, 304
Chubb & Sons 69
Chu, Bela xviii, 169, 265
Chung Chi College 15
Cigna Insurance 131, 139, 173, 175, 176, 200
Cisco 225
Citibank xvii, 30, 62, 64, 65, 66, 67, 68, 69, 70, 71, 73, 74, 76, 78, 80, 83, 86, 87, 88, 89, 90, 91, 92, 94, 95, 96, 97, 98, 105, 115, 117, 125, 132, 215, 300, 303
Citic Capital 254
Citicorp 277, 340, 343
Citic Pacific 180
Citigroup 339, 340
City Investing 60
Clark, Jack 69
CLSA 178, 181, 251
Columbia University ix, 5, 28, 29, 30, 35, 205, 303, 335
Commerzbank 276
Computer Associates 60
Connors, Jimmy 149, 300
Costanzo, Al 91
Credit Suisse 274
Cultural Revolution 41, 281, 283, 288
Curtis, Mallet-Prevost 155

D

Daewoo 105, 107, 218, 228
DEC 60
Deira 76, 79
Dell 225
Deng Xiaoping 114, 120, 136, 297
Derkx, Henri 76

DMT 162, 200
DMT Securities 162
Dodd, David x, 335
Dollar Credit 114
Donald, David Herbert 313
Doosan Infracore 344
Drexel Burnham 134, 138, 300
Dubai xvii, 75, 76, 77, 78, 79, 80, 81, 82, 83, 84, 86, 87, 88, 89, 90, 91, 93, 94

E

Edberg, Stefan 300
Electro Voice 26, 320
Enron 238, 243, 247, 327
Ernst & Young 155
Estrada, Francis 135, 140
European Central Bank 272

F

Fairchild Audio Equipment 320
Fallon, Robert 300
Fangda Building Materials 176
Fastow, Andy 247
Federal Deposit Insurance Corporation 342
Federal Reserve 127, 166, 170, 173, 206, 230, 238, 263, 277, 340, 343
Federer, Roger 300
FF Ball 152
Fiduciary Trust 175, 202, 207, 209
First World War 5, 312, 313
Fleming, Tom 54
Flex 143, 144, 147
Flex Holdings 143
Flextronics 145, 176, 207, 212
Fok, Lawrence 180
Friedlander, Jesse vii, xviii, 302
Fromkin, David 313
Fujian xvi, 292, 293
Furama Hotel 152

G

Galadari family 87, 88
Gansi 292

Garcia Marquez, Gabriel 313
GE Computer Services 56
General Electric 56, 111
General Motors 29, 126, 340
General Reinsurance 69
GIC 340
Gilbert, Martin 313
GITIC 209
Gleick, James 314
Global Crossing 243
Goldman Sachs 123, 134, 179, 343
Goldstein, Elliott vii, 158, 264, 302
Gooden, Dick 62, 64
Graham, Benjamin x, 335
Graham, Katharine 313
Grand Teton 198, 227, 304
Grass, Martin 245
Great Depression 4, 30, 248, 295, 343
Greenberg, Larry 98
Greene, Brian 314
Greene, Jim 98, 111
Greenspan, Alan 253
Guangdong 251, 292, 293
Guangzhou 180, 292

H

Hana 146, 147
Hang Seng Index 125, 126
Hanmi Pharmaceutical 248
Han, Richard 146, 291
Hansen, Louisa Wah xviii
Heathkit 318
Hepburn, Katharine 58
Hewlett Packard 145
Hitachi 57
Ho, Alan 132
Hochschild, Adam 312
Hoffman, Ed xvii, 68, 74, 75
Hohner 316
Holbrooke, Richard 313
Honeywell 60
Hong Kong Country Club 181, 300
Hong Kong Special Administrative Region 145
Hopewell 114
Hopkirk, Peter 312

HSBC 120, 144, 155, 168, 213
HSBC Private Equity 144
Hsin Chu Science Park 201
Huaneng 257
Huang, Chamber 20, 316
Huang, Peter 60
Huang, Powen 305, 306
Hubei xvi, 48, 290, 292, 293
Hui, Michael 301
Hunan 292, 293
Hutchison House 213
Hu, Yaobang 136
Hwan, Chun Doo 106, 128
Hyundai 105, 248, 257

I

IBM 30, 32, 33, 34, 35, 37, 38, 39, 40, 42, 43, 44, 47, 53, 54, 56, 60, 61, 74, 126, 145, 146, 262, 302, 303
ICBC 344
IDS 65, 66
Imclone 245
IMF 108, 194, 195, 197, 199, 200, 208, 218. *See also* International Monetary Fund (IMF)
INDA 43, 56, 59, 62
Indover Bank 122
Institute of Private Investors (IPI) 175, 255, 260
Intel 225
International Data Applications 43, 142
International Data Services (IDS) 65
International Monetary Fund (IMF) 108, 194, 248
Iyenga yoga 309

J

Jackson, Peter 181
Jacob, Fabrice 269, 273
Jakarta 119, 142, 196
Jardine Fleming 179
Jardine Fleming's Private Equity 144

Jardine Matheson 146
JDS Uniphase 233
Jiang, President 182
JK Asian Invest, LLP xvii
JKC Advisors 341
JK Capital Management 273, 275, 276, 341
Johnson, Al 61
JP Morgan xv, 339, 340
Jumeira Beach 80, 84

K

Kaixian xvi, 4, 281, 282, 283, 284, 288, 289, 292, 294, 295, 323
Kalyck, Mike 180
Kamen, Henry 313
Kao Un Road 8
Kaplan, Robert 312
Kashyap, Pradeep 89
Kennedy Road 15
KFTCIC 131, 141
Kim Dae Jung 198
Kim, Jiyoung 274, 341
King, Roger 145, 146, 301
Klingenstein, Lee 158
Knief, Byron 72
Korea Development Bank 106
Korea Exchange Bank 300
Kozlowski, Dennis 245
KPMG 141, 142
Kriwaczek, Paul 314
Krug, Guy 111, 112
Kruthoffer, Jan 95, 98
Kuala Lumpur 219
Kuok, Robert Hock-Nien 301
Kuwait 75, 131, 138, 139, 141, 263
Kuwait Foreign Trading, Contracting and Investment Corporation (KFTCIC) 131
Kuwait Investment Authority 340
Kwei, Amy 35, 302, 319
Kwei Beng Ying 297
Kwei Chen Hua 295, 296
Kwei Chen Yu 296
Kwei Chung Hue 292
Kwei Chung Shu xiii, xvi, xvii, 4, 5, 6, 7, 8, 12, 14, 15, 16, 17, 18,

19, 21, 23, 25, 28, 44, 45, 46, 47, 48, 109, 124, 185, 190, 239, 240, 267, 271, 281, 282, 283, 284, 285, 286, 288, 289, 290, 293, 294, 295, 296, 297, 298, 311, 323
Kwei, Clarence x, xvii, 72, 74, 80, 85, 86, 95, 97, 102, 110, 116, 124, 138, 140, 153, 170, 189, 191, 205, 223, 233, 234, 265, 266, 282, 300, 304, 330, 342
Kwei, Kathy x, xvii, 66, 67, 71, 72, 74, 80, 86, 95, 97, 100, 102, 110, 116, 124, 136, 138, 152, 153, 160, 161, 167, 168, 189, 191, 205, 222, 223, 241, 248, 249, 265, 266, 271, 287, 309, 319, 330, 341, 342
Kwei Ling Kui. *See* Kwei Xiao San
Kwei Tang 292
Kwei, Teresa x, xv, xvii, 58, 62, 63, 66, 67, 68, 71, 73, 77, 80, 87, 93, 95, 97, 114, 124, 128, 153, 161, 191, 205, 223, 234, 241, 250, 303
Kwei, Tom xvi, 3, 4, 8, 10, 11, 13, 14, 15, 16, 17, 18, 20, 21, 22, 23, 25, 27, 30, 33, 35, 39, 186, 187, 191, 239, 240, 241, 267, 289, 290, 293, 299, 302, 315, 316, 318, 319
Kwei Wen Hui xvi, 293
Kwei Xiao San 294
Kwei You Yue 292
Kwei Zheng 291, 293
Kwei Zhi Lan 292
Kwei Zhong Wu 292
Kwei Zhong Zheng 294, 295
Kwok, Raymond 114

L

Lane Crawford 271
Lan Kwai Fong 153
Laver, Rod 300
LBO 134, 138
Leckie, Stuart 180
Lee, David 60
Lee, John 160, 261, 267
Lee, Linda 7, 8, 9, 12, 14, 15, 109, 172, 185, 239, 240, 241, 281, 282, 290, 311
Lee, Ming 273, 278, 307, 308, 310, 344
Lehman Brothers 339, 343
Lendl, Ivan 300
Lenovo 262
Leung, Alex 270
Lifescan 145
Li & Fung 257
Li Ka-Shing 114, 132
Lindskog, David 155
Lingzhou 291
Lin Yutang 5
Lloyd, John 149
Long Term Capital Management 206
Lo, Tony 132
Lo, Y. S. 131
Loy, Tan Sri 139, 140
LTCM 206
Lu 282, 283, 284, 285, 289, 294
Lucent Technologies 225
Lu Zheng Ying 294

M

Macmillan, Margaret 313
Magee, John 100, 111, 112
Mahathir, Prime Minister 195, 219
Malaysian Central Bank 140
Malone, Tom 56, 59
Manchester, William 312
Marconi 233
Marks, Mike 145
MARS project 37, 38
Maryknoll Seminary 21, 299
Mason, Bob 98
Massie, Robert 313
Mauchly Associates 42, 43, 53, 54
MBF 139, 140, 141
McCullough, David 313
McDougall, Walter 313
McEnroe, John 300
McQueeney, Tom 64, 67

Merrill Lynch 158, 161, 277, 304, 339, 340, 343
Merszei, Leslie 140
Meyer, Frank 160
Milliken, Michael 134
Ming Dynasty 287, 292
Monroe, Marilyn 24
Moore, Charlie 160
Moore, Vernon 180
Moreschi, Jack 35, 39, 303
Morgan, Edmund 313
Morgan Stanley 134, 138, 231, 248
Mount Marcy 305

N

Nanjing 14
National Semiconductor 147
Nationwide Consumer Finance 73
NCR 60
Neuberger & Berman 158, 177
New Century Financial 272
New York Times, The 5
Nissho Iwai 131
Northern Rock 277
N.T. Butterfield Bank & Trust 155
Nuland & Arshad 158, 168
Nuland, Jamie xvii, 158

O

O'Connor, Cynthia 271
ODSSPI 145, 146
Okinawa 103, 104
Omar, Mullah Mohammed 243
O'Neal, Stanley 277
Opium War 293
ORIX 131, 168, 169, 173, 176, 197
ORIX Financial 131
ORIX Investments 168

P

Pacific Capital Management Ltd (PCML) 128, 131, 141, 142, 144, 160, 162, 168, 200, 212, 215, 216, 217
Pagels, Elaine 314
Pangilinan, Manny 99, 102, 108

Pao, Peter 121, 122
Pao, Sir Y.K. 121
Paribas Bank 181
Paro Valley 307
Peregrine Investments 200
Pernoud, Régine 313
Petain Road 8, 9
Petronas Towers 219
Pewin, Bernard 174
PIMCO 274
Ping An Insurance 270
Poon Bun Chak 178
Prince Charles 182
Prince, Chuck 277

Q

Qatar 75, 263
Qin Dynasty 291
Qing Dynasty 5, 48, 281, 290, 292, 323
Qwest 244

R

Rashid, Sheik 78, 81, 82, 83, 84, 89, 90
RCA 9, 29, 55, 60, 61, 63, 315
Reed, John 67, 75
Republic National Bank 117
Repulse Bay xv, 149
Rho Psi 25, 305
Ridley, Matt 314
Rigas family 244
Rinpoche, Guru 307
Rite Aid 245
Robinson, Jim 111
Roh Moo-hyun 249
Roh Tae Woo 107
Roswell, Ken 300
Roxas, Ting 96, 98
Russell Reynolds 117, 301

S

Safra Bank 117
Safra, Edmund 116
Sai Kung 307
Sampras, Pete 300

Samsung 105, 229, 257
Santayana 225
Sarda, Runny 111
Sarnoff, Bob 60
SARS 249, 250, 251, 252, 254, 257
Sartre, Jean-Paul xiv
Scholar Kwei 287
Schroders 200, 207
Scientific Resources Inc. 54
Securities and Exchange Commission 214, 274, 341
Securities and Futures Commission 141, 216, 273
Security Pacific Bank 144
SemiTech Holdings 135
Shangri-La Hotel 180
Shansi 291
Shan Zheng. *See* Kwei Zheng
Shaw Kwei & Partners 212
Shaw, Kyle 176, 207, 212, 213
Shearson Loeb Rhoades Inc. 110
Sheehan, Neil 313
Shui On 181
Sichuan xi, xvi, 4, 201, 271, 281, 282, 290, 292, 293
Siemens 145
SIFL. *See* Summa
Singer Group 136
SLORC 174
Smith, Al 111, 112
Soeryadjaya 117, 120, 122
Song Dynasty 292
Soros, George 179, 193
Spence, Jonathan 312
Sperry Rand 60
Spitzer, Eliot 248
Standard Bank 344
Standard Chartered Bank 121, 122
Starr, C. V. 7, 25
Steiner, Henry 155
Stern, Bob xvii, 43
St. John's Preparatory School 16, 19, 35, 233, 317
Suharto 202, 217
Summa 117, 118, 119, 120, 121, 122, 151, 154
Summa International Finance Ltd (SIFL). *See* Summa

Summers, Lawrence 262
Sun Hung Kai 114
Sun Microsystems 225
Surabaya 119
Suu Kyi, Aung San 174
Suzhou University 6
System 360 33, 34, 37

T

Tai Ping Revolution 312
Takefuji 103
Taktshang Monastery 307, 310
Tang Dynasty xvi, 291, 311
Temasek Holdings 340
Texwinca 178, 180
Thadani, Anil 132
Thai Central Bank 179
Thaleen, Bob 132
Three Gorges Dam 282, 283, 285
Time Warner 232, 265, 342
Ting, James 135, 136
Ting, Simon 180
Trade Development Bank 116, 117
Trauman, Jacques 181
Truman, President Harry 26
Tuchman, Barbara 311
Tung, Alice 145
Tung, C.C. 301
Tung Chee Hwa 145, 301
Tyco 245

U

UBS 180, 219, 237, 243, 277, 339, 340
United Arab Emirates 75, 78, 79, 89, 263
Univac 42, 60
U.S. Federal Reserve 228, 248, 253, 259, 267, 270, 272. *See also* Federal Reserve

V

Varn, Bob xvii, 158, 162, 175, 203
Venter, Steve 76, 82
Vietnam War 40, 41, 313
Vlachos, Peter 157

Voitja, George 91
Volcker, Paul 343
Vtech Holdings 131

W

Wachovia 339, 340
Wah Sang Gas 247
Wah Yan College 16
Waksal, Samuel 245
Wanchai 15, 64
Wan, Charles 54, 56
Wang, An 60
Wang, Charles 60
Wanghou 292
Wang Laboratories 60
Wanzhou 282, 284, 285, 286, 294, 296
Washington Mutual 340, 343
Weill, Sandy 110, 111
Wharf Holdings 121, 122, 123, 127, 128
WHO 251. *See also* World Health Organization
Wilson House 168, 169, 213
Wilson Sports 148
Women's Wear Daily 271
Wong, Allan 131
Wong, Frankie 181
Wong, Teddy 342
Woo, Peter 121, 122
WorldCom 244, 245
World Health Organization 250
Wriston, Walt 91
Wu, Gordon 114

Y

Y2K 214, 216
Yale Alumni Association ix
Yale University ix, xvii, 21, 22, 23, 25, 26, 30, 41, 44, 45, 156, 158, 160, 162, 171, 213, 232, 233, 301, 302, 306, 307, 312, 318, 320
Yamaichi 198
Yangtze River 7, 14, 201, 283, 285, 292, 294

Yeh, Ching Ju 219, 220, 222, 226, 227, 243, 254, 261, 265
Young, Ti Sheng 180
Yue Yuen 256
Yu, Willie 114

Z

Zhang, Mr. 285, 286, 287, 288, 294
Zheng 286, 287, 288, 290, 291, 297
Zhongdian 310
Zhou Dynasty xvi, 291

LaVergne, TN USA
06 November 2009
163393LV00002B/5/P